THE COLLECTED WRITINGS OF MURRAY STEIN

VOLUME 9

GENERAL EDITORS

STEVEN BUSER

LEONARD CRUZ

JUNGIAN STUDIES

MURRAY STEIN

CHIRON PUBLICATIONS • ASHEVILLE, NORTH CAROLINA

www.ChironPublications.com

Interior and cover design by Danijela Mijailovic
Printed primarily in the United States of America.

ISBN 978-1-68503-522-8 paperback
ISBN 978-1-68503-523-5 hardcover
ISBN 978-1-68503-526-6 electronic
ISBN 978-1-68503-524-2 limited edition paperback
ISBN 978-1-68503-525-9 limited edition hardcover

Library of Congress Cataloging-in-Publication Data Pending

TABLE OF CONTENTS

Jung's Vision of the Nature of the Psyche and Analytic Practice[1]

The Nature of Healing

A wit once proclaimed that the art of the physician is to entertain the patient while nature heals. This may be as true for analysis as it is for medicine. "The best the analyst can do is not to disturb the natural evolution of this [healing] process," Jung wrote in a letter in 1960. "The process consists in becoming whole or integrated, and that is never produced by words or interpretations but wholly by the nature of Psyche itself."[2]

Today most experienced analysts of all theoretical persuasions would agree that they are not healers of psyche but at best only allies of the healing processes that are to be found within it. All but the most inflated clinicians recognize their limitations of skill and technique in the therapeutic process. What actually heals in psychotherapy remains a mystery. Perhaps it is a certain kind of love.

What some commentators have seen as a holdover of German nature romanticism in Jung's works actually turns out to be a realistic assessment of what can happen in analysis. Jung's reliance on "nature" to supply the healing forces is not some sort of woolly mysticism but a physician's recognition that human art and science

---

[1] Originally published in P. Marcus and A. Rosenberg (eds.), *Psychoanalytic Versions of the Human Condition*, 1998.
[2] G. Adler and A. Jaffé (eds.), *C.G. Jung Letters*, vol. 2, p. 583.

have their limitations. The analyst is not omnipotent and certainly requires the cooperation of nature if healing is to occur.

Yet the practiced skill and masterful technique of the trained analyst are also important in analysis, and in some cases, they are even crucial. Otherwise, training would be unnecessary and training institutes an egregious waste of energy. While there may be "natural therapists" and healing personalities, the difficult analytic cases require a great deal of expertise and skill. This seems to have been true since time immemorial, as evidenced by shamanic healers, who were and are also highly trained technicians. Hurtful experiences in early life prevent nature's healing processes from having much effect.

It is often the case that the pathways by which nature does its healing are blocked and need to be opened and cleared of obstacles. Often, weak bridges need to be built up into solid, workable psychic structures, and in some cases a whole new psychic infrastructure must be constructed if nature is to have a chance to work its healing effects. Faulty and malignant conscious attitudes and developments, acquired usually through traumatic and hurtful experiences in early life, prevent nature's healing processes from having much effect.

Actually, many things can get in the way of the psyche's natural healing processes. To quote Jung from a very late work titled "Symbols and the Interpretation of Dreams,"

> "through dreams, intuitions, impulses, and other spontaneous happenings, instinctive forces influence the activity of consciousness. Whether that influence is for better or worse depends on the actual contents of the unconscious. If it contains too many things that normally ought to be conscious, then its function becomes twisted and prejudiced; motives appear that are not based on true instincts, but owe their activity to the fact that they have been consigned to the unconscious by repression or neglect. They overlay, as it were, the normal

2

unconscious psyche and distort its natural symbol producing function."[3]

This overlay of repressed psychic material is maintained and held in place by all the psychic splits, vertical and horizontal, that are revealed through the careful scrutiny of analysis. In large measure, the work of analysis has to do with bringing together the psychic pieces (the so-called opposites) that have been split and pushed apart, so that the normal psychic equilibrating force can take over and offer its creative and healing potential. This knitting together of bits of consciousness is the work of integration in a Jungian analysis.

The Nature of the Psyche

Jung's vision of the psyche and his approach to the theory and practice of analysis unfolded over a period of some 60 years. Beginning with psychiatric studies in 1900 at the Burgholzli Clinic in Zurich and continuing through his close collaboration with Freud between 1907 and 1913, Jung went on to extend the scope of what he believed to be the true range of the unconscious from a one- (or two-) drive theory to a theory that encompasses a wide array of instinctual and archetypal foci. He also reconceptualized the relations between conscious and unconscious in a more dynamic and less mechanical way than had Freud. His early argument with Freud about the nature of libido (is it purely sexual or more general psychic energy?) turned into a thorough going revision of the psychoanalytic theory that he had received in Vienna.

The nature of the human psyche embraces, in Jung's view, instinctual somatic elements (i.e., impulses) at the one end of a spectrum and spiritual archetypal elements (i.e., images and ideas) at the other. At both extremes, psyche fades through a psychoid barrier into nonpsychic areas: into physical matter at the somatic end and into pure spirit at the archetypal end. The psyche itself is

---

[3] C.G. Jung, "Symbols and the Interpretation of Dreams, CW 18, para. 512.

defined by the range of the will: whatever the will can affect or influence in principle belongs to the psychic realm, and whatever it cannot reach even in principle (e.g., autonomic system functions) lies outside the psyche. The psyche is bounded by instincts on the one side and by spirit on the other: "[T]he will cannot transgress the bounds of the psychic sphere: it cannot coerce the instinct, nor has it power over the spirit, in so far as we understand by this something more than the intellect. Spirit and instinct are by nature autonomous and both limit in equal measure the applied field of the will."[4]

The view much bandied about that Jung was a "mystic" is a distortion of the truth that he did take spirit into account in his theory of the psyche. And in analytic therapy it is as important to release spiritual elements as it is somatic instinctual impulses. But contrary to the popular opinion that Jung denied or downplayed the biological and instinctual side of psychic life, he actually gives it equal weight to the spiritual and archetypal. Jung's is not a purely spiritual psychology, although it takes spiritual matters more seriously perhaps than any other of the modern depth psychologies.

For Jung the unconscious contains much more than the sexual drive (the famous *Lustprincip* of Freud) and its associated materials, and more even than the total mass of repressed psychic contents of all kinds. The unconscious contains thoughts and images, impulses and desires that have not yet been experienced in an individual's life, as well as those that have been experienced and rejected for one reason or another. Certainly, Jung did not deny the existence and importance of sexuality, but he found that other somatic instinctual factors also play on the psyche, not to mention the panoply of contents and factors that have more a spiritual or purely psychological identity than a biologically based one.

Jung theorized that there are a number of instinct groups, in fact, five of them. In a significant but much neglected essay titled "Psychological Factors Determining Human Behavior," which was

---

[4] C.G. Jung, "On the Nature of the Psyche, CW 8, para. 379.

written in 1936 for presentation at the Harvard Tercentenary Conference of Arts and Sciences (where he received an honorary doctorate), Jung postulated that the five "instinctive factors" are hunger, sexuality, activity, reflection, and creativity. These deep human impulses, which lie beyond the levels of acculturation and cannot be controlled by the will, belong to human biological nature itself. They influence human behavior and supply energy and motive force ("libido") to the psyche. They are in turn shaped by several other physical, psychological, and cultural factors, which Jung calls "modalities" in the Harvard paper. These include the physical factors of gender, age, and hereditary disposition and the more psychological ones of typology, spiritual vs. physical orientation to the world, and the degree to which a person behaves consciously or unconsciously. Culture and history play a role in forming these latter three modalities and thereby influence the ways the instinct groups may be deployed in an individual's life. For Jung, history and culture play a large role in shaping and forming the deployment of both instinctual and archetypal factors in the psyche.

Jung's Harvard paper therefore also underscores his appreciation for the multitude of ways the individual psyche is embedded in and influenced by the surrounding social world. The individual is subject to social forces from both internal and external sources. As history and culture shape family life and attitudes, so family shapes the individual and, through the process of introjection, affects the ego from within the psychic matrix itself. Social disruption, war, and economic hardship are factors that contribute to the construction of an inner world that the individual carries throughout life. Jung's theory is nonsolipsistic in another sense as well: Through the psychological functions, such as sensation, thinking, and feeling, the ego is able to make adjustments to the environment and to fashion a conscious response that is not fatalistically determined by the instincts or complexes. Jung's vision is profoundly appreciative of the importance of the psyche in making judgments and formulating responses and ideas about the world, but it does not see the human being as locked into a dark box from which only projections can emanate and grope at a totally unknown and unknowable "outer world." For Jung, the human being is an adaptive animal who takes cues both from intrapsychic factors such as instinctually based impulses and archetypally derived ideational processes and from the surrounding environment.

It should be noted here as highly significant that Jung does not list aggression (Freud's second drive, thanatos) or the wish for power (Adler's core drive) as basic human instincts. In this, his conception of the human condition differs from Freud's more pessimistic view, not to mention Melanie Klein's further extensions of thanatos theory into earliest childhood and infancy, as for instance in her theory of envy. He also sets himself apart from Adler, for whom the power drive was the key force in psychological life and who saw the human experience of inferiority and powerlessness as central.

This is not to say that Jung's conception of the human condition is one-sidedly and naively optimistic or depicts a psyche that is free of internal conflict or power needs. It is not. He recognizes in many places that the instincts often compete (e.g., "the system of instincts is not truly harmonious in composition and is exposed to numerous internal collisions,"[5] and that constellations of the opposites and internal conflict within the psyche are inevitable. He also is cognizant of the power issue and its importance, especially for introverts. In fact, the existence of inner conflict is bedrock in Jungian doctrine. Conflict, inner and outer, is a normal part of human life and even provides the necessary condition for ego growth and development; politics is inevitable and universal because of the insecurity of the ego, but not instinctual. Politics are driven more by the ego's need for power and grandiosity than by instinct.

If Jung does not root aggression and the need for power in instinct, he does nevertheless have a strong conception of evil. The shadow (for Jung a technical psychological term) belongs to the human personality at all levels, personal and impersonal, individual

---

[5] Ibid., para. 378.

and collective. But ·the shadow is not invariably defined by "sex and aggression," the Freudian Id. It is mercurial; it depends on the particular aspects of personality that individuals and their culture choose to denigrate and attempt to eliminate. The shadow is that which does not belong in polite company, is shaming and embarrassing, and is rejected by the individual and by society as unacceptable and even intolerable. It is made up of the traits, feelings, and harbored fantasies analysands confess to their analysts with great shame and reluctance. The shadow is complementary to the persona (another technical term), a person's official psychosocial identity: One side is the face we want to have seen, the other the face we want to conceal. Both exist inevitably as shadow twins. But the shadow is not drive-based and is not associated or shaped by a specific instinct.

There is in Jung's theory, then, no specific drive toward destruction or aggression for its own sake, and the shadow does not inevitably tend in that direction. Destructiveness and aggressiveness are universal among humans, or so it seems, but they are the byproducts of other factors: frustration, traumatic childhood, the need to create, the urge to mate, and so on. There is no inherent human need to destroy. For Jung, this Freudian notion (the Thanatos myth) simply did not make sense from a biological or psychological standpoint, even though the idea seems to have originated with his early student, Sabina Spielrein, who passed it on to Freud.

Belonging to the same deep level of the psyche as the instinctive factors are the archetypes. Instincts are the drives, archetypes the shapers of the drives. Together they make up the famous Jungian collective unconscious. In an essay titled "On the Nature of the Psyche," which is perhaps his greatest single theoretical paper, Jung speculates about the relation between instincts and archetypes. He concludes that they are best conceived as lying along a spectrum, like the color spectrum, with the instincts at the infrared end and the archetypes at the ultraviolet end.[6] But

6 Ibid., para. 414.

7

archetypes and instincts are also intimately related to one another, the first shaping and giving form to the second. By themselves the instincts would be without form and void, like the biblical *te'hom* (Genesis 1:1); the spirit (archetype) broods above this amorphous chaos and gives it shape. The archetypes structure the deep unconscious, where matter and spirit come together and meet as instinctual urge and archetypal image. In fact, one never meets an instinct without an archetypally formed structure in the psyche. Jung would sometimes hold that the archetype is the image of the instinct. So intimately are they related that Jung often refers to archetypes and archetypal patterns without explicit or even implicit reference to instinct, simply assuming the link between instinct and archetype that drives the "pattern of behavior" that is the archetype.[7] Without such a source of somatic energy, archetypal images would be lifeless and without embodiment, pure mental specters that float around in the psyche without emotional connection or impact. Taken this way, archetypes become mental abstractions and schemata for thinking rather than the numinous powers that Jung had in mind whenever he used the term "archetype."

Without an image, on the other hand, an instinct would lack direction, it would be diffuse, it would not know how to find a suitable object. While instincts give energy and drive to archetypal images, archetypes generate the images that allow instincts to become object-related, to come into contact with fitting objects, which is what they inherently seek.

In Jungian theory, this linkage between instinct and archetype is the presupposition for all satisfactory object relations, beginning with the infant-breast unit (nurturance), extending through the formation of a love bond with a mate (sexuality), and including the discovery and recognition of a vocation (activity, creativity), and the persons involved and tools used for deriving meaning from experience (reflection). For Jungians, these key of a "fit" experiences in life are "archetypal," meaning that there is a good match between

---

[7] Ibid., para. 352.

internal and external worlds (between need and fulfillment) and between nature and culture (between self and other, individual and society). There is also the factor of innateness: These fittings are not learned, they are discovered.

Jung would not reject the point of the object relations theorists who wish to insist that humans are innately and inherently object-oriented and object-related from the beginning of life, but he would add that the ground for this relatedness lies in the still more fundamental link between instinct and archetype. When this linkage is disrupted or broken, object relations are inevitably disturbed, perhaps even from the first moments of intrauterine life but certainly from the moment of birth onward. Without the guidance of the archetypal image, the psychic energy pouring in from the somatic base is disorganized and unfocused.

Neither instincts nor archetypes are contained within the psyche itself, according to Jung's theory, and therefore they cannot be experienced directly. The instinct groups are rooted in the somatic base, and the archetypes are formative factors that exist in a realm beyond the range of the human psyche, which Jung calls "spirit."[8] From both extremes of the spectrum, the psyche receives signals: From the instinct groups these come as feelings of desire and as impulses, and from the archetypes they appear in consciousness as images, fantasies, ideas, visions, and intuitions. By the time they reach the psyche and even more so when they reach ego-consciousness, both types of signals have been "psychized" and related to the other type.

The empirical consciousness of individuals tends to slide back and forth between the somatic and archetypal poles of the spectrum, now experiencing desires, impulses, and the libidinal fires of passion more strongly, now images, ideas, and intuitions more intensely. Emotion can equally attach itself to either end of this polarity and either one can at times overwhelm or swallow the other. But in the healthy psyche, which is the balanced psyche for

---

[8] Ibid., para. 420.

Jung, consciousness holds instinct and archetype in tension, where they are coordinated and can work together, the one providing the impulse and drive and the other contributing direction and meaning. Precisely how this coordination comes into being and operates or fails to operate successfully was a topic pursued by Jung late in life, particularly in his last great opus, *Mysterium Coniunctionis*. The great "union of opposites" that the psyche is asked to host is that between matter and spirit. The human condition as we experience it at this point in evolution is fundamentally shaped by this tension of opposites between the soma-based instincts and the spirit-based archetypes. The meeting place (or the battleground) where they converge is the psyche. As Jung saw it, the meaning of human existence in the temporal universe lies in this precise function of the psyche: to unite spirit and matter within the space-time continuum of an individual human life.

When these two poles of the psyche, the material body and the transcendent spirit, are adequately coordinated, it makes for healthful psychic compensation from the unconscious. Jung's view of compensation is vastly different from Adler's. The term "compensation" for Jung does not refer to the outcome of a sense of inferiority or the attempt to overcome the feeling of smallness by imagining the opposite: It is not a "protest." Rather, compensation is conceptualized by Jung as a psychic mechanism that aims at directing a balanced dynamic movement toward individuation and wholeness. Ego-consciousness needs this compensation, which is a coordinated blend of impulse and idea, from the unconscious because on its own and without benefit of such a relationship with "nature," it becomes rigid, sterile, and one-sided. "True instincts" or "nature" can adjust, balance, and heal the conscious personality if the way is clear for psyche, the material body and the transcendent spirit are adequately coordinated, it makes for healthful psychic compensation from the unconscious. Jung's view of compensation is vastly different from Adler's. The term "compensation" for Jung does not refer to the outcome of a sense of inferiority or the attempt to overcome the feeling of smallness by imagining the opposite: It is not a "protest."

Complexes, Pathology, and Analysis

Since its beginnings in Freud's late 19th-century clinical workshop, psychoanalysis has been concerned with the dynamics and contents of repression and the problems created by this defense mechanism. Repression was, however, only the first indication of psychic splintering and fragmentation. Early in his psychiatric career, Jung noticed the wonders of dissociation in his psychotic and neurotic patients. Repression is but one of several means by which consciousness is prevented from integrating parts of the psyche and extracting meaning and benefit from experience.

What the early pioneers of psychoanalysis recognized clearly from the outset was that individuals who seek treatment block much of their psychic wholeness from their conscious self-perceptions, usually in order to avoid psychic pain. The price for this strategy of pain avoidance and defensiveness is other kinds of suffering, namely, symptoms, fragmentary one-sidedness, and lack of emotional fulfillment. The way to health, as both Freud and Jung recognized, lies in removing these blocks to consciousness, facing the necessary pain, and constructing a container of consciousness that can hold the pieces of psyche together and keep the defenses from splitting them apart. Simultaneously, Jung believed, this would also release the healing powers of the natural psyche into consciousness.

Thus, that which has been excluded from ego-consciousness and remains unintegrated is a key issue for psychotherapeutic theory and also, or especially, for analytic practice. For Freud, the chief content of repression was sexuality in its most basic, original, and instinctual forms as he understood them. Oedipal sexuality and its attached contents of fantasy, memory, and thought were the prime targets of the repression dynamic. This accounted, in Freud's view, for childhood amnesia. Moreover, the repression of Oedipal

11

sexuality lay at the heart of culture, and for Freud this was the root of civilized humanity's psychic discontents and miseries.

Jung rather quickly recognized the inadequacies of Freud's view about repressed contents. He found that there are many other elements in the unconscious besides those that have to do with sexuality (i.e., other instincts and archetypes). Umberto Galimberti, a contemporary Italian Jungian analyst, suggests that the more damaging and far-reaching repressions in our time have to do with the spiritual end of the psychic spectrum rather than the instinctual:

Actually, repression is carried out not so much on the level of instincts as, much more, on the level of meanings. Opinion is decided in such a one-sided and rigid fashion that the individual does not retain the possibility of expressing himself in a different way, one that could even perhaps be definitive...More than being a playground for impersonal instincts, the human being is defined by the openness to meaning, and freedom is demonstrated much more by the extent of this openness than it would be by the full deployment of the instincts.[9]

According to Galimberti, the task of psychoanalysis is to extend the range of possibilities for interpretation of psychological material and experience and of the meanings that a patient might otherwise refrain from considering, meanings that would consequently remain locked away in the unconscious.

These contents of the unconscious, its unthought thoughts and images, would have, if released into consciousness, the potential to transform the subject's self-concept and self-perception and provide a new map for meaning. We must understand that potential "meanings" and "ideas" can be as much the targets of repression and other splitting mechanisms as are instincts such as sexuality.

This notion vastly extends the scope of an adequate psychological hermeneutic. Not only does interpretation have the obligation of unearthing hidden sexual motives and other instinctual

---

[9] U. Galimberti, "Analytical Psychology in an Age of Technology," p. 91.

material, it also has the duty to expose obscured ideas and possible meanings, occluded images and experiences of the soul that are buried in the debris of personal and cultural prejudices toward what is to be allowed as true and valid for the individual. The rejection of a reductionistic hermeneutic was an essential move in Jung's break with Freud. In its place, he erected an interpretive method that could embrace a much broader range of meanings and significance.

This is not to say, however, that Jung abandoned reductionistic interpretation altogether. Rather, it was put to a different use. It was clear to him that the main hindrance to the smooth functioning of nature's psychological ecosystem lies in the personal complexes. These are psychic bodies that are developed throughout a person's life history, and most importantly in childhood. They are instigated by interpersonal traumata like emotional abandonment, sexual abuse, and lack of adequate mirroring, and then they grow by gathering associations of a similar nature around themselves and by binding them to the core of the complex with emotion. The complexes are highly charged with affect, behave autonomously (i.e., are not under the ego's control), and possess a kind of consciousness of their own. They are highly reactive to external stimuli, and when stimulated, they cause both physiological and psychological distress and confusion. They are our emotional "triggers"; when pushed, they can drive us to the brink of irrationality and beyond. In analysis they are interpreted reductionistically, although not necessarily bio-reductionistically. That is, the emotional reactions generated by complexes are placed in the context of their point of origination, usually childhood.

As important as their interference with the ego's so-called reality testing may be, however, a perhaps more severe problem comes about as the result of their eventual buildup into a sort of psychic barrier, often impenetrable, between the ego and the deeper, instinctive/archetypal levels of the psyche. It is this barrier of complexes that can severely block the healing compensations of the natural psyche from reaching ego-consciousness.

The complexes also form fracture points in the structure of the developing ego. They allow for ego fragmentation and dissociation along certain predictable lines of cleavage. When strongly stimulated, they splinter the psyche and cause splits within consciousness and between consciousness and the unconscious. When this happens, a person experiences a state of dissociation, high affectivity, and physiological stress. Consciousness is disturbed, and the integration of experience is blocked. Memory, too, is disrupted, and distortions of every variety intrude in the ego's account of reality.

These points of vulnerability in the psyche engender ego defenses that are meant to distance the subject from suffering and pain. Unfortunately, at the same time they distance the person from valuable psychic experience and from parts of the self that are called into play at the moment of the complex stimulus. They interfere with useful instinctual responses to stressful and even dangerous situations, and they cut down on the ego's capacity to take advantage of opportunities in the environment with adaptive responses. The resultant defenses against psychic pain prevent integration and foster the chronicity of psychic patterns and partiality. The self is not unified but rather becomes compartmentalized and dissociative. This is the problematic situation found, for example, in borderline personality disorder.

As much as the fragmentariness of a poorly formed and vulnerable ego interferes with healthy functioning and utilization of healing compensation from the deep unconscious, the existence of a thick, unbreachable layer of complexes between ego-consciousness and the deeper layers of the unconscious, along with the defenses employed by the ego to keep psychic pain at bay, creates a psyche that cannot utilize the healing powers of the unconscious even when they happen to break through in dreams, impulses, or fantasies. In analytic practice, it is not uncommon for a person to report a numinous archetypal dream that should have the effect of moving the subject toward greater wholeness and meaning but which the analyst sees as having no discernible effect. While such a dream should have a profound healing influence on consciousness, not even the added weight of the analyst's most empathic and inspired interpretation will move consciousness very far in the direction of health. Here, both dream and interpretation carry too little force within this undeveloped psychic matrix to make much difference. Psychic reality has little weight when thrown in the balance against the habits of consciousness and the power of the complexes.

The instincts, too, like the archetypes, may be ignored, overridden, or distorted by ego-consciousness and its governing complexes, or they can be turned to perverse and corrupt ends. The instinct for nurturance can be twisted into binging or anorexia (which actually denies instinct for an obsessive involvement with spirit); sexuality can be twisted into perversions by the complexes formed in childhood; activity can wither or become exaggerated, and so can reflection; and creativity can run amok in Dionysian dismemberments or cancerous inflations. Or the instincts can become so occluded and blocked off that almost nothing passes through from this level of the unconscious to ego-consciousness, at least in some of the instinct areas. Thus, we find a person with no creativity, or no sexuality, or very low levels of activity or reflection or nurturance. And it is not that one of these areas is capturing all of the libido; rather, the complexes are absorbing and thwarting the impulses, and the ego is more or less bereft of energy or motivation in any direction whatsoever. This is the problematic situation the therapist often faces in neurotic chronic depression.

These various clinical pictures are the result of personal developments that have created a fragmentary ego, considerable blockages between ego-consciousness and the unconscious through the accumulation of complexes, and pathological one-sidedness in the ego's attitude. Such developments also foster and promote defenses like splitting, projection, and repression. They interfere with the way the unconscious would otherwise normally influence the ego and provide it with life-giving, healing energies from the natural instinctive/archetypal psyche. The normal and optimal function of the unconscious is to compensate the ego and to orient it thereby in the direction of psychic equilibrium and balance, but this is thwarted by faulty ego development and the formation of complexes. This is what needs to be rectified by analytic treatment. At the heart of treatment lies the analysis (ana-lysis = dismemberment) of the complexes and the synthesis of an ego attitude that can support what Jung called the transcendent function, the bridge between ego-consciousness and the deeper layers of the unconscious.

Ego and Self in Analysis

The ego is, of course, the primary object of all practical therapeutic and analytic endeavors. It is to the ego that we must answer, for it is the ego that defines a person's consciousness and is the felt center of a life. It would be foolish to attempt the healing of the psyche without healing the ego: The procedure might succeed, but the patient would not know the difference!

And yet we also know that the ego is but a partial aspect of the whole psyche. The whole, of which the ego is a part, consists of the self in its totality of polarities, the most essential of which is the spectrum that stretches between the instinctual-somatic and the archetypal-spiritual extremes. This mind-body totality is what Jung conceived of as the self. The self is the God principle, as it were, and the ego is the human reality principle.

The ego is defined as a complex that constitutes a focal center for consciousness. Like all other complexes, the ego has an archetypal core, and in the case of the ego, this archetypal core is very special. It is the self. This sets the ego apart from the other complexes. The ego's consciousness is privileged within the psychic universe because of its unique link to the self.

Being a complex, however, means that the ego is also deeply constituted by trauma. In fact, Jung theorizes that the ego comes into being through the "collisions" that inevitably take place between an individual and the world. He was familiar with Otto

Rank's notion of the centrality of the birth trauma for ego development, and while he did not give this early experience quite the weight that Rank did, he would concede that traumata suffered at birth have a fundamental constituting force in ego formation. The ego is born in and through pain, and at its heart lies anxiety. The "reality principle" (by which the ego is supposed to operate according to Freud) in fact amounts to little more than an anxiety principle, but this is (for Jung, too) constitutive of the ego.

Like all complexes, the ego is made up of a variety of associated contents clustered around a bipolar core, and as such, it is subject to fragmentation and to splitting processes that can easily break it apart into states of dissociation. In a sense, modern depth psychology begins with the study of ego dissociation. Mesmer and his followers employed "artificial somnambulism," or hypnosis, to create special altered states of consciousness and to induce intense rapport between "magnetizer" and subject.[10] What these early practitioners of depth therapy had stumbled upon was the phenomenon of ego dissociation through hypnosis. Hypnotism became what Ellenberger has termed a "royal road to the unknown mind,"[11] because it opened a way through the normally defended rational ego into uncharted territory. From Mesmer the trail leads to Janet, who explored the phenomena of dissociation in great detail at the Salpetriere and is often credited as the founder of modern dynamic psychiatry (Ellenberger, 1970, p. 331).[12] Jung, like Freud and Adler, studied Janet's methods and employed some of his techniques and theories in his early work.

The existence of variety in ego states fascinated Jung from early on. His doctoral dissertation was the study of a medium (who was, in fact, his cousin Helene Preiswerk) who had an amazing ability to acquire personalities, during seances, that had vivid historical characteristics, about which she consciously knew nothing. These

---

[10] H. Ellenberger, *The Discovery of the Unconscious*, pp. 112ff.
[11] Ibid.
[12] Ibid., p. 331.

states of possession by foreign psychic bodies (complexes and archetypal images), as Jung found in his later investigations with psychotic patients at the Burgholzli Clinic in Zurich, can be transitory or relatively long-lasting. One goal of therapeutic analysis is to become aware of these various states of dissociation and part-personalities and to knit them together into a state of relative cohesiveness, so that an umbrella of consciousness can surround the parts and hold them together. This is different from merging them into a hybrid. Jungians speak of containing the opposites within consciousness, of maintaining the tensions inherent in the interplay and dynamics between the various pieces of the psyche and not allowing them to fall into dissociation.

As the virtual center of consciousness, the ego is responsible for playing the role of container of these polarities and splinters of consciousness within the larger psyche, as well as having the adaptational role of responding to changing environments. At its archetypal core (i.e., the self), the ego complex first comes into being even before the physical birth of the infant. This virtual center of incipient consciousness is in place and functioning already in utero, as the fetus orients itself to its environment and begins to sense the world. The self, which is the central organizing archetype of the psyche as a whole, imparts to the ego this same quality of centrality as the organism emerges into the world and gains more consciousness.

The deep connection to the self at the ego's core makes it a paradoxical psychic object. On the one hand, it is the seat of anxiety and pain, receiving its personal birth and awakening through trauma. On the other hand, it is divine and godlike because of its identity as the self. The ego is the place where time and eternity meet most intimately and crucially. The ego is at once the incarnation of the self in the time-space continuum and the fragile resister of existential anxiety.

Clustered around this central bipolar core at the heart of the ego are associations that make up a person's remembered history and personal identity. Experiences of self with mother, with father, and with other significant figures in the surrounding world are introjected and woven into the fabric of consciousness and ego identity. These can be supportive and life-enhancing associations, or they can be debilitating and toxic ones. Analysis attempts to separate the ego from the pathological associations trapped into the structure of the ego complex and to recover and support the beneficent ones.

Being a complex, however, also signifies that the ego is of only relative size and importance in the psyche's universe, not its center and not even a major body. As the putative center of consciousness, it easily succumbs to the illusion that it is the center of the whole psychological universe and has control over the other splinter psyches. This state of inflation, which is based on too close an identification between the individual ego and the archetypal self can lead to psychic symptoms, dangerous overestimation of self-mastery and control, and illusions of grandiosity vis-a-vis the world at large. While inflation of this sort is normal in early childhood, such a state of fusion of ego and self, if it continues too long, lays the groundwork for narcissistic personality disorders. This development is seen today as being caused by inadequate relations with a primary caretaker (the "mother"); the child is abandoned (emotionally if not physically) and so compensates for the absence of the suitably mirroring "other" by clinging to an archetypal structure that replaces the person. A lack of sufficient differentiation between ego and self on the internal level is then projected into the world, where the narcissistic individual assumes an unreal and usually very fragile position of centrality and entitlement. The ego must learn through hard experience and much analysis that it is not the master of the psychic household and that it is subject to fluctuations in the psychic economy. This hard-won knowledge is the sought-for outcome of analysis.

The ego that has not disentangled itself sufficiently from the self can behave like the executive of an organization who fails to realize that he needs the cooperation of even the humblest workers in order to function well. This ego takes too much credit for the success of the organization and usually tries to avoid blame if the organization fails. The workers, on the other hand, also need the executive; if sane executive decisions and judgments are made, all may survive and prosper. This perception of interrelatedness among the parts of the intrapsychic world is where the ego needs to arrive in its awareness in order for sanity and optimal functioning to become possible. It is a position of humility and large responsibility rather than the glorification expected by an inflated ego.

If, because of its deep internal association with the self, the ego has a tendency to assume centrality in the world and to fall into grandiose illusions of specialness and importance, it can also suffer the opposite problem if the connection between ego and self is too tenuous and distant. Then the ego feels abandoned and unmoored in a frightening world of impersonal forces. It feels inadequate and suffers from low self-confidence and high self-doubt.

The proper balance in this relation between ego and self is discussed in Jungian literature under the heading of the ego-self axis. If the ego-self axis is sufficiently and properly developed, a person has the feeling of possessing a solid core of inner strength, identity, and value and has access to resources for self-esteem and confidence, but the ego is not puffed up and unrealistically inflated.

The ego develops, according to Jung, through suffering collisions with the environment. These collisions, if they are not too severe and injurious, bring challenges rather than debilitating traumas. If the ego responds positively to the challenges posed by the environment, it develops strength and mastery and begins to show increasing autonomy. It gains self-confidence and adapts more and more effectively and forcefully to the world around. For this reason, some analysts will, after having established a sound working relationship with an analysand whose ego is relatively sound and healthy, deliberately create tension in the relationship in order to facilitate ego strengthening. Some will "rotate typology," that is, assume the opposite typology from the analysand, in order to challenge the ego. Or they will play devil's advocate or make demands for adaptation that they assume the analysand can reach.

This technique is, of course, not suitable for every case; with more fragile and disturbed egos, which may fall easily into mistrust or paranoia. For this technique empathy is needed in large and steady quantities.

If the ego is severely damaged or overcome by the collisions with the environment, the traumata result in the development of split-off complexes. The traumatic event may become largely repressed because of the psychic pain involved, but the wound will leave a point of fragility in the ego where it can easily fragment and become defensive. These points of vulnerability are carefully noted in analysis, appearing typically in transference reactions and often in dreams. Interpretation and supportive insight into their origins and functioning are the usual means of treatment in Jungian analysis.

The complexes of the personal unconscious are organized around a discrete number of archetypal cores, for example, images of archetypal Great Mother and Father. These can be identified over time as they make their appearance in the transference and through reflection on life situations as they arise in the course of analysis. The simple rule of projection is that what is unconscious can be projected, and the parental projections typically land on the analyst. When this happens, the analyst accepts it as an opportunity to allow the analysand to rework a relationship with parental complexes that has long since been in place and has controlled many of the ego's choices and decisions. Since complexes are distinguished by a high degree of affectivity and volatility, this work with transference is usually fraught with great emotional intensity. The analyst also can become "infected" (Jung's term) with the transferential material and can actually assume the feelings and roles projected onto him or her by the complex (see Stein, 1992a). In analysis this is much more easily observed than controlled. What it does is give the analyst a firsthand experience of the intrapsychic conflicts suffered by the analysand, and this can be extremely useful for empathic interpretation of the analysand's struggles.

No experienced analyst labors under the illusion that complexes can be eliminated or mastered. They can be worked on and to some degree "worked through," but they are like the old bulls of the bull ring: tough, experienced, and unlikely to give in to the matador under any circumstance. They function independently of the ego and will continue to do so even after many years of intense focused analysis. But knowledge about the complexes, how they work, and what stimulates them can extend the ego's range of options so that a person knows how to stay away from likely sources of complex stimulation and learns or masters certain techniques for calming down after the inevitable complex discharge. Through analysis some of the energy is drained from the complexes, too, and can be used for ego purposes. Learning about how one's personal complexes function is a part of the educational process that analysis engenders and is considered an important aspect of analysis by most Jungians.

In its history of interacting with the environment, the ego employs and develops certain characteristic features and manners of coping and self-protection. Some tools are at its disposal innately and are provided by nature. The ego inherits a specific "typology," that is, a characteristic tendency to assume one of two attitudes (introversion or extroversion) and one of two main functions (thinking or feeling, sensation or intuition). As this innate combination of attitude and function(s) matures in the course of development, it produces a typical cognitive style. There are introverted intuitive thinking types (the philosophers among us), and there are extroverted sensate thinking types (the managers); extroverted or introverted intuitive feeling types (the therapists and artists); and extroverted sensate feeling types (the designers and decorators). Typology forms an aspect of the personality's character structure that helps the ego cope with the environment and with the collisions that take place between itself and the surrounding world. Of course, this typology can also distort a person's reading of the environment and can, like projection, get in the way of adequate ego functioning and adaptation to the demands of life.

Ordinarily a person's typology will unfold quite naturally if supported and encouraged by parents and schools. If not, a "cross-type" development can take place, which occurs when the natural typology is not accepted, and the individual tries to adapt to social pressures and expectations by assuming another typology more in keeping with collective norms and expectations. This may lay the groundwork for psychological problems later in life.

Some Jungian analysts make extensive use of typology theory in their analytic work. One initial goal of therapy is typically to restore a person to natural, innate typological functioning if this has become distorted during development. In an extroverted society, for example, introverts need permission to be themselves as introverts. The depathologizing of certain typologies has a powerful therapeutic effect and goes a long way toward allowing an ego to find its own natural way of containing psyche, handling reality, and dealing with the environment. This job of ego restoration usually requires the dismantling of the parental complexes that maintain the twists in typology.

In addition to attitude and functions, the ego possesses defenses to help it cope with the world and with relationships. Typology is not seen by Jung as defensive in and of itself, but as a functioning of psychic wholeness. The movement toward wholeness would seem to demand as a first condition the overcoming of defenses that prevent integration from taking place. Some recent work by Jungian analysts has focused somewhat more extensively on the question of analyzing defences (H. Dieckmann, M. Fordham, N. Schwartz-Salant, J. Van Eenwyk).

This is especially crucial in the therapeutic analysis of neurotic conditions. In neurosis, the one-sidedness of the conscious attitude is so entrenched and the repressions so tightly wired into the structures that have developed historically that the deeper unconscious activities of symbol formation and instinctual percept creation are severely blocked. The evolutionary movement toward wholeness is stunted to the point of psychic invalidism. The symptoms, which are symbolic cries for help and indicators of what is needed, are compromise formations that cannot effect actual change or have significant influence on ego-consciousness even while they speak. Here the skill and technique of the analyst in interpreting defenses are necessary and can be beneficial.

By hearing the soul's cry for help and taking a stand on the side of the wounded and distorted individuation drive, the therapist can also aid and abet the deeper unconscious processes that are striving for health and wholeness. What Jung refers to as "soul" (the anima and animus in his writings) is a level of psyche that forms a link between ego-consciousness and the instinctual-archetypal, natural psyche, which ultimately is also the link between the ego and the self (Stein, 1992b). The anima/ animus structure is a "function" that corresponds to what Jung elsewhere calls the transcendent function, and its purpose is to provide a channel of communication between the ego and the deepest levels of the collective unconscious. It is also roughly equivalent to the ego-self axis if one imagines the axis as a function. To advance this cause of establishing a vital contact with the soul, almost any technique that does the job is good technique. In analytic practice, the usual Jungian move in trying to facilitate this recovery of the soul connection is to work intensively on dreams and to engage in active imagination.

Dream Analysis and Active Imagination

Dreams and fantasies are classic subverters of collective orthodoxy. They are also subverters of hardened and entrenched neurotic structure. Many dreams bypass the blockages created by the complexes and reach to the layer of soul, of anima and animus in Jung's terminology, which is the connecting link to the depths of the instinctual/archetypal psyche. It is not surprising that collective orthodoxies of all kinds seek to discount the value that might be placed on these products of unconscious process, nor is it surprising that neurotic analysands will resist bringing dreams into analysis or giving them much credence when they do. This is the resistance to soul.

The Jungian approach to analysis of the unconscious and to therapy of ego-consciousness is oriented largely by working with dreams and inner images and taking cues from them as to what kinds of intervention would be useful on the analyst's part. Dream analysis was and remains the cornerstone of classical and also of much neoclassical or post-Jungian analysis.

Dreams require interpretation and a method for rendering their often-puzzling themes and images psychologically useful in analysis. Jung's hermeneutic for dream interpretation is basically twofold: reductive and synthetic. If the clinical picture and the dream themes point to the need to interpret dreams reductively, that is, in terms of the past and especially of childhood and pathological developmental issues, then the analyst takes this approach. This is particularly recommended for character disorders and conditions implying ego inflation. Where the clinical picture and the dreams point toward the need for a prospective, synthetic approach, the analyst will interpret in terms of future possibilities, untapped potentialities, and larger symbolic meanings. This is usually recommended for cases of depression and chronic low self-esteem and feelings of victimization. Striking the balance between these two approaches, which are typically both used at one point or another in most lengthy analyses, is a clinical art. Timing and appropriateness depend greatly on the analyst's trained intuition and the accuracy of empathic knowledge of the analysand's inner states.

In a departure from Freud's theory of interpretation, Jung did not place much value on free association as a means for discovering the meaning of dreams. Free association, he felt, does not break free of the controlling complexes and the dominant ego attitude. It goes in a circle of the already more or less known. For Jung, the dream is not meaningful until it is brought to the point of telling the dreamer something new. If you can think the thought, he felt, you do not need to dream it. So, the interpretive strategy is to stay with the dream images as presented until they begin to reveal ideas, insights, patterns, or feeling states that are not already familiar to the ego. At that point, the ego can begin to benefit from the compensatory function of dreaming and can open a pathway to the deeper healing influences of the natural psyche, the instinctual and archetypal layers. The dream then begins to function as a pathway to the soul of the analysand.

A second method besides dream interpretation for reaching past the personal complexes and ego defenses into the deeper layers of the psyche was discovered by Jung in his use of active imagination. In active imagination, the analysand (in private, not in the analytic session) opens a dialogue with figures of the unconscious as they have appeared either in earlier dreams or in the active imagination itself. These imaginal figures do not represent the personal complexes—for example, mother and father—but rather figures of the archetypal, collective unconscious. Figures in active imagination function much like icons on a computer screen, opening the way to programs locked deeply away in the hidden layers of the unconscious. By stimulating these iconic images, the ego is exposed to a stream of messages and information from sources of energy and insight in the unconscious that lie beyond the individual's neurotic patterns, acquired complexes, and conventional ego attitudes.

Active imagination was classically a technique invoked in analysis to help resolve intransigent transferences. It does this by replacing an outer icon (i.e., the analyst) with an inner one. As an analytic technique, active imagination may be used throughout treatment or become more emphasized toward the end of analysis as a way of preparing for termination.

Practice follows vision and theory in Jung's psychology, but practice also feeds theory and keeps it growing and evolving. The Jungian vision is a continuously expanding one. What Jung himself lays down is a powerful and compelling view of the wondrous complexity and nuanced subtlety of the human psyche. Based in two polarities, the body and the spirit, it receives material and energy from both ends of this spectrum. The human being is both an animal and a spiritual agent. Jung's theory of the psyche therefore spans the heights and depths of human experience and accounts for the similarities and differences we find among human beings throughout recorded history. The rich territory where instincts and archetypes meet is the psyche, a vast and nearly inexhaustible wonderland of figures and energies.

Jung's is also a theory that allows for human evolution and emergence. Neither the individual nor the race is a static, "given" entity but rather an evolving process in motion. The final goal is unknown and can only be surmised on the basis of what is known about the basic structures of the psyche as we can come to understand them. What Jung concluded is that there is in the individual an implacable drive toward wholeness.

Pathology is caused by a departure from this basic ground plan. In its milder forms, it amounts to simple one-sidedness that needs correction. In its more virulent forms, it presents obstacles to living a full existence that need serious, sustained analytic treatment. Even in such cases, however, assistance is usually from nature itself, for healing has its deepest source in nature rather than in the healing ministrations of therapists.

For Jung, the fundamental human struggle is to become oneself as fully and completely as possible. What this means is living the basic plan of the psyche, which is written into the fabric of nature itself. This is not without many inherent conflicts that produce necessary suffering (as opposed to neurotic suffering) and severe limitation. The narrative that unfolds from this struggle is the story of individuation, a story of limitation but also of the realization of potentials that lie hidden in the depths of the unconscious from the beginning, awaiting the quickening summons of auspiciously timed constellating life events.

C.G. Jung as Writer in Dialogue[1]

Jung, the Writer

There exist numerous images of Carl Gustav Jung: scientist, physician, prophet, mystic, artist. Each one lures somebody to claim its centrality. None of them is definitive or exhaustive of his reality. The whole man always proves to be greater than the sum of his parts. And yet each of the pieces is needed to complete the full portrait.

I wonder if we have paid enough attention to Jung the writer. To me, it seems this prominent feature of his life has been neglected or overlooked in many of the studies now available on his life and work. In Jung's active life as an adult, beginning in his early 20s and continuing to his death at the age of 86, the importance of writing and publishing can hardly be exaggerated. He published enough individual works in the form of books, articles, forewords, and prefaces to fill 18 volumes in the assembled *Collected Works*, and this does not include his truly masterful autobiography, *Memories, Dreams, Reflections* (written with Aniela Jaffé), or the five big volumes of now published letters (not to mention the many still unpublished letters). While he was not a professional writer like

---

[1] Originally published as "The Role of Victor White in Jung's Writings" by The Guild of Pastoral Psychology, Guild Lecture No. 285, 2005. Somewhat modified for this edition.

Thomas Mann, he was keen with publishing contracts and made sure his rights and royalties were up to par.

As a writer, Jung was not perhaps a great stylist, because for him content was paramount and always more important than the niceties of phrasing. Often, he wrote in a hurry under pressure of deadlines and many other professional duties. From what I have seen of his manuscripts, he did not make many corrections in the original drafts. His writing was meant primarily to communicate ideas, many of them new and bold. He was not always subtle and nuanced, but certainly he could be when he took the time. Unlike Freud, he was not inclined to play the novelist nor was he gifted in that kind of writing. But rhetoric certainly did play an important part in his work, and he could be eloquent. Often, he was inspired as a writer, as an idea would take hold of him and give him words to infect others with the same spirit. Some said he was charismatic as a lecturer. I believe he was. He could have been a great preacher. And I daresay he produced as many good and memorable one-liners as almost any other 20th-century writer. He was a master of the pithy sentence, such as: "We must recognize that nothing is more difficult to bear than oneself"[2]; "Concepts are coined and negotiable values; images are life"[3]; "God can be loved but must be feared."[4] Today one often sees short quotations from his works on social media platforms, and always they are provocative and arresting. In reading and rereading his work, I have often underlined sentences and long passages and have stopped to marvel at the profound penetration of a phrase, or to listen to the spiritually uplifting song in a line of his prose. His writing can be tediously argumentative and laden with cryptic references, but rarely is it boring for long. Typically, a mass of amplifications and convoluted thoughts will come to a sudden climax in a stunning sentence that forces the reader to ponder a subject from a completely new angle. Jung wrote

---

[2] C.G. Jung, *Two Essays in Analytical Psychology*, CW 7, para. 273.
[3] C.G. Jung, *Mysterium Coniunctionis*, CW 14, para. 226.
[4] C.G. Jung, *Answer to Job*, CW 11, para. 732.

from a deep place in himself, and rarely is he superficial or mundane.

Writing was a central creative activity in Jung's life. This is a given, a "fact" to use one of his favorite words. Writing is where he put much of his most productive energy. But writing was not only a creative outlet for this gifted man. It had to do with his personal individuation process and with his relationships to specific people and to the broad cultural world of his day. The publication of his writing was as important as the act of writing because Jung did not write primarily for himself (except in his journal and the now famous Red Book), but for an audience. The immediate context which his writings addressed should be kept in mind. Jung is speaking to someone in particular in many of his works. The critical role of personal relationships in his written oeuvre has been largely overlooked.

In *Memories, Dreams, Reflections*, where he provides a great amount of detailed information about how his writings came about, he mentions almost no names except for Freud and his father. One gets the impression of almost hermetically sealed off and profoundly introverted creative acts. Actually, this turns out to be not altogether true. Jung needed and enjoyed audiences, such as the gatherings at the Eranos conferences. He also was greatly stimulated by individuals, and these relationships engendered some of his most important writings. He was a writer in dialogue.

Two Relationships of Importance

I want to consider how writing a book and publishing it grew out of and affected two of Jung's important relationships, the famous one with Freud and the less well-known one with Father Victor White. The parallels are quite remarkable. Out of both relationships a large correspondence grew, enough to fill a thick volume with often long and thoughtful letters. In both instances, Jung formed a close and complex relationship with the other man after the other had read one or more of his published works. In the case of Freud, the book was *Über die Psychologie der Dementia Praecox: Ein Versuch*, which was translated into English as *The Psychology of Dementia Praecox*. White had read quite a number of Jung's writings that were available in German and English before the early 1940s, when the outbreak of World War II isolated Switzerland from the rest of the world. Finally, and most importantly, the relationships and the correspondences culminated in the publication of a book by Jung that proved to be a breaking point.

The break with Freud came immediately after the founder of psychoanalysis read the Second Part of *Wandlungen und Symbole der Libido* in the *Jahrbuch* (edited by Jung) in 1912 (the complete work was translated as *Psychology of the Unconscious* in 1916 and later revised and published in the *Collected Works*, Vol. 5, *Symbols of Transformation*.) This book was decisive in what had already become a shaky relationship and for many reasons. In it, Jung challenged several central tenets of psychoanalytic theory, among them Freud's interpretation of the incest wish and his sexual theory of psychic energy. With Victor White, it was the publication of *Answer to Job* that proved disruptive. At first, it seemed to create no more than a ripple, but later when it was translated into English and began to be read by White's fellow Roman Catholics, the effect surged into a tidal wave. Here one major issue was their difference regarding the problem of evil, but beyond that, as was true also in the relationship with Freud, the book revealed fundamental differences between the men in philosophical grounding and worldview.

For Jung, these writings represented a kind of climax of the relationship, in that differences became openly and decisively clarified. Writing was Jung's way of conducting an *Auseinander-setzung* (an essentially untranslatable word meaning roughly, "a differentiating encounter" or "dialogue") with a partner. Publishing a book in this manner, however, also had the effect of throwing down a gauntlet. The relationships, which stimulated his thinking and creativity to an almost feverish pitch, fed directly into his writing and publishing, and what he wrote played a key role in ending them, although this was not his conscious intention.

With Freud, Jung was from the outset in the role of the younger student, a beginner in the art and science of psycho-analysis. Freud received a strong idealizing father transference from Jung, which complicated their relationship, especially around the issue of Freud's authority and his need for control over psycho-analytic doctrine. Jung proved himself to be a rebellious son, seeking his own path in life and needing to affirm his own creativity. He demanded space for autonomy and freedom in his thinking, and he refused to knuckle under to what he perceived to be Freud's anxious need for control. *Wandlungen* represented his declaration of independence. The split, which became formalized in 1913, proved to be irreconcilable.

With White, Jung held the opposite position, namely that of teacher and older authority figure. He was celebrating his 70th birthday when he received the first item of correspondence from the younger English Dominican priest (b. 1902) living in Oxford. It was August 1945, just after the end of the Second World War. White was well established in his career as theologian and teacher when he first contacted Jung to wish him a happy birthday, but in psychology he was far less advanced and easily accepted Jung's superior wisdom and guidance in this area. The idealizing father transference now ran in the other direction, with Jung as the recipient. Jung responded with an equally positive counter-transference, embracing White enthusiastically from the beginning: "You are to me a white raven inasmuch as you are the only theologian I know of who has really understood something of what the problem of psychology in our present world means."[5] Jung saw in White an ideal conversation partner for deepening his long-standing dialogue with Christian theology and history. He often complained that local Protestant ministers and theologians showed no interest in his work. White's keen interest in psychology and his

---

[5] A. Lammers and A. Cunningham (eds.), *The Jung-White Letters*, p. 6.

reading knowledge of Jung's ideas would facilitate a genuine intellectual engagement, Jung thought.

White's agenda from the beginning and clearly laid out in his writings was to build a bridge between theology and psychology. This project was modeled on the Thomistic idea of theology finding a handmaiden in human scientific knowledge (for Aquinas that was the philosophy of Aristotle, for White it would be the analytical psychology of Jung). In contemporary times, White hoped, theology and a human science (i.e., psychology) would be able to meet and manage a rich cross-fertilization, and from his point of view the chief beneficiary would be theology. Theology, in his view, needed some updating to come into the 20th century.

For Jung, the agenda at the outset could have been stated in quite similar terms. He also thought that Christian theology was badly in need of further development, particularly in the areas of its teachings on evil and "the feminine." But he was quite conscious that as a "modern person" his worldview was shaped fundamentally by psychology, whereas the classical Christian theologian, who is bound to continue making metaphysical assertions and who typically clings to a faith in unproven doctrines based on revelation, belonged to another historical era, the Middle Ages. Jung regarded theologians as premodern. As he saw it, the dialogue between himself as a psychologist and a theologian was bound to be an exchange between a contemporary person and an anachronism. But in White's case, Jung foresaw a possible chance to influence the other. At any rate, he was willing to give it a try.

Among Jung's most thoughtful letters are those he wrote to White. In them, he carried on the dialogue that began between them during the weeks spent together at Jung's tower in Bollingen. Many of them addressed theological matters, and especially they circled around the issue of "evil" and what Jung found to be the quite irritating doctrine of evil as "*privatio boni*" ("the absence of good"). Try as they might, the two men could never quite get past their contrary view on this doctrine. For Jung, a religious teaching could not be valid unless it was backed by evidence showing that it was archetypal (this was a fundamental rule laid down by psychology). If it met this criterion, he would consider its psychological merits on the same level as other archetypal images (i.e., mythologems). For *privatio boni*, however, he could find no evidence of archetypal backing.[6] It falls much more into the psychological category of rationalization. As a psychologist, Jung considered it nothing but a dodge from accepting the responsibility for immoral behavior.[7] It amounts to a type of denial, a familiar ego defense mechanism. Evil is not the absence of anything, Jung argues, but the active and indeed often dramatically impressive *presence* of something quite psychologically substantial in its own right, such as an impulse or an instinct.

At the level of medieval psychology, evil would be personified and named the Devil. In modern times, however, evil is a moral judgment that we apply to certain types of behavior and attitude, and this judgment is based upon current ethical understanding and consciousness. Immoral behavior and attitude (i.e., evil) are rooted in psychological reality, for example, in envy. To say that envy is merely the absence (*privatio*) of gratitude misses the psychological factor because it glosses over the reality of envy as a force in its own right. For Jung, making moral judgments was an essential human duty, as context-bound and relative as this might be in particular cases. Much depends on which side of a conflict one is standing! But to avoid making the judgment altogether would be tantamount to reneging on ethical responsibility.

While Jung could find no archetypal backing for the notion of evil as *privatio boni*, he certainly could find plenty of it for evil itself in the many mythologems that tell of devils, demons, and sundry other evil characters. Evil should therefore be considered a real force in the world and in the human soul and not be written off as a mere absence of its opposite. Evil actively opposes the good, and the two principles are locked in an eternal struggle for the upper hand. If

---

[6] C.G. Jung, "Foreword to White's God and the Unconscious, CW 11, para. 459.
[7] Ibid., para. 457.

they were to be united in a single God figure, moreover, this monotheism would need to conceive of God as combining both good and evil in one Being. White, steeped in classical philosophy and Thomistic theology and deeply influenced by Roman Catholic doctrine, could not accompany Jung down this path. And in his rational mind, he saw no particular need to do so.

He thought he could use the basic tenets and findings of analytical psychology in a way that met his own need for a constructive dialogue partner for theology without compromising a keystone of Christian theology, namely the doctrine that God is light and in Him there is no darkness.

This was the grain of sand in the relationship between the two men that yielded what some people judge to be the greatest pearl-of-wisdom literature Jung ever produced, *Answer to Job*. One may well argue that the writing of *Answer to Job* is a product of the Jung-White relationship. White was the catalyst for this incandescent piece of writing, just as Freud was the stimulus for Jung's earlier works, *Wandlungen und Symbole der Libido* (*The Psychology of the Unconscious* in the English translation) and *Psychological Types*.

As a piece of writing, *Answer to Job* occupies a unique place in Jung's published oeuvre. Typically in his written work, Jung assumes the persona of the empirical scientist or the medical doctor. These were his professional calling cards. He held a degree in medicine from the University of Basel and was trained as a psychiatrist and scientific researcher by Eugen Bleuler at the Burghölzli Klinik in Zurich. These were top-drawer professional credentials. But Jung the writer can often be seen bursting at the seams of this tightly woven professional fabric, and frequently he could not keep his passion and enthusiasms confined within such narrow limits. In much of his writing, one can sense both the firm intellectual commitment to scientific method and the barely checked sounds of another kind of writer, a poet or a preacher. This comes strongly to the fore in his letters.

In *Answer to Job*, these stirrings in the background took the first chair. In tone, this work is closer to the letters, personal and human. The authorial voice is not dominated by the professional persona, although that remains, albeit tempered in the background. We know that he wrote this work in a short period of time and while recovering from an illness.[8] In a letter to Henry Corbin, dated May 4, 1953, he writes (in response to Corbin's comments on *Answer to Job*): "You say you read my book as an 'oratorio.' The book 'came to me' during the fever of an illness. It was as if accompanied by the great music of a Bach or a Handel. I don't belong to the auditory type. So I did not hear anything, I just had the feeling of listening to a great composition, or rather of being at a concert."[9] The work had been writing itself in Jung's unconscious for quite some time, and its birth into written language was fast and furious. In it, Jung allowed himself the freedom to express his thoughts and feelings boldly. He is by turns angry, intemperate, aggressive, didactic, and prophetic. As a sort of biblical scholar, his persona in *Answer to Job* picks up on his father's unfulfilled vocation as a specialist in Old Testament languages and literature. In *Memories, Dreams, Reflections*, Jung recounts a dream in which he hears his father interpreting the Bible with great intensity ("his mind was flooded with profound ideas"[10]) and links this directly to the composition of *Answer to Job*. At the beginning of *Answer to Job*, Jung explains:

I shall not give a cool and carefully considered exegesis that tries to be fair to every detail, but a purely subjective reaction. In this way I hope to act as a voice for many who feel the same way as I do, and to give expression to the shattering emotion which the unvarnished spectacle of divine savagery and ruthlessness produces in us.... I shall express my affect fearlessly and ruthlessly in what follows, and I shall answer injustice with injustice, that I may learn to know why and to what purpose Job was wounded, and

---

[8] See G. Wehr, *Jung: A Biography*, pp. 382ff.
[9] G. Adler (ed.). *C.G. Jung. Letters*, vol. 2, p. 116.
[10] C.G. Jung, *Memories, Dreams, Reflections*, p. 218.

what consequences have grown out of this for Yahweh as well as for man.[11]

He then goes on to deliver this promise in full measure.

Much of what Jung wrote in *Answer to Job* he had said before in other published writings, also in his letters and in his many seminars. It is not so much the content that is new and unique as the style. Others have recounted the general background of the ideas in the work.[12] It is important to recall that as a youth Jung had read Goethe's *Faust* and had been indelibly impressed by it. *Faust* and The Book of Job share a similar frame story and are based on the same premise: God and Satan/Mephistopheles make a bargain, by which God allows the Evildoer to test and to have his way with a chosen human being but only up to a point; the Almighty then intervenes and rescues the object of this experiment in virtue. Jung's book, *Answer to Job,* might be considered a further contribution to this genre, now delivered on the psychological and not on the mythological/theological or literary/poetic plane.

More to the point, however, is that *Answer to Job* is Jung's answer to Victor White and to the tradition in which Father White stood and with which he was identified. The discussions with White, which are partially recorded in the correspondence, constituted the decisive stimulus that provoked Jung's creative outburst. He was in dialogue.

---

[11] C.G. Jung, *Answer to Job*, paras. 561-63.
[12] See P. Bishop, *Jung's Answer to Job* for a detailed scholarly account of the background.

Of Texts and Contexts[1]

In November 1932, the city of Zurich surprisingly awarded Jung its Literature Prize.[2] About this he joked in a letter to a friend: "There are great news happening here. Last week I got the 'Literaturepreis der Stadt Zurich,' which means that I'm no longer a prophet in my own country. A sad end to a hopeful young prophet's career. It is always sad when one loses a perfectly good reason for grumbling."[3] The *Neue Zürcher Zeitung*, the city's leading newspaper, reported on the award, commenting that it was unprecedented to give this literary prize to someone who was not identified as primarily *Belletristik*, but also defending the award on the grounds that Jung's writings had had great influence on important literary figures like Hermann Hesse. The *NZZ* article went on to mention Jung's recent review of James Joyce's *Ulysses* in its own pages, saying: "The uninhibited way with which he imbues a work like *Ulysses* by Joyce with importance and value is so stimulating and fresh that we are

---

[1] Originally published in *The Journal of Analytical Psychology* 52:3, 2007. Here somewhat revised.

[2] On the occasion, Jung gave a talk titled "Über Psychologie," which was published in May 1933 in *Neue Schweizer Rundshau*. Later he expanded and revised it as "Die Bedeutung der Psychologie für die Gegenwart" (1934), translated as "The Meaning of Psychology for Modern Man," *CW* vol. 10.

[3] G. Adler, *C.G. Jung Letters* I, p. 109.

forced to admire such critical prowess and fructifying energy even if its judgment misses the mark."[4]

Although Jung did receive this Literary Prize from the city of Zurich, he did not get it for his own literary accomplishments. Jung has not been widely regarded as an accomplished stylist in the German language. His books tend to be heavy. Quotations are too many and too long, and frequently in antique languages. For Jung, content was paramount and counted for more than a nice literary style. He was not a fussy writer; if anything, his style was rather a bit rough and ready. This preference for content over style partly explains the remarkable ease with which he wrote in foreign languages, like English and French. Subtle nuances and niceties of expression—the music of language—did not preoccupy him a great deal. From his letters, it is evident that he wrote mostly in a hurry and under severe time pressure, with many other professional duties clamoring for attention (this is especially vivid in his correspondence with Freud). He intended his published writings primarily to communicate ideas, many of them fresh and audacious, and there was a sense of urgency to get them out to the public in a timely fashion. Often, he wrote against deadlines. While his writing is not generally deemed elegant, it is almost invariably surprising and unique. And rhetoric occupies a place there, too. He could be eloquent. There are many moving sentences and passages in his work. Often his writing seems inspired, as an idea takes hold and words flow forth that can impregnate readers with new insights. As the *NZZ* writer said, his writing has "prowess" and "energy."

Some people said he was charismatic as a lecturer. In an earlier age or a different cultural context, he could have been a brilliant preacher, like his grandfather Preiswerk, who held forth from the big Cathedral pulpit in Basel. And he produced many memorable and pithy one-liners: "We must recognize that nothing is more difficult to bear than oneself"[5]; "Concepts are coined and negotiable

---

[4] NZZ, 27 Nov. 1932, my translation.
[5] C.G. Jung, *Two Essays on Analytical Psychology*, CW 7, para. 373.

values; images are life"[6]; "God can be loved but must be feared."[7] In reading and rereading his work for many years, I have underlined countless sentences and passages and have often stopped to marvel at the profundity of a phrase, or to feel the spiritual lift in a line of his prose. His writing can induce tedium for a time but it is rarely boring for long. Typically, a tangled mass of amplifications and convoluted thoughts will resolve into a brilliant passage that is dazzlingly clear.

Writing was an essential creative activity in Jung's life, and through it, he established himself as an author and an authority. The English word "author" derives from the Latin *auctor*, meaning "enlarger, founder" and "one who causes to grow." An author is a writer who founds something, enlarges a field, and causes ideas to grow. Jung belongs to a very small company of modern thinkers who have created a body of published texts that founded a field and consistently caused modern consciousness to grow. Authors in this sense of the word are usually figures whose writings include much more than technical matters pertaining to an academic specialty (in Jung's case, this would be psychiatry); they cover as well social and culture criticism, and even, as in Jung's case, religious criticism and reflection. Freud, too, was such a figure. Authors get and hold onto authority. Their ideas and perspectives have force. Their writings inspire confidence and induce personal commitment. They change people. This is what makes authors, as distinct from ordinary writers, outstanding. For them, moreover, creating written work is nonnegotiable. Jung spoke of the force that compelled him to author his works as a *daimon*.

This, then, is what makes Jung an author. Through the medium of writing, he authored. His writing is not only expository, entertaining, or academic. Whether one likes it or not, agrees with him or not, practically everything Jung published bears the imprint of his forceful personality. It may be that he identified a little with

---

[6] C.G. Jung, *Mysterium Coniunctionis*, CW 14, para. 226.
[7] C.G. Jung, *Answer to Job*, CW 11, para. 732

his putative ancestor, Goethe, the archetypal author of German literature. Like Goethe's works, Jung's continue to be read and used long after his death. Their generative effects do not diminish with time. They do not become outdated. Today the field of analytical psychology is authorized by his published work, and these texts provide the authoritative charter for its enterprises. This is not said out of idealization. It is simply a fact.

It should not be misconstrued that writing was primarily a creative outlet for Jung, a kind of hobby carried on beside his other more urgent professional occupations. The publication of his work was critically important to him because in it he was creating something for the world. As an author, his work was not conceived primarily as a monument to himself. Nor did he write only to please himself (except perhaps in his journals and in the now-famous Red Book, where he took pains to script the texts and paint beautiful pictures). He wrote for an audience. At a rather early age, Jung already had a public in Europe and internationally. By his mid-30s, he was writing for more than the small circle of medical specialists and psychological researchers who used his ideas in their practices and academic studies. Many people outside the fields of medicine and psychology read his books and articles. When he published in popular journals, magazines, and newspapers—which he did quite frequently—he was addressing a very broad range of readers. Writing gave him a position in culture, a platform, a resounding voice that he could use to author further works. It also induced in him a sense of social responsibility and obligation. In the final analysis, his authoring, in all the variety of forms it took, stood in the service of a single overarching and impersonal cause: the growth of human consciousness. Authoring through writing was his way of paying back to society and humanity for what he had received and taken for his own individuation,[8] and his work was meant to benefit and

---

[8] In a lecture given to the Psychological Club in Zurich in October 1916, titled "Adaptation, Individuation, Collectivity," Jung speaks of this responsibility. The individuating person, he says, "must bring forth values which are an equivalent

to help others on their own individual paths. Jung's close friend Fowler McCormick told the following story at the Memorial Service held for Jung in New York on December 1, 1961:

> Two or three years ago, when Jung was attending an art exhibit in Zurich, a woman introduced herself to him and expressed her gratitude for what he had done for her. Dr. Jung asked her if this had come about through reading his books. Her reply was: "Those are not books. That is bread."[9]

She had grasped the point of Jung's authorship as a writer.

While Jung would not have placed himself in a literary Guild among professional writers like Thomas Mann, for instance, his neighbor in Küsnacht for a time and then across Lake Zurich in Kilchberg, he was nevertheless busy with producing written texts for most of his adult life. Most of these were not about medical subjects per se, although he would always identify himself as a medical man. Medicine was his official Guild. He did bother, however, with publishers and contracts from early on in his career and took pains to make sure his rights and royalties were up to par. In this sense, he was also a professional writer. His work sold well, and publishers were eager to have more of it.

Until recently, students of Jung surprisingly did not pay much attention to this feature of his life, even though he himself devotes a whole chapter of his autobiography to giving an account of his written work and to how it came into being.[10] Susan Rowland has remedied this deficit somewhat with her book *Jung as a Writer*. There she analyzes the ingenious strategies evident in his arguments, using the techniques of modern literary criticism to elucidate several of his most important texts and to discuss a range of meanings for contemporary students. What I am speaking of,

---

substitute for his absence in the collective personal sphere. Without this production of values, final individuation is immoral and – more than that – suicidal." CW 18, para. 1095.

[9] F. McCormick, "A Memorial Meeting," p. 16.

[10] C.G. Jung, *Memories, Dreams, Reflections*, Chapter 7, "The Work."

however, is more about the psychological issue of identity, the high value and purpose that writing and publishing held for Jung's conscious sense of himself. In his career, these were anything but marginal activities. This should be obvious given the sheer volume of his production. He published enough work in various forms— books, articles, lectures, forewords, prefaces—to amount to 18 large volumes in the assembled *Collected Works*, and this does not include his autobiography (written with Aniela Jaffé), *Memories, Dreams, Reflections,* or the five big volumes of now published letters (not to mention the many still unpublished letters). One can only conclude that Jung spent a good deal of his waking life engaged in writing. This activity doubtless held great meaning for him.

There have been many attempts by now to paint Jung's portrait and to capture the essential features of the man's life and work. Each one ends up highlighting specific attributes while discounting or ignoring others. As a personality and a looming cultural figure, Jung presents a daunting kaleidoscope of complexity. He is not easy to capture in a single portrait. Some of the personae put forward to date have been Jung as scientist (Bennet), as theoretical psychologist (Shamdasani), as psychotherapist to individuals and to Christianity (Stein), as artist (Gaillard), as visionary mystic (Schlamm), as haunted and misguided prophet (Stern, Noll), as creative personality (Jaffé, von Franz), as avatar (Edinger), and as religious thinker (Dourley). Phases of his life have been put on stage and film as well. Novelists too have used him for their own ends. None of these depictions is definitive on the one hand or totally devoid of value on the other. Some of them are extremely one-sided and polemical (positively and negatively), while others are more balanced and objective. Each of the numerous images cast off by Jung in his lifetime, it seems, has persuaded someone to use it to bring him into focus, whether in a glowing or harshly critical light. But none of them turns out to be totally convincing or exhaustive of his reality. The whole man has so far proven to be too complex and more even than the sum of his many parts, and so he continues to baffle and defeat his biographers and likewise the novelists and playwrights who try to conjure him. While each of his personae adds something to the dramatization of a potentially full and rounded dramatization of Jung the man, it seems there are always more characters in the wings clamoring for attention than can be put on a single stage. Until now, no one has, in my opinion, captured Jung in his full complexity on paper, stage, or film. Perhaps it is not possible to do so at this point in history. It seems well nigh impossible to get the proportions and the spaces right in this complex personality.

Putting the image of Jung as author to the fore, I see him sitting at his desk in the study of his house in Küsnacht, busily and intently putting his ideas down on paper, looking up passages in books from his library in the next room, checking details among the papers scattered across his desk, and pondering psychic life with his intellect and imagination. He mumbles under his breath, arguing with somebody not in the room but in the center of his mind. His writing carries him forward and takes his thought beyond where it had gone before. He becomes gripped by the images and ideas that flow from his hand, and he follows his flight of intuition as his pen scrapes across the pages. He ends up writing things he did not know he was thinking, and he says them in a clearer or a more forceful way than he has spoken or thought them before. Authors surprise themselves as they push on. They discover what they are thinking by writing.[11] Writing is a means for thinking and for becoming conscious, as well as a creative act and a recognized cultural mode to express and to share one's thoughts with others. An author's

---

[11] To Victor White, Jung writes: "Not very long after I have written to you, I simply had to write a new essay I did not know about what. It occurred to me I could discuss some of the infer points about Anima, Animus, Shadow and last not least the Self. I was against it, because I wanted to rest my head. Lately I had suffered from severe sleeplessness and I wanted to keep away from all mental exertions. In spite of all I felt forced to write on blindly, not seeing at all, what I was driving at. Only after I had written about 25 pages in folio, it began to dawn on me, that Christ—not the man but the divine being—was my secret goal. It came to me as a shock, as I felt utterly unequal to such a task." A. Lammers and A. Cunningham (eds.), *The Jung-White Letters*, p. 103.

writings are a link to the world and especially to some particular people in that world.

Assessing Jung's audience, though, is complicated. Whom was he writing to? Often there was a concealed and more specific target for his writing than the general reading public or the professional world at large would have recognized or known about. In many works, he was arguing with someone in particular or answering a specific person's challenge. Reading him, it is always instructive to know the immediate context in which a text appeared and specifically to whom it was addressed. The critical fact of personal relationships is often not always obvious in his written oeuvre. He does not often tell the reader outright that in a particular essay or passage he is speaking, for example, to Freud, Martin Buber, Victor White, Erich Neumann, or another of his colleagues. In *Memories, Dreams, Reflections*, where he provides detailed information about how his writings came into being, he mentions almost no names. One gets the impression that his authoring was almost hermitlike, a genre of profoundly introverted authorship. In fact, this is not the complete picture. It leaves out his interlocutors. Jung needed and enjoyed specific audiences, such as the scholars who gathered annually at the Eranos Tagungen in Ascona, for instance. He was greatly stimulated by certain individuals, and his relationships with them engendered some of his most exciting and far-reaching reflections. The result is that his writings are, in addition to being publications of scientific or general cultural interest, also a continuation of private conversations, dialogues, arguments, or disputes. They are not abstract argumentation delivered into a void. Jung had someone in mind as he authored them. His texts have contexts.

Two Relationships as Context: Freud and Victor White

As prime examples of this point, I will consider two instances where authoring and publishing grew out of the context of important relationships, affected them, and then contributed importantly to ending them. The first is the famous early one with Freud; the second is the less well-known and later one with Victor White, the Dominican priest and theologian.

The parallels in how these relationships unfolded and ran their course are striking. Both relationships stimulated a large correspondence, enough to fill a heavy volume with often long and thoughtful letters. In both instances, Jung formed a close and complex relationship with the other man after the other had read one or more of his published works.[12] Finally, and most importantly, both relationships and the respective correspondences culminated in the publication of a critical book by Jung that sparked a strong negative response from the other and proved to be a breaking point.

With Freud, the break came almost immediately after the founder of psychoanalysis read the Second Part of Jung's *Wandlungen und Symbole der Libido* in the Jahrbuch, of which Jung was editor, in 1912.[13] This book proved decisive in what had already become, for many reasons, a shaky relationship earlier. In *Wandlungen*, Jung challenged several major tenets in standard psychoanalytic theory of the time, among them Freud's interpretation of the incest wish and his libido theory. In this publication, Jung was showing his authorial flag and openly stating his differences with Freud in public. He had kept some of these disagreements to himself until then, but many of his points of difference had been made earlier and repeatedly in the letters he had written to Freud. Freud reacted dismissively to Jung's new contribution and made some disparaging comments about its

---

[12] In the case of Freud, the book was *Über die Psychologie der Dementia praecox: Ein Versuch*—in English, *The Psychology of Dementia Praecox*. Jung had sent Freud a complimentary copy. White had on his own read quite a number of Jung's writings that were available in German and English before the early 1940s, when the outbreak of World War II isolated Switzerland from the Allied countries.

[13] Jung was the founding editor of this first psychoanalytic journal. In it, he published *Wandlungen* in two parts, the first in 1911, the second and critical part in 1912. The complete work was first translated by Beatrice Hinkle, a student of his, as *Psychology of the Unconscious* in 1916 and later extensively revised and published in the *Collected Works*, Vol. 5, as *Symbols of Transformation*.

meager importance for psychoanalysis. Jung responded with a series of angry letters, thus provoking the actual break. He was wounded and deeply insulted by Freud's remarks and in a letter accused him of letting his "neurosis" get the better of him and causing him to fail to recognize the value of Jung's new ideas.[14] Freud replied a short while later by pointing out a slip of the pen that Jung had committed, to which Jung retorted with fury. After that, the curtain fell on their relationship quickly and decisively.[15]

With Victor White, it was Jung's publication of *Answer to Job* that proved highly disruptive and finally terminal. White read this work originally in draft form and later in the German edition, and at first, it seemed to create no friction between them. In fact, White seemed quite enthusiastic about it. The topic of "evil" and the Catholic doctrine of "*privatio boni*" had been, and continued for some years longer to be, at the center of their conversations. When the work was later translated and published in English and then read by White's fellow Roman Catholics in England and the United States, however, the negative effects of the work surged and overwhelmed White.[16] Still an active Dominican priest, White found himself in the

---

[14] The letter is dated 3 December 1912: "My very best thanks for one passage in your letter, where you speak of a 'bit of neurosis' you haven't got rid of. This 'bit' should, in my opinion, be taken very seriously indeed because.... I have suffered from this bit in my dealings with you, though you haven't seen it and didn't understand me properly when I tried to make my position clear. If these blinkers were removed you would, I am sure, see my work in a very different light. As evidence that you...*underestimate* my work by a very wide margin, I would cite your remark that 'without intending it, I have solved the riddle of all mysticism, showing it to be based on the symbolic utilization of complexes that have outlived their function.' My dear Professor, forgive me again, but this sentence shows me that you deprive yourself of the possibility of understanding my work by your underestimation of it.... This insight has been self-evident to us for years.... It is only occasionally that I am afflicted with the purely human desire to be understood *intellectually* and not be measured by the yardstick of neurosis." W. McGuire (ed.), *The Freud/Jung Letters*, pp. 525-6.
[15] Freud's short letter is dated 16 December 1912, and Jung's angry reply is dated 18 December 1912.
[16] For a full and detailed account of White's various reactions to *Answer to Job*, see A. Lammers, *In God's Shadow*, pp. 89-113.

awkward position of having to answer agitated questions from fellow Roman Catholics about Jung's position vis-à-vis Christian doctrine and faith, which appeared highly unorthodox (to say the least!) in this work. Finally, White reacted aggressively by writing a scathing review in the Dominican publication, *Blackfriars*.[17] There he vigorously upheld the conventional Catholic position regarding Scripture and distanced himself decisively from his mentor, whom he depicted as making a pitiable fool of himself in his dotage.[18] Although he offered a gesture of apology to Jung for his outburst,[19] severe damage was done to the relationship, and it ended not much later in painful silence.

In both of these cases, Jung's published work expressed in public what had mostly been discussed previously in private, either in the letters that passed between the men or in long conversations. In both cases, too, it was the other man's reaction to Jung's writing that paved the way for damaging the relationship beyond repair. Jung's publishing was the precipitating factor. Why did he do it?

For Jung, these writings would have represented a climax of the dialogue that had been generated within the respective personal relationships. The differences that had arisen in these private exchanges and conversations had come to a head and now became openly and decisively stated in a published work. Writing was for Jung a way of conducting an *Auseinandersetzung* ("confrontation"). Publishing a book had the additional effect, however, of throwing down a gauntlet. This put the issues on the table in public view and

---

[17] *Blackfriars*, Vol. 36, No. 420 (March 1955). Reprinted in A. Lammers and A. Cunningham (eds.), *The Jung White Letters*, Appendix 6.

[18] He writes: "It [i.e., *Answer to Job*] has—and this is the most distressing feature— the ingenuity and power, the plausibility and improbability, the clear-sightedness and blindness of the typical paranoid system which rationalizes and conceals an even more unbearable grief and resentment." A. Lammers and A. Cunningham (eds)., *The Jung-White Letters*, p. 355.

[19] He wrote a letter to Jung from aboard the Queen Mary en route back to Europe and before the review was published: "...there are some passages I would now wish to have kept to myself." A. Lammers and A. Cunningham, *The Jung-White Letters*, p. 259. In a later version of this review, he dropped the more offensive passages.

constituted a challenge. In setting up this problematic, Jung's writings proved to be divisive. Differences that could perhaps have been managed in private became intolerable when ventilated in public. The relationships with Freud and White, which had stimulated Jung's thinking and brought his authorial creativity to a feverish pitch of intensity, fed directly into his publishing. But then, the published works severely damaged relations with the very men who helped to instigate them, although this result was not Jung's conscious intention in writing these works.

The two relationships were different in many respects, but structurally they have notable parallels. With Freud, Jung was from the outset in the position of the younger man, a student and beginner in the practice of Freud's psychoanalysis. Freud was clearly the author, Jung the apprentice. At first, Freud was the object of an intense transference from Jung.[20] Freud appeared to Jung as a unique genius, an intellectual hero, and a cultural pioneer; his vivid personality made a deep and lasting impression on the young psychiatrist from Zurich. Freud for his part happily stepped into the role of mentor and father figure to Jung. As the creator of a new movement in the treatment of mental illness, he adopted Jung as an heir and quickly came to favor him as his "crown prince"—to the irritation of his other "sons" in Vienna who immediately became envious of Jung's privileged position. This quasibiblical (think of Joseph and his brothers with father Jacob showing favoritism toward the youngest son) dynamic complicated their relationship beyond their capacities to manage and work through the subsequent emotional entanglements. Jung proved on his side to be a difficult and rebellious son (as he had been also to his biological father, Paul Jung), seeking his own intellectual path and claiming procreative and authorial energies for himself. Freud eventually detected in Jung a death wish toward himself. As the younger man increasingly and

---

[20] In a letter (dated 28 October 1907), Jung confesses to Freud: "I have a boundless admiration for you both as a man and a researcher...." W. McGuire (ed.), *The Freud/Jung Letters*, p. 95.

somewhat secretively requisitioned space for autonomy and freedom in his thinking, he began also stubbornly to refuse to knuckle under to what he perceived to be Freud's anxious need to stay on top.[21] *Wandlungen* was both a testament to his gifts as a psychoanalytic theorist and a declaration of independence. Authoring and publishing it was an act of individuation, which always proves to be a risky business and often puts important relationships to the test, if not to the knife. Moreover, the field of psychoanalysis was too small at the time to contain two such authors.

In the relationship with Victor White, Jung held the contrary position vis-à-vis the younger man. Shortly after celebrating his 70th birthday in 1945, Jung received the first item in what would become an extensive correspondence with the then 42-year-old English Dominican priest living in Oxford. At 70, he was the elder mentor figure. Their contact began just at the end of World War II in Europe, and Jung was beginning to feel released from the confinement of the war years, like Noah finally free to exit the ark at the end of the Great Flood. White was busy, if not happy, in his career as theologian and teacher at Blackfriars, the Dominican house in Oxford, when he first contacted Jung with a packet of his writings and a slightly belated birthday greeting. He was familiar with the Jungians in England and had studied with and been in analysis with John Layard, Toni Sussman, and Gerhard Adler. It was at Adler's suggestion that he made bold to contact Jung personally. While highly regarded and far advanced in theological and Thomistic studies, White thought of himself as a relative beginner in psychology and readily accepted Jung's authority in this area.[22]

---

[21] "You go around sniffing out all the symptomatic actions in your vicinity, thus reducing everyone to the level of sons and daughters who blushingly admit the existence of their faults. Meanwhile you remain on top as the father, sitting pretty," Jung screamed at Freud in one of the last letters (18 December 1912). W. McGuire (ed.), *The Freud-Jung Letters*, p. 535.

[22] See White's letter to Jung on 23 October 1945: "For some time past I have found myself ploughing a rather lonely furrow, painfully aware of the inadequacy of my

Though not lacking a critical intellectual attitude, White made a strong emotional transference to Jung, who became the recipient of White's idealization. Jung responded with a warm reply to White's initiative (similarly to how Freud had responded to Jung's initial contact), embracing White with enthusiasm[23] and commenting positively on his writings and saying he wished White were "at my elbow"[24] so conversation would be easier. When White indicated an interest in visiting Switzerland, Jung invited him to be his guest at his retreat in Bollingen.[25] In White, Jung hoped he had come into contact with an ideal partner for deepening his longstanding psychological dialogue with Christian theology and tradition. White's keen interest in "psychology and religion" and his surprisingly extensive knowledge of Jung's writings to date could facilitate a genuine intellectual encounter, Jung thought. He was eager to try. If Freud had hoped that Jung would help him break out of his restrictive Jewish circle of medical colleagues and students in Vienna into the wider European medical world of psychiatry, Jung now may have thought that White might help him similarly to break out of his sense of alienation and separation from fellowship with members of his religious tradition, Christianity.

White's agenda was from the outset of the relationship stated in his letters and writings. It was to build a bridge between Catholic

---

experience on the psychological side, and of my need for expert and understanding guidance—at least to the extent of some reassurance that I was not positively on the <u>wrong</u> lines from the psychological standpoint." A. Lammers and A. Cunningham, *The Jung-White Letters*, p. 15.

[23] In his letter to White of 5 October 1945, Jung wrote: "You are to me a white raven inasmuch as you are the only theologian I know of who has really understood something of what the problem of psychology in our present world means." Ibid., p. 6.

[24] Ibid., p. 5.

[25] In a letter dated 13 April 1946, Jung writes: "I should like you to consider yourself as my guest during your stay here. I shall be in the country, on the upper part of the lake of Zurich, which I have a little country place. If you are a friend of the simple life you will have all the comfort you need. If your tastes should be too fastidious you would find it a bit rough." Ibid., p. 32.

theology and modern psychology basically for theological purposes. This notion followed the Thomistic model of theology, a divine science, having a working relationship with a human science as a "handmaiden" to theology. For St. Thomas, the working partnership was with the philosophy of Aristotle, while for Father White, it would be analytical psychology. In modern times, White suggested, theology could use the empirical science of depth psychology to make it more relevant and intelligible to people. Theology needed assistance (a "handmaiden") to engage with intellectual life in the 20th century in a fresh and convincing way, as White saw it. That theology would retain the senior position in this partnership was an unspoken assumption left in the shadows.

For Jung, the agenda at the outset of this adventure in dialogue could have been stated in quite similar terms, up to a point. He also thought that Christian theology was badly in need of revision, particularly in the area of its teaching on "the problem of evil" and its attitude toward "the feminine." But the similarity was deceptive. Jung was quite aware that his worldview was shaped fundamentally by Kantian and post-Kantian philosophy and modern psychology, whereas he saw classical Christian theologians, not without reason, as people who are bound to continue making metaphysical assertions and who typically assume a stance of faith in unprovable doctrines based on revelation. Jung therefore regarded theologians as belonging to another historical era, the Middle Ages. Theologians are essentially premodern, as he saw them. They continue to live in a world controlled spiritually and intellectually by myth, not by science or reason. As Jung would have known from previous experience with theologians, the dialogue between himself as a psychologist and White as a theologian was bound, at least to a degree, to be an exchange between a contemporary thinker and a historical anachronism. But in White's case, because this unusual theologian had taken psychology seriously, Jung saw a possible chance to reform the other and to connect, through him, to many more people who needed to enter the modern world without completely losing contact with the tradition of soul and spirituality that Christianity has represented. If White could make this transition, then his theology would change significantly, and this was a risk well worth taking. Jung was excited by the challenge. In this perspective, Jung might have intuitively anticipated the kind of theology created later by figures like the Protestant Paul Tillich (whom he met and heard in 1936 at the Eranos Tagung) and by Catholic theologians like David Tracy and John Dourly. This is a very different kind of theology from that commonly known and practiced in the Catholic Church in the middle of the 20th century. It is open, questioning, psychologically astute, and fully cognizant of the implications of modernity for the contemporary theologian.

Some of Jung's most thoughtful and passionate letters were written to Victor White. In them, he continued and sharpened the discussions that took place during the weeks spent together in Bollingen and at the Eranos Conferences. Many of the letters addressed theological topics, especially the reality of "evil" and what Jung found to be the most irritating Catholic doctrine of "*privatio boni*" (evil defined as "the absence of good"). Try as they might, the two men could never get past their contrary views on this teaching of the Church. For Jung, a religious notion or image did not make sense psychologically unless it was backed by empirical evidence showing that it was archetypal, i.e., universal. The metaphysical was for him an unavailable domain; it looked arbitrary to him, controlled by powers in authority and not by free reason. If a doctrine were based on archetypal psychological foundations, he could assess and consider its merits. This was a limiting condition to the dialogue between psychology and theology laid down by psychology. If a doctrine met this criterion, he would consider its psychological merits on the same level as other archetypal images. For *privatio boni*, however, he could find no evidence of archetypal backing.[26]

---

[26] In his Foreword to White's book, *God and the Unconscious*, Jung wrote: "It seems to me, however, that the existing empirical material, at least so far as I am acquainted with it, permits of no definite conclusion as to the archetypal background of the *privatio boni*. Subject to correction, I would say that clear-cut moral distinctions are the most recent acquisition of civilized man. That is why such

This doctrine could more reasonably be considered under the psychological category of denial, a defense mechanism of the ego. As a psychologist, Jung considered *privatio boni* nothing but a dodge from accepting the responsibility for immoral behavior.[27] Evil is not the absence of something or a space empty of Being, Jung argued, but the active and indeed often dramatically impressive *presence* of something psychologically substantial in its own right, like an impulse or an instinct.

In Jung's reflections, evil medieval psychology was personified and named the Devil, while in modern times evil is not imaged. It is a moral judgment that one applies to certain types of behavior and attitude, and this judgment is based upon current ethical understanding and consciousness. Immoral behavior and attitude (i.e., evil) are understood today as rooted in psychological reality, for example in emotions like hatred, envy, or lust. To say that evil in the form of envy, for example, is a *privatio boni* (namely the absence of something good like gratitude, for instance) is specious because it denies the psychological reality of envy as a force in its own right. This is the psychological, not a metaphysical, argument put forward by Jung in his critique of the *privatio boni* doctrine.

---

distinctions are often so hazy and uncertain, unlike other antithetical constructions which undoubtedly have an archetypal nature and are the prerequisites for any act of cognition." C.G. Jung, "Foreword to White's 'God and the Unconscious,'" *CW* 11, para. 459.

[27] On this point, Jung comments: "...I was called upon to treat a patient, a scholarly man with an academic training, who had got involved in all manner of dubious and morally reprehensible practices. He turned out to be a fervent adherent of the *privatio boni,* because it fitted in admirably with his scheme: evil in itself is nothing, a mere shadow, a trifling and fleeting diminution of good, like a cloud passing over the sun." Ibid., para. 457. In a letter to White dated 31 December 1949, more than a year before he wrote *Answer to Job,* Jung wrote fiercely: "As long as Evil is a, μὴ ὄν *nobody will take his own shadow seriously.* Hitler and Stalin go on representing a mere 'accidental lack of perfection.' *The future of mankind very much depends upon the recognition of the shadow.* Evil is psychologically speaking—*terribly real."* A. Lammers and A. Cunningham, *The Jung-White Letters,* p. 143. (Jung's emphases).

Jung could find no archetypal backing for the notion of evil as *privatio boni*, but he certainly could find plenty of it for evil. Mythologems universally tell of devils, demons, and sundry other shadowy characters. Evil should therefore be considered a real force in the world and in the archetypal levels of the human soul, not be written off as a mere absence of its opposite. The psychological dynamics and motivations that one can group under the heading of "evil" actively and energetically oppose those that would be named "good," and the two groups are locked in a protracted competition for expression in behavior. The urge to destroy is powerful, as is the urge to create. They are a pair of opposites in the human soul. If they were to be projected into the transcendent realm spoken of by theology and brought together within the image of a single unifying and all-encompassing ultimate God figure, then this is a monotheism that would conceive of God as containing the tension of these opposites within a single Being. This was Jung's preference, although he was not a theologian and shied away from mythological statements. The alternative, in his view, would be a radical Dualism, with an all-good God locked in eternal struggle with a contrary all-Evil God.

White, steeped in classical Catholic theology and Thomistic thought and deeply formed by Catholic habits of belief, could not comfortably follow Jung to such conclusions. And in his theologically trained mind, he saw no particular need to do so. In his view, analytical psychology was a human science and limited to the empirical dimension of psychological existence, where evil is certainly a verifiable factor, but it had nothing to say about the Divine (the privileged territory of theology, a science based on revelation), where evil has no reality. He wanted to use the basic tenets and findings of analytical psychology in a way that met his own need for building a bridge between theology and psychology, faith and reason, and he certainly had no interest in dissolving what is probably the keystone of Christian theology, i.e., the doctrine that God is the *Summum Bonum* in Whom there is no darkness. Psychology could thus serve theology if it stayed on the ground at the human level and did not challenge theology on the own higher domain of Being itself. For Jung, this separation between psychology and theology was unacceptable. Theology had no reality for him apart from psychology. By itself and without backing from the archetypes, it was nothing but empty and arbitrary speculation and mere words.

This was the intellectual and cultural nub of the problem between Jung and White, and it turned out to be the grain of sand in the oyster that yielded what some people judge to be the greatest pearl-of-wisdom literature Jung ever authored, *Answer to Job*. I would argue that we owe Jung's authorship of this controversial text in great part to his relationship with Victor White. White was the immediate catalyst for this incandescent piece of writing, just as Freud provided the stimuli for Jung's earlier ventures in authorhood, *Wandlungen*, and, even more importantly for analytical psychology in the long run, the massive tome, *Psychological Types*, which is, in a more complete sense than the former work, Jung's answer to Freud.

Jung's Authorship of *Answer to Job*

As a piece of writing, *Answer to Job* occupies a unique place in Jung's published oeuvre.[28] Typically, in his writings Jung assumes the persona of the empirical scientist or the medical doctor. These were his professional calling cards. He held a degree in medicine from the University of Basel and was trained as a psychiatrist and scientific researcher by Eugen Bleuler at the Burghölzli Klinik, a branch of the University of Zurich. These were top-drawer professional cre-dentials. But as an author, Jung can often be seen bursting at the seams of this tightly woven professional suit of clothing, and frequently he could not keep his passions and enthusiasms within

---

[28] I do not consider pieces like *Septem Sermones ad Mortuos* and the Red Book as belonging to this category of published work, although they are part of Jung's written legacy. They were not published for public consumption but were rather kept private and shared with only a few close acquaintances.

such narrow confinements. This is because he was an author, not merely a writer or a reporter of scientific results. In much of his writing, one feels both the firm intellectual commitment to scientific method and the barely checked sounds of another kind of writer in the background, sometimes a poet or a preacher, certainly a passionate author and a creative personality. The latter comes through resoundingly in many of his letters.

In *Answer to Job*, these authorial markings normally kept under wraps break out in full display. In tone, this work is closer to his letters—personal, impassioned, and human. *Answer to Job* could be read as a letter addressed to the public in post-World War II Western societies, or better yet as an impassioned sermon. In it, Jung consciously puts aside his professional inhibitions and lets fly a dazzling display of authorial virtuosity and rhetorical fireworks. The voice of this author is no longer dominated by the persona of the professional medical man, although that remains in the background. We know that Jung wrote this small work in a short period of time when he was recovering from an illness.[29] *Answer to Job* possesses a kind of musicality often absent in his more scientific writings. In a letter to Henry Corbin, dated 4 May 4 1953, Jung writes (in response to Corbin's comments on *Answer to Job*): "You say you read my book as an 'oratorio.' The book 'came to me' during the fever of an illness. It was as if accompanied by the great music of a Bach or a Handel. I don't belong to the auditory type. So I did not hear anything, I just had the feeling of listening to a great composition, or rather of being at a concert."[30] The work had been incubating for a long time, and its birth into written language and coherent text was fast and furious. Here finally, Jung allowed himself the freedom to express his feelings openly, even recklessly. He is highly emotional, by turns angry, intemperate, aggressive, didactic, and prophetic. His passion here is related to his father's unfulfilled vocation as a specialist in Old Testament languages and literature. In *Memories, Dreams,*

---

[29] See G. Wehr, *Jung, A Biography*, p. 382.
[30] G. Adler (ed.), *C.G. Jung Letters*, Vol. 2, p. 116.

Reflections, Jung recounts a dream in which he hears his father interpreting the Bible with great intensity ("his mind was flooded with profound ideas"[31]) and links this directly to the composition of *Job*.

At the outset, Jung apologizes: "I shall not give a cool and carefully considered exegesis that tries to be fair to every detail, but a purely subjective reaction. In this way I hope to act as a voice for many who feel the same way as I do, and to give expression to the shattering emotion which the unvarnished spectacle of divine savagery and ruthlessness produces in us.... I shall express my affect fearlessly and ruthlessly in what follows, and I shall answer injustice with injustice, that I may learn to know why and to what purpose Job was wounded, and what consequences have grown out of this for Yahweh as well as for man."[32] He lets the text work on him emotionally, and then he interprets it using his powerful, frequently confused, and highly charged transferential feelings and reactions. The net result is a combination of hermeneutics and sermonics, and an *Auseindersetzung* with the biblical God. In this writing, Jung achieves mythographic authorship. He retells the biblical story and in this creates a new mythic version of who God is and what He is doing and becoming.

Much of Jung's argument had appeared in various forms before in other places—in published papers, in lectures and off-the-cuff remarks recorded by his followers, in various letters, and in his many seminars. It is not the content per se that is brand new and different for his published work so much as the authorial voice. Since other scholars have adequately recounted the general background of the ideas in the work,[33] I will not dwell on this matter here. It is necessary to know, however, that as a youth, Jung had deeply read Goethe's *Faust* and had been indelibly marked by it. *Faust* and The

---

[31] C.G. Jung, *Memories, Dreams, Reflections*, p. 218.

[32] C.G. Jung, *Answer to Job, CW* 11, paras. 561-3.

[33] See for instance, G. Wehr, *Jung, A Biography*, Chapter 24, and P. Bishop, *Jung's Answer to Job: A Commentary*.

Book of Job are based on the same premise: God and Satan/ Mephistopheles make a bargain to put a human being to the test, and God allows the shadowy Trickster to have his way with him up to a point. In the end, God intervenes with a rescue. *Answer to Job*, like these, is a reflection on God's ways with humankind. Going further, however, it is also a sharp and direct critique of God's ways and methods, and it images God as developing dramatically as the story unfolds into New Testament times. It was this critique and remythologization that White found so problematical in the work.

Jung's *Answer to Job* represents his answer to Victor White and to the religious tradition in which the Dominican stood and with which he remained strongly identified. The discussions with White, as placed on record in the correspondence, roused the authorial daimon in Jung from his slumbers and prepared the way for the creation of this text at this particular moment in Jung's life.

Throughout his long life, Jung was engaged with Christianity in one way or another. In the same letter to Henry Corbin cited above, he wrote: "Schleiermacher...is one of my spiritual ancestors. He even baptized my grandfather—born a Catholic—who by then was a doctor. This grandfather became a great friend of the theologian de Wette, who had connections of his own with Schleiermacher. The vast, esoteric, and individual spirit of Schleiermacher was a part of the intellectual atmosphere of my father's family. I never studied him, but unconsciously he was for me a *spiritus rector*."[34] (Significantly, de Wette, a professor of theology at the University of Basel, was one of the 19th century's giants of Old Testament scholarship. He too must have given The Book of Job a great deal of thought.) In *Jung's Treatment of Christianity*, I detailed much of this background and the reasons for Jung's long dialogue with Christian doctrine and its theological representatives. Briefly stated, I argued that Jung in his mature years took it upon himself to offer Christianity psychotherapeutic treatment for its deeply ingrained tendency to split good and evil on the one hand, and the materially

---

[34] *Letters*, Vol. 2, p. 115.

grounded and spiritual aspects of the human psyche on the other. Jung diagnosed a classic neurotic psychological structure in Christianity. And as it turned out, the Dominican priest who was so aptly named White, represented the very malaise Jung was struggling to correct. Jung's encounter with White, poignantly and richly detailed in the many letters that passed between them, engaged him profoundly. White's struggle for individuation came to matter deeply to him. By entering into such an intense relationship with White, he gained a further emotional purchase on the essential conflicts raging within the traditional Christian soul generally. *Answer to Job*, addressed to White in part, is also meant for all of Christendom. Its audience includes everyone who lives within the context of Christian culture and tradition.

What is the message that the author of *Answer to Job* is trying to communicate? Basically, it is a radical notion: that the burden of the drama depicted as taking place on the level of the transcendent Divine in the Bible and in Christian theology has now shifted from the metaphysical and mythical to the psychological plane, and that human beings are now responsible for the reconciliation of the opposites and not an objective God or any other metaphysical entity. Salvation is no longer from above. The age of the psychological is now upon us. This is the burden of modernity, as Jung understood it.

Answer to Job is anything but objective scholarship regarding the biblical text. As biblical interpretation and commentary, it stands outside any particular religious tradition on the one hand and is similarly unfettered by conventions of historical inquiry and scholarship on the other. It is neither religious nor academic. It is psychological. A particular reading of history and a theory of the development of human consciousness, which sees humankind as having emerged from the mythical and the metaphysical era of premodern consciousness and as now having entered into the psychological, govern its conclusions. The psyche replaces heaven and hell and all such mythological beings as gods and goddesses, angels and devils, as the field of action on which the essential conflicts rage and must be won, lost, or endured. And with this comes the ethical responsibility for ordinary humans to take on the challenge of what Jung calls "incarnation."

Incarnation is reinterpreted as a here-and-now psychological process, basically as the individuation process as described by Jung in many places, not as a mythic or unique historical event as Christian doctrine has it. For modern men and women, incarnation means entering actively and consciously into the battle of the opposites (good vs. evil, masculine vs. feminine, etc.), submitting to the extreme suffering of this cross as Jesus Christ suffered on his, and enduring this agony until a *unio oppositorum* is born in their individual souls. Each person is called upon to incarnate the full complexity God, in other words. This means that individuals must now bear the conflict of opposites inherent in God's nature. And this also means that modern people cannot dodge such fundamental conflicts by embracing a comforting notion like "evil is the absence of goodness" and "if I just let God take care of it, things will be OK." That would be to shrink from the essential task. The shadow cannot any longer be projected into the metaphysical realm or swept under the carpet but must be taken on board consciously. Evil must be faced within each individual soul. This is the book's deepest argument.

As Jung lays out his psychological interpretation of The Book of Job and the rest of the Christian Bible, he creates an astonishing story. In this writing, he achieves his supreme act of authorship. In effect, he rewrites the supreme fiction of Christendom, the Bible. In Jung's *Answer to Job*, we find what Harold Bloom would call a "strong misreading" of the Bible, which creates the possibility of a great poem. Here is a summary of Jung's misreading. He tells us that God, after recognizing his embarrassing display of unconsciousness in front of his servant Job, came to feel morally inferior to humankind and had to take a dramatic decision that would advance his level of consciousness to that demonstrated by his creature. In his servant Job, God recognizes human consciousness as superior to His own. The human had suddenly outstripped the divine and shifted the balance. This marks a new level of consciousness in the human and an equivalent low grade for God. So in compensation and to answer Job for the purpose of regaining his standing, God incarnates himself and experiences, in the life and death of Himself as Jesus Christ, a degree and quality of suffering equal to that which He inflicted upon Job. On the assumption that suffering tests and increases consciousness, this act of empathic mirroring will upgrade God's standing and bring Him to a position of equality with the human. The critical issue is shadow awareness. God's action culminates in the crucifixion, when Jesus utters, "My God, my God, why hast Thou forsaken me?" At this moment, the myth that Jesus had trusted in his identification with an image of God as a wholly good Father figure is shattered, and he (and God himself, in and through him) suffers the same betrayal that servant Job had suffered at the hands of Yahweh. The shattering of the Good God myth is the critical piece in this narrative. This is God's response, his "answer to Job." God shatters the God-is-good myth about Himself but paradoxically confirms it at the same time. In this fashion, God advances and brings His moral and conscious standing up to the standard set by the human figure Job. God is reborn from this ordeal as a more integrated consciousness.

According to Jung's understanding of modernity, humans have now arrived at stage of postmythic consciousness. Bereft of comforting myths to live by, humankind is now at the place where Job stood, and where Jesus hanging on the cross found himself: alone and abandoned, with myths shattered and evil starkly revealed. How can individuals cope with this horror? To return to myth and religious belief is impossible for modern consciousness because it has advanced beyond that stage into a new territory, and there is no way back. The way forward must be psychological, which means a new kind of conscious attitude toward individual life, and responsibility must come into being that does not depend on the backing or comfort of myth.

For the traditional Christian (Victor White was on the fence for a time and then retreated to orthodoxy in his blistering response to

Jung's *Answer to Job*), the Church offers protection from such anguishing dilemmas. The essential battle between good and evil has either already been won through the victory of Christ over Satan and by his resurrection, or it will be won by God in the end times when Satan will be defeated and locked away forever. The major opus of salvation is completed on the mythic level. The believer must only have faith that God has done (or will do) the job, get on board the collective vessel of the Church, passively accept the gift of grace, and cling to the assurance that all will be well.

What Jung announces in his *Answer to Job* is the bad news that this is not good enough any longer. Today, everything decisive hangs on the balance of the human psyche. Will the human psyche endure the conflict and resolve the tension of the opposites, or will it split and violently unleash the awesome powers delivered by science to destroy the earth? "Everything now depends on man: immense power of destruction is given into his hand, and the question is whether he can resist the will to use it, and can temper his will with the spirit of love and wisdom."[35] Jung's powerful sermon invites people who are no longer secured in the big vessel of Church to get into their small individual boats and deal with the high seas on their own. But is the frail and vulnerable human individual capable of surviving the crashing waves of the warring opposites? This is the giant dilemma that faces humankind today. What can deliver us?

The major book to follow *Answer to Job* was *Mysterium Coniunctionis*, subtitled "An Inquiry into the Separation and Synthesis of Psychic Opposites in Alchemy." This can be read as Jung's answer to the anguished question raised by *Answer to Job*. This is a work that shows faith in the capacity of the human psyche to transcend the conflict between the warring opposites paired off in the self. Coming out toward the end of Jung's long career as an author, *Mysterium Coniunctionis* is the culmination of the alchemical studies he began in the late 1920s. The first piece of it was published separately as the clinical essay "Psychology of the Transference."

[35] C.G. Jung, *Answer to Job*, CW 11, para. 745.

Mysterium Coniunctionis completed the line of thought begun there. It is all about the inner resolution that takes place when psychological conflicts are honestly suffered and a new consciousness is born from their union. This is tantamount to the process of Christification and incarnation that he wrote about in *Answer to Job*. It is what God achieved through the life of Jesus.

By the time Jung published *Mysterium Coniunctionis*, he and White were no longer in regular communication. Their relationship foundered over White's violent reaction to *Answer to Job*. Clearly, he opted for the security of tradition and the Church. For some reason still unknown (perhaps due to a wishful thought), White started to believe that Jung had told him he would not publish *Answer to Job* but would rather share it with only a chosen few, similar to what he did with the Red Book and the *Septem Sermones ad_Mortuos*.[36] He must have sensed that it was addressed to him personally, as it was in part, but failed to recognize that Jung the author also had a larger readership in mind. This was a fateful misunderstanding. Jung felt compelled to share his burning Job thoughts with a much wider public. It was an important piece of the edifice he was building through his authoring. It was also in line with his vocation as a therapist to Christianity to offer the patient the results of his reflections. Beyond that, the work is addressed to all who claim modernity as their level of consciousness. This was not therefore something to be kept hidden away in a drawer and brought out only for the select few. In fact, one of the main thrusts of the message in *Answer to Job* is the notion of the "Christification

---

[36] This is what he says in the letter to Jung dated 17 March 1955, though he had earlier said (23 April 1951) that he was excited he hear of the book's publication in German and eagerly waited to have it to read again. When he did receive a copy from Jung, he wrote excitedly: "Thank you a million for 'Hiob.' Though I have countless things to do, I can hardly put it down. It is the most exciting and moving book I have read in years: and somehow it arouses tremendous bonds of sympathy between us, and lights up all sorts of dark places both in the scriptures and in my own psyche." A. Lammers and A. Cunningham (eds.), *The Jung-White Letters*, p. 181.

of many."[37] *"God wanted to become man, and still wants to,"*[38] Jung writes in italics for emphasis. For him this was not something to be kept quiet.

In authoring and publishing *Answer to Job*, Jung was delivering himself of a work that had been growing in him for decades. It was the culmination of the energy he had devoted specifically to interpreting Christian doctrine and history, which included the two essays, "A Psychological Approach to the Dogma of the Trinity" (1942) and "Transformation Symbolism in the Mass" (1942), and the major book, *Aion* (1951). Consistently, throughout all of these writings, Jung argued that Christian doctrine and practice do not sufficiently deal with the problem of evil or with the split between body and spirit. What the stimulating relationship with Victor White contributed was the spark that ignited the passion so hotly expressed in *Answer to Job*. It is as though Victor White brought the author in Jung up to a state of high excitement. What Jung initially greeted as a white raven when White appeared on the scene turned out to be *un homme inspirateur!*

---

[37] C.G. Jung, *Answer to Job*, *CW* 11, para. 758.
[38] Ibid., para. 739.

"Divinity expresses the self…"
—An Investigation[1]

Jung's Self Concept

One does become weary with the question of whether the term "self" should be capitalized or not. I have struggled with this and gone back and forth. My fond hope is that in this investigation I will be able to conclude once and for all that there is one self only, not two. And let's not capitalize it, lest we confuse the self with Divinity. I have to add at the outset that I think "self" is an excellent term for what it is meant to denote, a real stroke of genius on Jung's part. Why? Because it is at once personal and impersonal, individual and universal. This is important because to tilt too far one way or the other would destroy its ability to capture the full scope of the meaning and psychological value it has when it retains this paradoxical unity.

Let me begin by observing that it is generally recognized by anyone even a little familiar with Jung's writings that he drew a critically important distinction between the meaning of the terms "ego" and "self." On this point, the author was clear and consistent throughout. This distinction is a matter of scale and perspective. As a term, self refers to a psychic domain that encompasses all aspects of the ego complex and the surrounding penumbra of actual and potential consciousness, and surpasses this nexus of psychic

---

[1] Originally published in the *Journal of Analytical Psychology* 53:3, 2008.

material in several respects: Its range and scope of reference are greater in extension, in that it subsumes all conscious and unconscious levels and aspects of the psyche under its domain. Its texture is therefore also more complex because it embraces all the polarities and tensions within the psyche as a whole and not only those within consciousness and the ego complex; and its center of gravity lies beyond the conscious/unconscious divide. The term self represents the unity of the psyche as a whole, whereas the term, ego, represents a center of identity in consciousness. The ego is, as Jung defines it, "a complex of ideas which constitutes the center of my field of consciousness and appears to possess a high degree of continuity and identity."[2] The relation of the terms ego and self is that of a part to the whole. The ego is a part of the self, so one should be careful not to think of them as two separate and distinct psychic territories. When I say "I," it is the self speaking, but not the whole self. It is the ego, which is the Latin word for "I." Other parts of the self, such as shadow or anima, would not be represented by "I."

For the adult personality, the ego is defined as the center of consciousness and therefore also as the subject within the self-conscious person, while the self is defined as a virtual center and also (paradoxically) as the circumference of the whole psyche, conscious and unconscious, and the source of its full potential and state of unity. The self accounts for the unity of the personality before the ego is formed as well as for its unity as a whole after ego formation and development have taken place.

With the notion of self, moreover, Jung was reaching intuitively and theoretically for a psychological dimension that far exceeds the limits of individuals' usual *conscious* self-awareness, identity, sense of self, and experience of psychic reality. It is this notion in particular that constitutes the essential link between analytical psychology and explicitly religious forms of spirituality because it stretches to infinity. The term self takes our thinking beyond an everyday secular

---

[2] C.G. Jung, *Psychological Types*, CW 6, para. 706.

range of self-knowledge—be it ever so psychoanalytically well informed about complexes, instincts, archetypal images, phantasies, alpha function, and beta particles, etc., etc. —toward the unknown-within, toward the mystery of existence, toward a personal relation to and possible inclusion in the infinite, toward the *numinosum*. All of this comes under the heading of the self in analytical psychology. Within the ego complex, we are focused, defined, and somewhat cognizant of our thoughts, feelings, and the grounds for our emotional conditions; we claim an identity more or less unified and singular, a sense of self that is bounded and unique. As the self, on the contrary, we are utterly indeterminate, infinitely potential, never fully realized, and linked to (even fused with) the Divine. The self links the ego complex to ultimate wholeness. It encompasses all the psyche's inherent inner oppositions and obscurities, the shadows, and the numerous contradictions and riddles one has to live with in respect to subtle and ever shifting foci of ego identity and identification. The self arches high up, rising above the abysses that cut through the personality, linking and containing the persona and the shadow (good and bad), the gendered ego complex and the anima/animus (masculine and feminine), and conscious and unconscious. Self is what we are above, beneath, and beyond all identities, identifications, and part-personalities—personal, cultural, historical, engendered, and moral. It is what we are when all that we know or suspect that we are is added together, *plus* what we are when all that is stripped away—a surplus of psyche. We can extinguish the ego, but it is doubtful that we can kill the self. It is especially this *extra* that we want to investigate when we direct our attention to the self. And this is the task I have set for myself in this essay.

An Ontological Grounding for the Self

Jung's *Mysterium Coniunctionis*, published as the last in a long series of works in which alchemy is centrally featured, is a literary and theoretical meditation on the union of the opposites in the self. In this late work, albeit in obscure and indirect terms, he summarizes his reflections on the self as psychic totality and provides hints that would indicate a much larger than individual and psychological, indeed an ontological and even metaphysical, grounding for the self. As the title indicates, the work is concerned especially with the self's polarities, as well as with the prospect for overcoming the psyche's chief divide, that between conscious and the unconscious. At the outset, Jung boldly announces "the polaristic structure of the psyche" as a given.[3] The opus of alchemy was to unite the opposites, Jung declares, and this too is the goal of analysis. From here on, however, his way forward is anything but direct.

Mysterium is, like the psyche itself, replete with ambiguities, and for the translator it is a full-blown nightmare. The text for this essay happens to be a most thorny passage, where Jung states a connection between the self and Divinity. It is one of many places in Jung's written work that links the human and the Divine, and it is a particularly significant one, which happened to produce a mistranslation.

In the chapter titled "Luna," where Jung explores the symbolism of the moon with reference to the symbolism of the Feminine in alchemy, there is a subsection called "The Dog." The image of the dog brings up for Jung the paradoxical definition of the self as something at once noble and base, as though one could think of it as the greatest treasure and a curse at the same time. In the original German, the text is:

Der Hundesohn des KALID ist der hochgepriesene "Sohn der Philosophen," und damit wird die Ambiguität dieser Gestalt hervorgehoben: sie ist hellstes Licht und tiefste Nacht zugleich, also eine vollkommene coincidentia oppositorum, als welche die Göttlichkeit das Selbst ausdrückt.[4]

[3] C.G. Jung, *Mysterium Coniunctionis,* CW 14, p. xvi.
[4] Ibid., German edition, GW, vol. 14:1, para. 171.

Hull translates this somewhat convoluted sentence as follows: Kalid's "son of the dog" is the same as the much extolled "son of the philosophers." The ambiguity of this figure is thus stressed: it is at once bright as day and dark as night, a perfect *coincidentia oppositorum* expressing the divine nature of the self.[5]

"Son of the philosophers" is for Jung, as we know, an alchemical term that represents the self. Because "son of the philosophers" is designated by Kalid as "son of a dog," its ambiguity is sharp and unmistakable. The German phrase that concludes this sentence—*als welche die Göttlichkeit das Selbst ausdrückt*— should read: "as the Divinity expresses the self," or "as the self expresses the Divinity." Hull's translation—"expressing the divine nature of the self"—is incorrect. Jung is not saying that the self has a divine nature. What would that mean? That the self is God, or a god? There are two distinct terms: Divinity and self. Divinity is not adjectival to self. Literally, *ausdrückt* means "expresses." The relation between them is not identity but a type of "expression" of the one (Divinity) in the other (the self). The relation is indicated in the term "expresses." It is a mirroring relationship, not an identity. One is the source, the other an expression (or mirror) of the source. The ambiguity (*coincidentia oppositorum*) in the Deity is mirrored in the self.

As Jung announced at the beginning of *Mysterium*, the psyche is structured as a polarity, and now he adds that this structure is a mirror of the Godhead. The structure of self-division into conscious and unconscious components, for instance, and into ego and shadow, noble and base, high and low, is not only human but also Divine. The one reflects, or expresses, the other. The self is an expression of something beyond itself (*die Göttlichkeit*) but is not identical with it or of the same substance. This will be important for any discussion of the self as a psychological and human factor, for if the self is seen as divine, it becomes critically separated from

---

[5] Ibid., English edition, para. 176.

historical processes in the individual, a floating specter within or above the messiness of finite lived life.

It is no doubt significant that Jung uses the term *die Göttlichkeit* here rather than the simpler *Gott* (God). The term *die Göttlichkeit*[6] does not translate easily into English. It is a noun made from an adjective: *göttlich* = divinelike, like a Deity, made of divine substance. I translate it as "Divinity." *Die Göttlichkeit* does not refer to a specific god or goddess. As a noun, the attribute is made into a substance, as when we make the move in English from high to Highness, as in "Her Highness." A quality is turned into a substance, a being with specific quality. *Göttlichkeit* is the quality all the specific gods and goddesses hold in common, something they all participate in. *Göttlichkeit* is the quality that makes them divine and distinguishes them from beings nondivine. In psychological terms, Divinity means "archetypal." All the gods and goddesses are archetypal images. All share the quality of archetypality.

Jung is making a claim that the self is archetypal and not personal. In this respect, it shares the feature of being a *coincidentia oppositorum*, which is a characteristic feature of Divinity. He is bringing the terms into a mirroring relation with one another. The idea is that the self reflects *die Göttlichkeit*. While the biblical God is not mentioned here, this is a restatement of the familiar biblical message that humankind is created in the image of God:

So God created humankind in his image,
in the image of God he created them;
male and female he created them.[7]

---

[6] I find 17 instances of the use of this and a related term (*das Göttliche*) in the *Gesammelte Werke*, but this is the only place where Jung uses it as an active noun, as the subject of an action. Otherwise, it is used adjectively. There are, on the other hand, many instances where Jung uses the terms *Gott* (God), *Götter* (Gods), and *Gottesbild* (God-image),

[7] Genesis 1:27. New Revised Standard Version.

Psychology or Theology?

Nevertheless, quite a few questions call for attention as one reflects on this passage. Is Jung subtly subsuming psychology under theology and setting up a kind of theologically based psychology with the *imago Dei* doctrine as its centerpiece? Clearly, he is not borrowing the standard Christian version of the God image in this reference to *die Göttlichkeit*. For classical Christian theology, God is pure light and goodness, and in Him there is no darkness or shadow at all. This was the very doctrine that Jung objected to so frequently in his writings on Christianity, furiously disputing the *privatio boni* doctrine of evil[8] and critiquing the Christ-image as one-sided since it splits off and leaves out the darkness of the shadow as represented in Satan. Jung argued that the Christian doctrine of God chooses to privilege one side of *die Göttlichkeit*, the light aspect, and to repress the other features. Jung's image of Divinity as "the brightest light and the deepest night at the same time, a perfect *coincidentia oppositorum*" is much closer as a figure of the Divinity to Abraxas, the Deity referenced in *Septem Sermones ad Mortuos* already in 1916: "Abraxas is the God who is difficult to grasp. His power is greatest, because man does not see it…. Abraxas produces truth and lying, good and evil, light and darkness, in the same word and in the same act."[9] This is what is mirrored in the self as Jung describes it in *Mysterium Coniunctionis*.

For Jung, psychology supersedes theology and can therefore inform theology about the nature of Divinity. It can, for example, guide theology away from one-sidedly privileging the light side over the dark. It is this pull toward tilting God images in the direction of the solar that has characterized the monotheistic religions.

It is not the case, however, that Jung is espousing a purely humanistic position opposed to religious faith and belief. The psychological position is different, in his view, as he explains in a

---

[8] Evil defined as "absence of good."
[9] C.G. Jung, *The Red Book*, Reader's Edition, p. 520-21. See also *Black Books*, vol. 6, pp. 213-14.

heated exchange with the Jewish philosopher and theologian Martin Buber, who had accused him of being one of the chief figures responsible for the decline of religious faith in modernity. Jung explains his position on the relation of psychology and the articles of religious belief as follows:

> The fact is that the ego is confronted with psychic powers which from ancient times have borne sacred names, and because of these they have always been identified with metaphysical beings. Analysis of the unconscious has long since demonstrated the existence of the powers in the form of archetypal images which, be it noted, *are not identical with the corresponding intellectual concepts.* One can, of course, believe that the concepts of the conscious mind are, through the inspiration of the Holy Ghost, direct and correct representations of their metaphysical referent. But this conviction is possible only for one who already possesses the gift of faith. Unfortunately I cannot boast of this possession.... What I have described is a psychic factor only, but one which exerts a considerable influence on the conscious mind. Thanks to its autonomy, it forms the counterposition to the subjective ego because it is a piece of the *objective psyche.* It can therefore be designated as a "Thou."[10]

Jung is here picking up on Buber's use of the term "Thou" to describe a type of relationship with a living other. Too often, calling these factors "merely psychic" reduces them to names and concepts and misses their living power and forcefulness, which Jung wants to emphasize.

The Self as *Imago Dei*

For Jung, *die Göttlichkeit* is a reference to an unconscious psychological force beyond the control of the ego. It is a living and

---

[10] C.G. Jung, "A Reply o Martin Buber," CW 18, para. 1505.

dynamic factor, as Jung stresses. It is the archetype of the self. The self is the ultimate, central archetype of order in the psyche. It is also a *coincidentia oppositorum*. The monotheistic God-image also is precisely such an inclusive figure. The two are mirrors of one another. The many gods and goddesses of polytheism, on the other hand, are lesser or subsidiary psychic forces, which in the end are united in and governed by the ultimate archetype of unity, the self. They represent the anima or the animus level of the psyche, while the God-image of monotheism represents the self, the ultimate psychic ground from which the lesser figures spring and by which they are united and controlled.

However, the term "self" also transcends the typical mono-theistic God-image, which inevitably tends toward one-sidedness and partiality due to the interventions of consciousness—of theologians, priests, religious officials. Jung says that he chose the term self "in accordance with Eastern philosophy, which for centuries has occupied itself with the problems that arise when even the gods cease to incarnate. The philosophy of the Upanishads corresponds to a psychology that long ago recognized the relativity of the gods. This is not to be confused with a stupid error like atheism."[11] Here the archetype of the self would be seen as the psychic agency responsible for any and every type of unifying image, theory, plan, or fantasy. In other words, it is the bottom line of any type of emergent orderedness. It is the monad behind multiplicity, as in dual-aspect monism.[12]

This line of thought, however, would seem to contradict the view that Jung takes in *Mysterium*, namely that the self is an expression of *die Göttlichkeit*. If the self is an *imago Dei*, the *Dei* of which it is an *imago* must have priority and be a deeper mystery, a more encompassing reality than the self. The interesting point here would be that if there exists this kind of reflected congruence

---

[11] C.G. Jung, *Psychology and Religion*, CW 11, para. 140.
[12] See H. Atmanspacher and D. Rickles, *Dual-Aspect Monism and the Deep Structure of Meaning.*

between the structure of the self and the *Dei* of which it is an *imago*, one can read traits of the one off the other. Since the self is a *coincidentia oppositorum*, the Divinity must be similar. Moreover, dynamically, they affect one another in this mirroring relationship. In *Answer to Job*, Jung asserts that the Deity gains consciousness of Itself by gazing into its human mirror image. There is a two-way passage of information. God can become conscious by looking in the mirror.

What is being advocated is a state of continuity and mirroring between the supernatural Divinity and the human self. For Protestant theology, however, God is radically other. Jung would say that the standard Protestant estimate of the human is limited to ego-consciousness and that he is moving vastly beyond this in his explorations of the infinite unconscious. Jung is proposing a kind of depth psychology in which the master feature of the human psyche, the archetype of the self, can be located and taken up as "Divinity within." The mystery of *die Göttlichkeit* as *"unerforschliche Wesen"* ("unfathomable being") is retained because the human mind cannot be certain that all is revealed in the psyche or that consciousness can ever apprehend the whole of reality, psychic or other.

I cite another instance of the *imago Dei* idea in Jung's writing. In one passage in the fierce exchange of 1952 with Martin Buber, who had characterized Jung as a modern Gnostic and in fact named him as a secret devotee of Abraxas, a God image that, as we have seen, fits the pattern of *coincidentia oppositorum* accurately, Jung replied with tongue in cheek:

> Here, just for once, and as an exception, I shall indulge in transcendental speculation and even in "poetry": God has indeed made an inconceivably sublime and mysteriously contradictory image of himself, without the help of man, and implanted it in man's unconscious as an archetype, an ἀρχέτυπον φως, archetypal light: not in order that theologians of all times and places should be at one another's throats, but in order that the unpresumptuous man might glimpse an image, in the stillness of his soul,

that is akin to him and is wrought of his own psychic substance. This image contains everything he will ever imagine concerning his gods or concerning the ground of his psyche.[13] The idea here is identical to the one expressed in *Mysterium*, written at about the same time, in the phrase: "*als welche die Göttlichkeit das Selbst ausdrückt.*" In both instances, *die Göttlichkeit* (or "God," as he says to Buber) plants the *imago Dei* (as ἀρχέτυπον φῶς or archetypal light in the reply to Buber) within the human psyche. Expressed in the psyche as an archetype, the self is the source and the point of origin of all humanly elaborated mythologies and theologies, even if it is not necessarily a complete or accurate description of "the unfathomable Being" itself. The self, as the fundamental psychic ground of all human images and ideas of Deity, is itself grounded in Divinity. As Jung says, this is "poetry," but this poetry speaks a deep truth about Jung's vision.

The relation between psychology and religion was also the basic theme under discussion in Jung's correspondence with the English Roman Catholic theologian Victor White. Responding to an article White had published on Gnosticism, Jung writes:

Have I faith or a faith or not? I have always been unable to produce faith and I have tried so hard, that I finally did not know any more, what faith is or means.... The equivalent of faith with me is what I would call *Respect*. I have respect of the Christian Truth. Thus it seems to come down to an involuntary assumption in me, that there is something to the dogmatic truth, something *indefinable* to begin with. Yet I feel respect for it, although I don't really understand it. But I can say, my lifework is essentially an attempt to understand what others apparently can believe.... My respect is—mind you—

---

[13] C.G. Jung, "Religion and Psychology: A Reply to Martin Buber," CW 18, para. 1508.

involuntary; it is a 'datum' of irrational nature. This is the nearest I can get to what appears to me as "faith."[14]

This project of understanding what others believe, which Jung claims here as his "lifework," was an important part of his explorations of the self.

The Self, the Body, the "World"

If the self is conceived as *imago Dei* and takes, as a consequence, the form of a *coincidentia oppositorum*, as Jung says in *Mysterium*, what about its relation to the body and the world? Is the self a cut-off, purely spiritual entity housed within an alien material form as the ancient Gnostics held, or is it much more intimately embedded in and conditioned by the social and cultural worlds and actually at home in the human body? The view of the self as *imago Dei* could pose a problem if the psyche is seen as essentially unattached from life in the flesh and in the natural and social worlds.

Jung advanced a possible answer to this question in a theoretical paper titled "On the Nature of the Psyche":

Since psyche and matter are contained in one and the same world, and moreover are in continuous contact with one another and ultimately rest on irrepresentable, transcendental factors, it is not only possible but fairly probable, even, that psyche and matter are two different aspects of one and the same thing.[15]

In this and other works of the same late period in his life, such as "Synchronicity: An Acausal Connecting Principle," Jung was conceptualizing a model for a unified field theory of psyche-soma-world, an essential unity of mind-and-matter, in which the archetypal patterns that emerge in the psyche correspond to patterns found throughout nature. *Die Göttlichkeit* would therefore be seen as an immanent player in the world of material and psychic

---

[14] A. Lammers and A. Cunningham, *The Jung-White Letters,* p. 119.
[15] C.G. Jung, "On the Nature of the Psyche," CW 8, para.418.

objects and processes and not be an arm's length observer as Deistic theology, for instance, would have it. The self as *imago Dei* is both material and spiritual. Marialuisa Donati has expounded on this in her paper "Beyond Synchronicity: The Worldview of Carl Gustav Jung and Wolfgang Pauli," which she concludes with the statement:

> As a result of their discussion of synchronicity, Pauli and Jung's investigation crosses the limits of single sciences such as physics and psychology, in order to take its place within the wider realm of the philosophy of nature.... Jung and Pauli's discussions on synchronicity shed light on the special need for a philosophy of nature today, emerging from a theoretical revision of the relation between mind and matter.[16]

In this regard, Jung was not in agreement in the least with the ancient Gnostic analysis of the human soul's state of bitter alienation in a hostile material universe.

If there is no break between psyche and the material world, a persistent danger lurks that psyche will be reduced to matter as a byproduct of neuronal activity in the body. Is the self "expressed" by *die Göttlichkeit* or by the neurons of the body? Is it the brain, consisting of 100 billion neurons working (still so mysteriously) in millions of organized networks, that is being reflected in the self concept that Jung puts forward as the containing, organizing, centering foundation of the psyche? Is the *imago Dei* in fact an image of our neuroanatomy rather than an expression of Divinity? Or can it be both, since in Jung's late view spirit and matter are two sides of a single reality?

Should *die Göttlichkeit* be found out to be the neuronal basis of the mind, and the *imago Dei* its psychic image, even this reduction, as radical and still improbable as it seems, would leave open the question: Does an even more fundamental pattern-generating factor underlie this base of the psyche? Is there a spirit-matter patterning energy that is active beneath this basement

---

[16] M. Donati, "Beyond Synchronicity," p. 728.

in what has classically been referred to as the *unus mundus*? Jung clearly thought that his studies on synchronistic phenomena pointed in this direction. Perhaps the self as we know it in the psychological realm is, even if it rests and depends critically on a neuroanatomical base, still a more or less reliable mirror of a general pattern in reality as such, i.e., in the Divinity. In Jung's writings we find the persistent intuition that a mysterious force is at work behind the scenes, putting its imprint on body and soul and creating the pattern of *"coincidentia oppositorum, als welche die Göttlichkeit das Selbst ausdrückt."* Jung often speaks of the hidden hand that guides our destiny in the course of individuation.

To extend this line of thought, one can venture that the Divinity that expresses itself in the human psyche with a psychological self also leaves imprints in the material world generally—in all animals, plants, man-made objects, and in the cosmos. The human self would be but one instance of the *imago Dei* in all things. Joseph Cambray has taken up the discussion of emergence and complexity theory in the natural sciences and specifically of "complex adaptive systems" (CAS) to reflect on the constellation of archetypal patterns in the psyche, and further to note that such patterns may be of the scale-free network variety, thus finding homologous expression throughout the natural world. "Complex systems," he writes, speaking of the psyche as such a system, "tend to exhibit 'scale-free' features, showing similar patterns in a homologous series, or nested emergent phenomena.... The self-organization manifesting in CAS appears transcendent from what is know about the behavior of the individual agents (and transcendent from the perspective of consciousness if the system is biological, including human)."[17] George Hogenson has similarly argued that symbol formation, of which the *imago Dei* would be an example, can in contemporary scientific terms be best explained using "...operative concepts... [like] dynamic self-organization, self-organizing criticality, fractals,

---

[17] J. Cambray, "Synchronicity as Emergence," p. 231.

and power laws".[18] These modern analytic tools would allow for a reasonable contemporary scientific account of "the interface of dream, symbol, and the material world that Jung intuited".[19] Referencing the research on dreaming of Harvard neuropsychologist Carl Anderson, Hogenson observes that "what is important about the fractal nature of the REM sleep brain patterns is that they follow a power law distribution with precisely the same mathematical structure as 'the flow of the Nile, light from quasars, ion channel currents, neuronal firing patterns, earthquake distribution, electrical current fluctuations in man-made devices, inter-car-intervals in expressway traffic, and in variations in sound intensity in all melodic music'".[20]

All of this tends to confirm the notion that the *imago Dei* in the human psyche, the self, rests for its constellation in a particular person upon transcendent self-organizing dynamics within the universe as such, which we could perhaps agree to call *die Göttlichkeit* if we mean by that the dynamic instigator and organizer. The human psyche thus stands in profound continuity with the world, as the world does with the psyche. This is what Jung intuited in his notion of psyche and matter being two sides of a single reality.

The Self Under Development

It might be wrongfully concluded that once the *imago Dei* takes form in a human being and is constellated as a core self, it resembles a static construct embedded in this discrete particle of flesh, perhaps repeating the same old songs from birth to death but not changing fundamentally. On the other hand, developmental psychology has long held that the human psyche is not a static entity but undergoes gradual and rapid developmental shifts throughout an individual's lifetime. Stages of ego and self development have

---

[18] Hogenson, p. 156.
[19] Ibid., p. 165.
[20] Ibid.

been discovered and discussed by Freud, Jung, Fordham, Erikson, Piaget, Klein, Winnicott, and a host of other theoreticians. Fordham speaks of deintegration and reintegration processes in the self that account for the building up of ego-consciousness, but do these bring about essential change or development in the self per se? Does the self change as a result of lifelong individuation? And if so, how does this affect its transcendent source, *die Göttlichkeit*? Is the transcendent somehow also brought into a developmental process as the *imago Dei* emerges in an individual person's life?

To forestall the notion that we are dealing with static entities in speaking of ego and self, Jung describes, a few pages later in the same section of *Mysterium*, "The Dog," two main steps, or phases, in the alchemical (i.e., the psychological) opus, which lead to the full emergence of the alchemical *lapis* (i.e., the self), the goal of the process. Psychologically, this work requires overcoming the radical polarity in the psyche between conscious and unconscious, a polarity that is endemic to the human personality and comes about naturally in the course of earlier developments of ego-consciousness. It amounts to a division within the self. Jung is speaking here of a further stage of individuation after ego has been formed, persona identity achieved, and the consolidation of conscious personality and character structure has been put into place and lived. Using the imagery of alchemy, he writes:

> [There are] two main divisions of the work, the *opus ad album et ad rubeum*. The former is the *opus Lunai*, the latter the *opus Solis*. Psychologically they correspond to the constellation of unconscious contents in the first part of the analytical process and to the integration of these contents in actual life.... The psychological parallel is the transformation of both the unconscious and the conscious, a fact known to everyone who methodically "has it out" with his unconscious.[21]

---

[21] C.G. Jung, *Mysterium Coniunctionis*, CW 14, para. 181.

The first piece of the analytic work (the Lunar opus— "whitening") involves the exposure of unconscious contents, which is followed by the integration of these contents into conscious and practical living (the Solar opus—"reddening"). First, there is the discovery phase, bringing up contents of the unconscious into consciousness—Jung names hypochondriachal obsessions, phobias, delusions, as well as dreams, phantasies, and creative forerunners. These must be "whitened," that is taken into the light of consciousness and accepted fully for what they are. Once these aspects of the self are made thoroughly conscious, the assimilation of them and their meaning into practical life can begin.

Together, these two phases of the work were seen to bring about the transformation not only of consciousness but also of the unconscious. In his seminal paper "The Practical Use of Dream-Analysis," Jung speaks of "mutual penetration of conscious and unconscious, and not—as is commonly thought and practiced—a one-sided evaluation, interpretation, and deformation of un-conscious contents by the conscious mind."[22] This mutual penetration changes both sides of the psyche, conscious and unconscious. The point here is that the self as psychic totality is actually a work in process, not an inner object simply waiting to become raised into visibility. Emergence of the self is a lifelong process, continuing into old age and especially so if the work of making it conscious is deliberately undertaken. The *imago Dei* develops in the course of individuation.

Nevertheless, no matter how far the development toward consciousness may advance, a region of mystery remains. A few lines later in *Mysterium*, Jung writes: "the salvation (*salus*) is one, just as the thing (*res*) is one…it is the fact of the self, that indescribable wholeness of people that cannot be made visible but is indispensable as an intuitive concept."[23] Jung designates the self here as "a fact" (*eine Tatsache)* that surpasses description. As a fact,

---

[22] C.G. Jung, *"The Practical Use of Dream-Analysis,"* CW 16, para. 327.
[23] C.G. Jung, *Mysterium Coniunctionis*, CW 14, para. 181.

it is indisputable and psychically real, and so one can speak of "an experience of the self" or "the self as experience." But, even as one recognizes and names the self as a "fact," it remains paradoxically out of reach as an intuitive concept (*intuitiver Begriff*). Intuitive concepts reach for the unknown and the ineffable, which in itself (*per se*) remains forever beyond the grasp of the conscious mind.

Experiencing the Self

How, then, can we speak of experiencing the self, this *imago Dei*, a transcendent psychological fact/concept, and of bringing it into view at least partially within our limited conscious horizon? What does it mean to *experience* the self?

Jung himself seemed to regard religious experiences as experiences of the self. In his view, an experience of the self is a religious experience, and vice versa. An account of these as found in all the cultures of the world—the many "varieties of religious experience"—would describe the self archetype per se from various cultural and traditional vantage points.

Rudolf Otto classically described this type of experience in his book *The Idea of the Holy* as numinous. From that extremely influential work, which was explicitly about *religious* experience and which Otto claimed was a unique kind of experience—*sui generis*—Jung borrowed the terms *numinosum* and numinous to describe experience of the archetypal images of the collective unconscious. Otto defined the numinous as a *mysterium tremendum*. Jung in turn regarded the numinous experience of the Holy as the religious expression of the psychological experience of the self because the self is so deeply related to *die Göttlichkeit*. It is the same experience with a different name. Religious persons beg to differ, under-standably, and claim that their experiences point beyond the *imago Dei* to the *Dei* itself, beyond the subjective to the objective. As a psychologist, Jung stopped short of ontological or metaphysical claims of this sort, but he could relate to them in his feeling as a human being and as the subject of similar experiences. Moreover, he links the self to Deity, as we have seen.

The religions of the world provide for their adherents a host of images, ideas, and names that may evoke the experience of the Holy in one or another mental or physical form. Each tradition shows a wide variety of religious experience. Religious icons, for example, provide an opportunity for numinous experiences, as do prayer, meditation, ritual actions, and pilgrimages. So do active imagination, intersubjective dialogue, and intimate psychophysical communion. All of these can lead to numinous experiences, to experiences of a *mysterium tremendum*, to a sense of awe that one may justifiably name an experience of the self.

There is another category of experience that we may name an experience of the self, and this has to do with energy flow and overcoming, or transcending, the barrier between conscious and unconscious aspects of the psyche. This type does not have so much to do with religious awe and numinosity, although Otto does write about "The Element of 'Energy' or Urgency" in *Das Heilige*, but can be described instead as moments of abandon and psychic fullness, when physical and psychic energy flow freely and without ob-struction into a channel formed by an impersonal "director," which is not the self-conscious, intentional, willful ego. Such moments are generally not without tightly prescribed form, although the form may be largely unconscious to the actor. Indeed, most frequently they are highly and formally structured and articulated with extraordinary finesse and refinement. A convincing religious ritual, for instance, is both indelibly scripted by tradition and learned by practice, but in the moment of performance it is filled with a flow of energy and spontaneous emotion that generates numinosity. So, too, with art. At St. Petersburg's Mariinsky Theater, the star ballerinas, who dance with and far beyond "technique," pouring their whole beings into well-practiced and now deeply ingrained habitual forms, incarnate the self in their effortless-looking movements. Those who can deeply see this and take it in also experience the self in and through them. It is a complete psychic and physical involvement without inhibition or restraint, holding back nothing, the full all-out abandonment to an impersonal form and style, which makes it "of the self" and not "of the ego." Sometimes we talk, read, run, work, play, cook, and eat like this. Life in the self means overcoming the divide between conscious and unconscious, being both at once. In this we also participate in the fullness of *die Göttlichkeit* as immanent within the space and time limitations of our physical world. One can think of incarnation of the Divine in these grace-filled and full-bodied moments.

Like the more familiar numinous experiences described as religious, these are also experiences of the *imago Dei* expressed by *die Göttlichkeit*, and they can take place in social settings or in solitude, when mental activity, feeling, and behavior become uninhibited and lead to unconsciously scripted unions and conjunctions—physical, psychological, and spiritual. One may come to these in "dialogues" that become "monologues with two voices" (duets); in reveries whether alone or with another; in solitary walks in nature or through urban landscapes when one's self-consciousness as a separate individual fades away and one becomes united with the surroundings; in athletic or artistic creation that "happens," beyond technique and conscious determination; in dreams that are symbolic and numinous. Here the ego joins with the self and becomes one with the *imago Dei,* approximating or perhaps even becoming fully fused with *die Göttlichkeit* behind it.

A third category of experiences of the self consists in the conscious containment of opposites (for example, the sublime and the shabby—the perfection of the Mariinsky Theater and the trashy parking lot behind the St. Petersburg hotel) in a single, undivided image. Jung draws on alchemy for this, in the image of Kalid's "son of the dog" who is also the "son of the philosophers." For the individual, this has to do with the immensely difficult task of holding in conscious awareness a fuller and more objective perception of oneself than is normal, which integrates in a single sense of self, or self image, the persona and the shadow (good and bad, light and dark, angel and animal), the gender-identified ego and the otherwise-gendered subpersonality within (a syzygy), and the superior with the inferior psychological functions and attitudes. This is heightened or expanded self-consciousness, as well as full self acceptance. It denotes psychological maturity, which may ripen with age and result in psychic objectivity about oneself, others, and the world at large.

Conclusion

"Yesterday I had a marvelous dream," Jung writes to Father Victor White at the end of 1946 as he is recovering from a heart attack.

"One bluish diamondlike star high in heaven, reflected in a round, quiet pool—heaven above, heaven below. The imago Dei in the darkness of the Earth, this is myself. The dream meant a great consolation. I am no more a black and endless sea of misery and suffering but a certain amount thereof contained in a divine vessel.[24]

It was from experiences like this that Jung drew when he penned enigmatic phrases like the one in *Mysterium*, *"als welche die Göttlichkeit das Selbst ausdrückt."* The Divinity, symbolized by a bluish star, is reflected in the endless sea of misery within the darkness of the experienced world, and here it expresses itself in a form, as *imago Dei*, reflected within the psyche. This imago is the sacred vessel that contains all our self-contradictions, polarized part-personalities, and confusing emotional states. It gives our specific individual life its impersonal divine form and meaning. Holding this vessel firmly in the mirror of consciousness must be counted as an experience of the self. This is what remains when all the specific contents and personal structures of one's psychic identity are erased. It is the surplus factor, the soul itself.

---

[24] A. Lammers and A. Cunningham, *The Jung-White Letters*, p. 60.

C.G. Jung, Richard Wilhelm and I Ching[1]

Our psychology would be very poor indeed if we did not regularly, systematically, and even thievishly borrow from the research and investigations of many other disciplines. Freud did this, and Jung did it even more. In a 1913 letter to Drs. Smith Ely Jelliffe and William Alanson White, the founders of a new journal called *Psychoanalytic Review*, Jung advocates "studying the remarkable analogies with certain ethnological structures.... It is beyond the powers of the individual...to master the manifold domains for the mental sciences which should throw some light upon the comparative anatomy of the mind.... We need not only the work of medical psychologists, but also that of philologists, historians, archaeologists, mythologists, folklore students, ethnologists, philosophers, theologians, pedagogues, and biologists...."[2] This is an impressive list of "others" to learn and to borrow from, but it is by no means complete or exhaustive. Jung left out comparative religion scholars and theologians as well as modern physicists, who we know would later become among his most important dialogic "others."

There is also the critically important matter (and today especially so) of dialogue among cultures, for clinical practice as well as for theory. More specifically, I will look at the results of the

---

[1] Originally given as a lecture in October, 2013 in Qingdao, China at a conference on "Richard Wilhelm and I Ching, I Ching and Jungian Analysis." Published in the *Chinese Journal of Analytical Psychology,* vol. 1, no. 1, 2015.

[2] W. McGuire (ed.), *Jelliffe: American Psychoanalyst and Physician*, p. 193.

dialogue Jung engaged in with Chinese thought. If any culture on earth presented the Eurocentric mind of Jung's day with radical otherness, it was the Chinese. The story of how Jung engaged Chinese thought is fascinating. He opened himself to profound influence, all the while maintaining his Western roots in scientific thinking and clinical practice. This influence entered his psychological world most strongly through his relationship with Richard Wilhelm, his friend and collaborator. I will recount this as an instance of how analytical psychology was deeply influenced and enriched by engagement with other cultures.

As we now know, many tributaries flow into the mainstream of Jung's psychological theory. In recent years there has been considerable scholarly interest in tracing these various sources. Evident among them is the psychiatric background, of course, with Eugen Bleuler as a key figure and followed strongly by Théodore Flournoy, Pierre Janet, and Jean-Martin Charcot. Then there is the general intellectual background of the Enlightenment and 19th century European thought—figures such as Kant, Schopenhauer, Goethe, and C.G. Carus are referenced frequently in Jung's published writings. It is evident that he read them deeply. Of course, Sigmund Freud also plays a central part in Jung's formation as a psychological theorist, and the Freudian influence remains important even after Jung's break with his mentor in 1913. Another group of tributaries began entering the picture already in the Freudian period: anthropologists like Lévy-Bruhl, psychologists like William James, ancient Gnostics, various Christian and pagan figures, scholars of mythology and religion, and thinkers from other disciplines as well. Later the alchemists, from whose works Jung absorbed so much, added their tinctures. Blended into the mixture from at least the time of the publication of *Wandlungen und Symbole der Libido* in 1912 was the (increasingly important) influence of non-Western thought—Egyptian, Indian, Tibetan, and most centrally for our purposes here, Chinese.

One way to get our bearings here is to look at the significant relationship between Jung and the important European scholar of

Chinese thought, Richard Wilhelm. This relationship began in the early 1920s, according to Jung, and lasted until 1930, when Wilhelm died. Thomas Kirsch, upon the occasion of a visit to China in 1994, in a talk titled "Jung and Tao," reminded the audience that Jung "claimed that Wilhelm had influenced him more than any other individual in his life. This comes as a surprise to many who would naturally have thought that Freud was the most influential person in Jung's development."[3]

A short correspondence exists between Jung and Richard Wilhelm, which is housed in the C.G. Jung Archives at the ETH-Bibliotek in Zurich. It is small but revealing. Some of Jung's letters to Wilhelm have been published in *C.G. Jung Letters 1906-1950*, but not all of them and none of Wilhelm's letters appear there. While this was not one of Jung's major correspondences and in no way rivals the extensive epistolary exchanges with Sigmund Freud (showing the influence of psychoanalysis), with Wolfgang Pauli (detailing the importance Jung gave to the relationship of analytical psychology with modern physics), or with Victor White (expounding his agreements and differences with Christian theology), it is nevertheless instructive and provides an important perspective on the significance of Chinese thought for Jung.

Let me introduce Richard Wilhelm before entering into a discussion of the correspondence. Wilhelm was born on 10 May 1873 in Stuttgart, Germany. (He was therefore two years older than Jung.) His father was a craftsman and died when Richard was 9 years old. After that, his mother and grandmother raised him. In 1891, at the age of 18, he began theological studies at the University of Tübingen. In 1895, at the age of 22, he was ordained, and he became a vicar in the German town of Wimsheim in 1897. There he met his future wife, Salome Blumhardt. They were engaged in 1899, just before he left for China to work in the East Asia mission (the Allgemein Protestantischer Missionsverein) in Qingdao, a German colonial city at the time. In 1900, Salome joined him in China, and

---

[3] T. Kirsch, "Jung and Tao," p. 1.

they were married in Shanghai. Four children were born in China in rapid succession.

From 1899 until 1920, with a couple of brief trips back in Germany (in 1907 with his family of by then four children and his wife; in 1911) for health reasons—he had contracted amoebic dysentery from Chinese food in 1910, Wilhelm worked in Qingdao as pastor, educator, and translator. Gifted with strong intellectual abilities and scholarly inclinations, he quickly developed a fascination for Chinese culture and religion. This was recognized by the German Mission, and he was allowed to spend much of his time on linguistic and scholarly studies. He soon became fluent in Chinese and began translating Chinese texts into German. His first set of publications, seven in number, among them works by Confucius, Da Hüo, and Tsai-Li-Sekte, date from 1905, the year his son, Helmut, was born. In 1920, Wilhelm returned with his family to Germany, but in two years he was back in China, this time in Peking, where he served as scientific counselor in the German embassy and taught at Peking University until 1924. Returning permanently to Germany in 1924, he became honorary professor of Chinese history and philosophy at the University of Frankfort and remained at this university until his death in 1930, just shy of his 57th birthday.

His production of works on Chinese culture was prodigious. Between 1910 and 1930, he worked on the translation and editing of an eight-volume series of Chinese literary works titled *Religion und Philosophie Chinas* ("The Religion and Philosophy of China"). After 10 years in close collaboration with the noted Chinese scholar and sage Lao Nai-hsuan, he produced his masterful if somewhat controversial translation of *I Ching*, published in 1924. After his final return to Germany in 1924, he became known as "the spiritual link between China and Europe."[4] He enjoyed friendly contact with numerous culturally prominent figures of the time—Rudolph Otto, Albert Schweitzer, Herman Hesse, Martin Buber, Tagore, and, most importantly for our purposes, C.G. Jung.

---

[4] K. Rennich, "Richard Wilhelm," p. 1301.

The correspondence on file in the ETH archives extends over a period of only about 10 months and contains 13 letters all told. Some letters between the two men are evidently missing from this collection. The first one is a letter from Wilhelm to Jung dated 28 December 1928. The letterhead reads "China-Institut, Frankfort a. M, Director: Prof. Dr. Richard Wilhelm." In a formal and typically "correct" style, Wilhelm asks Jung if he would be willing to let his name be used as a sponsor of the newly founded International Institut für Buddhismusforschung. This institute was founded by a committee at the Musée Gaimet in Paris. S.E. Tai Hsü, the president of the Chinese Buddhist Union, had come to Europe to found this organization, which also had centers in Nanking and Singapore.

It is unclear from the available correspondence what sort of relationship Jung and Wilhelm had prior to this letter. Nor is it evident why Wilhelm would have wanted to ask Jung to add his name to the list of sponsors of this organization. It must have been the case that from their previous encounters and discussions Jung had struck Wilhelm as someone with a deep interest in Eastern, and particularly in Chinese, thought and religion. Also, it was true that Jung's reputation and intellectual standing in Europe at the time was such that the leading European scholar of Chinese religion and philosophy would want his support. We know from many sources that Jung had a voracious appetite for the study of religious symbols and concepts from all corners of the world. In his Foreword to the Baynes English translation of the Wilhelm translation of the *I Ching*, Jung writes that he met Wilhelm in the early 1920s. They probably first encountered one another in person in the circle of Count Hermann Keyserling, founder of the "Schule der Weisheit" (the "School of Wisdom") in Darmstadt, Germany. In 1921, Wilhelm lectured at the Psychological Club in Zurich on the *I Ching* (*"Der Jking"*), during which he gave a demonstration on how to use the book of oracles. In 1926, he presented two lectures at the club, titled "Chinesische Jogapraxis" ("Chinese Yoga Practice") and "Chinesische Seelenlehre" ("Chinese Spiritual Teachings"). So, it is clear that by the time the first letter in our extant correspondence arrived on

Jung's doorstep, the two men had had a considerable exchange of views and would have built up a solid working relationship.

The second letter in the series is from Jung to Wilhelm, dated 6 April 1929. Earlier that year, on 29 January, Wilhelm again lectured at the club, this time on "*Einige Probleme der buddhistischen Meditation*" ("Some Problems in Buddhist Meditation"). This letter is published in *C.G. Jung Letters*, Volume 1. Reading between the lines, it seems that a great deal had transpired between the two men since the first letter was written some three months earlier. Jung addresses Wilhelm as "Mein lieber Professor," (My Dear Professor), a somewhat more familiar form than the more usual formal German greeting, "Sehr geehrter Professor" ("Highly Esteemed Professor"). His letter is friendly and casual, and he says that he hopes Wilhelm is feeling better: "It was surely the cold mayonnaise at X's [the Schlegels, a part of Jung's circle in Zurich] which ruined our care."[5] Jung goes on to say that he will be passing through Frankfurt on his way to Bad Nauheim for a Psychotherapy Congress (the fourth General Medical Congress for Psychotherapy) where he delivered the much referenced lecture, "The Aims of Psychotherapy," and says that he would like to meet with Wilhelm if possible, however briefly—he would have a three-hour stopover in Frankfurt between trains. He also mentions a joint project: "I shall soon be able to make a start on our MS."[6] This is a reference to the work that would be published as *Das Geheimnis der goldenen Blüte* (*The Secret of the Golden Flower*), a translation of an ancient Chinese alchemy text by Wilhelm. Wilhelm sent this translation to Jung sometime in 1928 with the request that Jung consider writing a psychological commentary. Here we find Jung and Wilhelm in an intellectual partnership.

Working on this text marked a critical turning point for Jung. In *Memories, Dreams, Reflections,* he writes: "Light on the nature of alchemy began to come to me only after I had read the text of

---

[5] G. Adler (ed.), *C.G. Jung Letters*, vol. 1, p. 63.
[6] Ibid.

the *Golden Flower*, that specimen of Chinese alchemy which Richard Wilhelm sent me...["7] Jung's fascination with alchemy had its major point of origin, according to Jung himself, in this Chinese treatise. From this point in his life on, the study of alchemy became one of the main resources in his psychological writing and thinking. Why? From at least 1913 forward, Jung was searching for the fundamental stratum of the human psyche in the depths of the collective unconscious. He was quite sure that Freud had not found it in his theory of the unconscious, with its emphasis on sexuality and the Oedipus complex. His quest for basic structures led him to postulate (eventually) the theory of archetypes, which he would later often define as the basic building blocks of the human psyche and common to all members of the species. What he found in the Chinese treatise that Wilhelm gave him was a set of images and experiences that ran parallel to what he had found repeatedly in the analysis of his Western patients. More importantly still, he glimpsed, perhaps for the first time, the common dynamic that points to individuation as the goal of psychological development. It was the process of transformation leading to individuation that drew him to alchemy. From Chinese alchemy he would go on and enter into a deep study of alchemical symbolism, primarily in Western sources, interpreting and translating them into psychological categories, and relating these symbols and images to the deep unconscious structures, processes, and symbolic representations offered by the psyches of modern people in analysis.

The third letter in this correspondence—from Jung to Wilhelm and dated 26 April 1929—shows Jung in an apologetic mode. He wants Wilhelm to know that he is sorry for intruding on his privacy by rushing over to his home while passing through Frankfort on his way to Bad Nauheim. He says that he was worried about Wilhelm's health. As an experienced and highly intuitive physician, Jung must have sensed Wilhelm's fragility. Wilhelm would, after all, die in less than a year from the date of this letter. Jung expresses his urgent

[7] C.G. Jung, *Memories, Dreams, Reflections*, p. 204.

concern by underlining: "You are *too important* to our Western world. I must keep telling you this. You musn't melt away or otherwise disappear, or get ill."[8] And then he comes to the point of the letter:

> The result of my lecture at the recent Nauheim Psychotherapeutic Congress is that, without my knowledge, the board of the Psychotherapeutic Society has decided to ask *you* to give a lecture next year (presumably in Baden-Baden) This will make history! Think what it means if medical practitioners, who get at person so brashly and in the most vulnerable spot, were to be inoculated with Chibnese philosophy! It is simply unbelievable. I am delighted and only hope that no devils will keep you away from this historic occasion. This really goes to the heart of the matter. Medicine is switching over to psychology with a vengeance, and that's where the East comes in. There's nothing to be done with the philosophers and the theologians because of their arrogance.[9]

Here we can see the weighty importance for Western medicine and psychotherapy that Jung attached to Wilhelm's translations of Chinese texts. The transformation of medicine that Jung speaks of here was his lifelong concern, namely to shift psychiatry and the mental health professions away from the dominant materialistic reductionism of the medical model (psyche = brain chemistry) to a psychological understanding. For this he had looked to many disciplines in the previous 30 years, and now he glimpsed a brand-new and powerful resource, Chinese thought. This perception that Chinese philosophy and religion would be such a potent and much needed tool in the transformation of Western medicine, especially with respect to mental health, was founded on Jung's conviction that in its deep historic introspective tradition, it had discovered the

---

[8] G. Adler (ed.), *C.G. Jung Letters*, vol. 1, p. 63.
[9] Ibid., pp. 63-64.

psyche in all its range and complexity, and this would now be revealed to Western minds through such universal symbols as the mandala.

At the end of this letter Jung states in passing: "The Lamaic mandala has been copied. I will send back the original soon."[10] In *Memories, Dreams, Reflections* Jung comments at some length on the importance of this mandala image for him. He relates that as a part of his own self-analysis and inner work in the years 1927-28, he painted a couple of images that he would later call mandalas: The first he titled "Window on Eternity" (which is reproduced in several places, e.g., in "Concerning Mandala Symbolism,"[11] and the second he says had an odd Chinese quality to it. Shortly after this, he writes, "I received a letter from Richard Wilhelm enclosing the manuscript of a Taoist alchemical treatise entitled *The Secret of the Golden Flower*, with a request that I write a commentary on it [this letter, incidentally, is not found in the correspondence in the ETH archives]. I devoured the text at once, for the text gave me undreamed of confirmation of my ideas about the mandala and the circumambulation of the center. That was the first event which broke through my isolation.... In remembrance of this coincidence, this 'synchronicity,' I wrote underneath the picture which had made so Chinese an impression upon me: 'In 1928, when I was painting this picture, showing the golden, well-fortified castle, Richard Wilhelm in Frankfort sent me the thousand-year-old Chinese text on the yellow castle, the germ of the immortal body.'"[12]

What this gift from Wilhelm provided for Jung was a way of understanding the meaning of what he had been doing spontaneously for about 10 years, i.e., drawing mandala images. The mandala represents circumambulation of the self, and therefore the individuation process. What the Chinese text taught him—or confirmed for him—was that psychological development is not

---

[10] Ibid., p. 64.
[11] C.G. Jung, CW 9ii.
[12] C.G. Jung, *Memories, Dreams, Reflections*, p. 197.

linear but rather "circular," a circumambulation of a non-representable center: "There is no linear evolution; there is only circumambulation of the self. Uniform development exists, at most, only at the beginning; later, everything points toward the center."[13] This notion of individuation as circular rather than linear, basically a Chinese one, would become a central feature of Jung's theory of individuation. Chinese thought, therefore, played a key role in coming to this understanding and formulation of a process that is perhaps the centerpiece of Jung's psychological theory. It was precisely the absence of linear thinking in Chinese philosophy that impressed Jung. His theory of synchronicity would also grow out of this.

At the time of the correspondence, of course, Jung had no idea of how important the long-range influence and effect of Wilhelm's friendship and gifts would be for him. His intuition led him, however, to use the word "historic" when speaking of Wilhelm's potential contribution to medical psychotherapy. This is because he sensed the power and depth of what Chinese thought had to offer to the one-sided rationalism of Western medical science, with its strictly causal explanations and exclusively linear perspective on growth and development. Chinese thought, as delivered by Richard Wilhelm, would further a historic transformation. With respect to Jung's own thinking, at least, this seems to have been the case.

The next letter in the correspondence is short but quite moving (25 May 1929) and marks a definite turning point in the personal relationship between the two men. Again, there seems to be a missing letter from Wilhelm to Jung in the extant correspondence, since Jung writes back to Wilhelm celebrating his acceptance of the invitation to give the lecture proposed by Jung a month earlier. For the first time in the correspondence, he addresses Wilhelm as "Dear Friend." He writes: "Dear Friend, It is lovely to hear the word 'friend' from you. Fate seems to have assigned us the role of being two pillars which support the weight of the bridge between East and

---

[13] Ibid.

West. I thank you with all my heart that you have agreed to give the lecture".[14] The lost letter from Wilhelm, it must be surmised, invited this new level of closeness between them—now friends, not collegial professors—and Jung responded with feeling and the image of a joint mission: to mediate East and West together. The remarkable thing is that Jung locates himself in this way. It was obvious that Richard Wilhelm was such a mediating figure for Europeans. But Jung? Jung's role would be somewhat different from Wilhelm's, as it turned out. Always he begins his reflections and interpretations of non-Western materials from the point of view of the Westerner, with his own experience as a primary reference point. Whereas Wilhelm, the learned Sinologist, had spent nearly 25 years living and working in China, Jung was a Western psychiatrist who spent his entire adult life in Zurich, Switzerland. But the meeting with Wilhelm struck a chord deep within him, and he was never the same afterward.

Jung's method in mediating East and West called for him to stick with the Western psyche and to find points of commonality with Eastern thought as revealed in its classical texts. Wilhelm was a Western Christian missionary who had so deeply immersed himself in Chinese thought that he engaged the West from a Chinese point of view. In a sense, he was a missionary who had "gone native." (He is supposed to have boasted to Jung that during his 20 years as a missionary in China, he had never baptized a single Chinese!) Knowing the philosophy and religion of both sides so well, he could critique his own original religious tradition from a Chinese perspective. And his translations of Chinese texts into German are more than literary translations; they transform the content in such a way that it can be effectively transmitted to Western intellects. This has, of course, been a point of criticism: that his translation of the *I Ching*, for example, is not literal and exact enough. But this transformation of texts also makes them accessible. Wilhelm was hermetic, more a transformer than a mere translator.

---

[14] C.G. Jung, *Letters*, vol. 1, p. 66.

In the same letter Jung again expresses his concern about Wilhelm's health. Given that Wilhelm had agreed to give the lecture the following year to the Medical Psychotherapy Society, Jung wanted to be sure that he would follow through. (In fact, he would not be able to give that lecture. He died a couple of months before it was due to be presented.) Jung also apologizes for not yet completing his commentary on "The Secret of the Golden Flower" and writes: "No harm has been done by my putting it off, because I have had a number of experiences that have given me some very valuable insights."[15]

In the months following this exchange, Wilhelm received some treatments for his health problems, and the correspondence turns to the minutiae of publishing—contracts, fees, etc., and some further projects being planned. Then on 10 September 1929 Jung writes to Wilhelm from his tower at Bollingen and announces that the commentary "is more or less finished."[16] It is longer than expected "because it represents a European reaction to the wisdom of China. I have tried my hand at interpreting Tao."[17] In the commentary as it is finally published, Jung offers a rich and nuanced psychological interpretation of the Chinese alchemical text and relates his own and his patients' inner development to the processes described in it. In both the Chinese text and the inner experience of Western patients, he writes, the goal of the work is consciousness and wholeness, i.e., realization of the self. Jung puts the emphasis in his commentary decidedly upon *living* the Tao rather than only interpreting it. (He acknowledges the several ways in which it has been translated, as "way," "meaning" [Wilhelm], "God" [Jesuits], "providence.") Jung's essay is a *tour de force* and must be ranked as one of his most brilliant and inspired works. The careful methodology he lays out and employs here is one that he will carry forward in his work over the decades to follow. While Wilhelm

---

[15] C.G. Jung, "Richard Wilhelm: In Memoriam," CW 15, para. 96.
[16] Ibid., para. 78.
[17] Ibid.

bridges from China to Europe with his translation, Jung bridges from Europe to China with his psychological commentary. Between them, they did truly create a splendid avenue for exchange and discourse between East and West.

It seems important to me that any further work on the dialogue between analytical psychology and Chinese thought begin with this text of Jung's. Here he offers a methodology that will betray neither side in the dialogue and will create numerous subtle and profound inner connections that can link the psychological theory of analytical psychology to the traditional insights of Chinese thought and philosophy.

In the penultimate letter of the correspondence, dated 24 October 1929, Wilhelm suggests some minor changes in Jung's text and in the contract with the publisher. He also confirms that the German title of the book will be *Das Geheimnis der Goldenen Blüte* ("The Secret [or Mystery] of the Golden Flower [or Blossom]"). A Chinese editor had previously changed it to "The Art of Prolonging Human Life," but they decided to go back to the original title.

In the final letter, the 13th in the series, dated 28 October 1929, Jung states his agreement with the changes and expresses his warm approval of the title. He also says that he is preparing a series of mandalas drawn by patients: "The pictures complement one another and reveal in their complexity an excellent picture of the efforts of the European unconscious spirit to grasp the Oriental eschatology" (my translation). What Jung means by "Oriental eschatology" is the goal of the individuation (or spiritual) process: wholeness and conscious realization of the self, "the diamond body" in Chinese alchemy. He closes the correspondence with the unforgettable sentence: "At any rate you must never forget the care of your body, since the spirit has the unfortunate tendency to want to devour the body" (my translation). The book was published at the end of 1929. Wilhelm died on 1 March 1930.

In May 1930, Jung delivered the principal address at a memorial service for Richard Wilhelm in Munich. In this moving speech, Jung expresses his deep gratitude for what he received from Wilhelm:

"Wilhelm's life-work is of such immense importance to me because it clarified and confirmed so much that I had been seeking, striving for, thinking, and doing in my efforts to alleviate the psychic sufferings of Europeans. It was a tremendous experience for me to hear through him, in clear language, things I had dimly divined in the confusion of our European unconscious. Indeed, I feel myself so very much enriched by him that it seems to me as if I had received more from him than from any other man."[18] Jung tells why he feels Wilhelm's contribution was so important: His translation of and commentary on the *I Ching* provides "an Archimedean point from which our Western attitude of mind could be lifted off its foundations."[19] Moreover, he "has inoculated us with the living germ of the Chinese spirit, capable of working a fundamental change in our view of the world."[20] The *I Ching* is based not on the principle of causality but on the principle of synchronicity, and this related, in Jung's view, directly to his work on the unconscious of his European patients.

The treasures that Jung found in Chinese thought, thanks to the work of Richard Wilhelm, continued to influence his thinking for the rest of his life. What began in their joint mission of holding up a bridge between East and West ended in a complex psychological theory that combines Western linear, causal, scientific thinking and Eastern (i.e., Chinese) noncausal, synchronistic, holistic thinking. In such works as *Aion*, "Synchronicity: An Acausal Connecting Principle," and *Mysterium Coniunctionis,* Jung proposes a view of (psychic) reality that is as compatible with Chinese Taoist thinking as it is with European scientific thinking.

In his life, too, Jung made himself an experiment in the uniting of these "opposites," East and West. He did attempt to live the Tao and not only to think and write about it. The influence of China entered into his everyday life as well as into his psychological theorizing. I believe this has continued, to some extent at least, in the clinical tradition that is so much a part of analytical psychology.

---

[18] C.G. Jung, "Richard Wilhelm: In Memoriam," para. 96.
[19] Ibid., para. 78.
[20] Ibid.

Creative Powers and Personalities[1]

A client of many years in analysis recalled a dream that he had several days earlier which had stayed with him ever since and retained a remarkable degree of vividness. This is the dream as he told it to me:

> I am in a group of people from the medical profession. These are outstanding scientists and inventors of new medical technologies. One of them signals me over to the side to show me a new creation. He holds out to me a device with two metal handles that are attached to a basketlike structure which is holding a beating heart. He tells me that this heart has been created purely with stem cells, and this represents a major breakthrough in medicine. I am astonished as I look at this miracle of laboratory creation. It is a real heart made of cells and tissues, and it is beating steadily. I reflect on the incredible recent history of medical technology, beginning with open-heart surgery in the 1950s and continuing in a rapidly accelerating pace through the recent decades with inventions like pacemakers and stints until now this breakthrough. It is as though we had climbed a high mountain and now look into the far distance at even higher mountains to climb. I cannot take my eyes off the beating heart. The creator hands it over to me, and I take

---

[1] Originally Published in K. Madden (ed.), *The Unconscious Roots of Creativity*, 2016.

the handles and carry the beating heart over to my young daughter to show her this miracle of science. I realize that it will be only in her generation and her children's generation that the full impact of this creation will be recognized and fully integrated into medical practice. As he tells me of this experience in the night, I sense his deep emotion. He continues to visualize the image of the beating heart, he says, and he has been meditating on it. He could not remember a more impressive dream, and he has been recording dreams for decades by now. To me, this symbol seemed to sum up a long span of personal development and inner creativity. The image at the center of the dream was numinous, in a strong sense of that loaded word: It was awesome and inspiring. It signaled a new creation.

This account strikes me as exactly to the point of what Erich Neumann describes in his essay "Creative Man and Transformation": "This is our situation. We stand before the creative principle. Wherever we find the creative principle...we venerate it as the hidden treasure that in humble form conceals a fragment of the godhead."[2] In this dream, the subject stands in awe of *human* creativity. It is Promethean. But there is recognition, too, that this new creation is the result of the mysterious creativity in nature, in the stem cells; it is not purely human, although humans participate in it. The new creation—this beating heart—is a result of an interaction between human and nature's creativity. It is this combination that produces the stimulus for wonder and admiration. It is miraculous and, as Neumann says, "conceals a fragment of the godhead." For Neumann, creativity and divinity are, let's say, synonymous, and somehow the godhead has come to reside in the human psyche as its creativity.

Neumann was obviously fascinated by what he calls "the vital principle" and sometimes "the creative principle." Considering his *oeuvre* as a whole, which began haltingly in the 1930s and then accelerated rapidly after the Second World War to reach full

---

[2] E. Neumann, "Creative Man and Transformation," p. 168.

authority by the time of his early death at the age of 55 in 1960, one cannot miss how much of it is dedicated to the theme of creativity. The works that focus explicitly on creativity and its expression in art are: "Kafka's 'The Trial.' An Interpretation through Depth Psychology" (1933/1958); "Art and Time" (1951); "Leonardo da Vinci and the Mother Archetype" (1954); "Creative Man and Trans-formation" (1955); "Creative Man and the 'Great Experience'" (1956); "Chagall and the Bible" (1958); "A Note on Marc Chagall" (195?); "Georg Trakl: The Person and the Myth" (1959); *The Archetypal World of Henry Moore* (1959); "Psyche as the Place of Creation" (1960). However, it must also be said that all of his works are in one way or another concerned with the topic of creativity and "the new." (As an aside, his name translates from German to English as New-man.) Creativity was a fundamental theme in all of Neumann's writings and is perhaps even the main trunk of his considerable body of work. He was deeply gripped by a sense of a new future coming into being in modern cultures and by new "forms" (Gr. *Gestaltungen*), inner and outer, arising out of a seemingly inexhaustible Source. His high respect for this Source is of a religious caliber. To say that Neumann is referencing implicitly *Ein Sof*, the Kabbalistic term for the wellspring of creation, would not be off the mark. (He was after all a student of Kabbalah and Jewish mysticism). His fascination with creativity and creative power was as evident with respect to his outer life as a young Zionist in Palestine as it was for his inner life as an individuating personality and for his brilliant contributions to analytical psychology.

Neumann was a theoretical thinker par excellence and did not hesitate to build metapsychological constructs of immense proportions. In this respect, he differed from his teacher, Jung, who as an "empiricist" was much more cautious in proposing his hypo-theses and mostly would only cast hints and suggest possible directions for more speculative thinking and further research. Jung recognized and admired Neumann's bold contributions, however, and considered them to be significant additions to his pioneer work. I think we would be well advised to agree with Jung on this point.

Sadly, much of Neumann's work has been overlooked or undervalued by the field of analytical psychology as it has developed since Jung's death. One hopes that this neglect will be rectified now with the publication of the extensive and revealing correspondence between Neumann and Jung, *Analytical Psychology in Exile*. As Jung writes in a sharp letter of rebuke to Jolande Jacobi, who was venomously critical of Neumann's early work: "I think that Neumann's work is excellent. It is not a dogmatic system, but a structured account, thought through in minute detail.... One needs to think with him, otherwise one is lost. I even recommend a careful reading of his lecture ["Mystical Man"]."[3] Thus Neumann came to be known as the "thinking Jungian." Jung supported and defended the work of Neumann consistently and throughout his years as a lecturer at Eranos (1948-1960) and as an author of such classics as *Depth Psychology and the New Ethic*, *The Origins and History of Consciousness*, *Amor and Psyche*, and *The Great Mother*. Indeed, there is evidence that Jung regarded Neumann as his most promising student and successor. At the Eranos Conferences, Neumann was well known to be Jung's stand-in as spiritual center and intellectual leader after Jung retired from regular attendance in 1952. In fact, Olga Fröbe-Kapteyn, the founder of Eranos and owner of its beautiful grounds on Lago Magiore, intended to leave the estate as a loan to Neumann upon her death for his lifetime.[4] Unfortunately, he died before she did.

What I would like to do in this essay is to give an account of Neumann's theory of creativity as expressed primarily in two essays, "Creative Man and Transformation" and "The Place of Creation" and with reference to some of his other works. These two essays were originally lectures presented at the Eranos Conferences in 1954 and 1960, respectively. I will not try to explain why the subject of creativity was so important to Neumann, since I have no documented sources or evidence for that and choose not to

---

[3] M. Liebscher (ed.), *Analytical Psychology in Exile*, p. xli.
[4] R. Bernadini, "Neumann at Eranos," p. 226.

speculate. Without question, however, the topic of creativity fascinated him and gripped him throughout his life with a kind of religious passion.

Creative Powers in Nature and Human Beings

I will begin by reading Neumann backward, from the high perspective of his essay "The Place of Creation." This was his last lecture at Eranos, presented in August 1960, only several months before his death in December. At the time, he did not know that he was seriously ill, so his demise came as a surprise to all, including his family. Even he was not aware that he was dying to the very end.[5]

In this densely packed essay, which summarizes much of his thinking on creativity and brings it to a culminating meta-psychological summit, he gives expression to a theory that is all-embracing, extending from the most primitive manifestations of created order in the mineral and plant worlds to the most sublime on the psychological level. Looking back from this vantage point, one can recognize how the earlier works fall into a consistent pattern. One of his intellectual guides in this endeavor was Adolf Portmann, the marine zoologist and fellow star Eranos lecturer; the other was, of course, C.G. Jung, his friend and most important mentor.

I summarize: For Neumann, it can clearly be said, all manifestations of creativity, whether purely natural, human or transpersonal (archetypal), are fundamentally expressions of what he calls the Vital Principle (VP), or sometimes alternatively the Creative Principle. This is the driving force behind all of creation and evolution, a sort of God-factor, which is why I capitalize it. In this late essay, Neumann delineates three aspects of this creative power. Within the Vital Principle, there is a mysterious center that is responsible for order and form. This is the Ordering Agency (OA), a second aspect of the God-factor. In itself, the VP would create an

---

[5] L. Neumann. "A Letter from Julie Neumann to Olga Fröbe-Kapteyn," p. 237.

excess of multiplicity. Its profligacy is delimited and shaped by the OA. This dual process is exemplified in the creation of "species" in the animal world, for example: Each individual animal belongs to a species, which contains the plentitude of living beings in that order. Without the effective operation of the OA and its form-creating potency, chaotic multiplicity would prevail and spill out of all boundaries beyond measure.

The combined action of the Vital Principle and the Ordering Agency is responsible for "creation" (in German, *Gestaltung*).[6] Neumann sees this whole process as further governed by a third factor, the Directing Agency (DA), which "arises out of the unitary 'field,' in which 'outside space with centers' and unicellular organisms distributed in the field are brought together in an orderly arrangement under unitary direction."[7] The DA is teleologically oriented and is the third factor in the Trinity of creation.

This interplay of factors—dynamic (VP), shaping (OA), goal-oriented (DA)—results in ceaseless creative activities that take place from the most basic levels of existence—Neumann uses the example of the slime mold to illustrate this process at the unicellular level[8]—to the most exalted plane in the human personality, which receives this Trinity into itself and gives it human and cultural expression. This stage, where the Trinity is humanized, was long in preparation. In the course of cosmic and planetary evolution, ever more complex and refined orders have come into being through the activities of the extraneous (to the human psyche) Trinity of creative forces. This has resulted, on our planet, in the formation of species within the animal kingdom. For animals in general, behavior is species-controlled. Inborn instinctive reaction-patterns rule behavior. Neumann describes this as a "migration-into-the-interior of knowledge,"[9] replacing the "extra-

---

[6] E. Neumann, "The Place of the Psyche in Creation," p. 320.
[7] Ibid., pp. 333-34.
[8] Ibid., p. 332.
[9] Ibid., p. 341.

neous knowledge" of the "field" that had previously ruled creation, which is made possible by developments in the sensory organs and nervous systems of members of the animal kingdom. When humans appear on the scene, the strict rules of species behavior are loosened in favor of consciousness in the distinctively human personality. In the human being (*Homo sapiens*), an organism has been created with the necessary means in its neuronal system to take up and extend the project of ordering, of adapting to environments, and indeed of creating new forms. In this, Neumann concurs, whether deliberately or unconsciously, with the biblical view that humankind is the high point (so far) of creation and indeed has received the gift of imago Dei, if one considers the three factors mentioned (VP, OA, and DA) as a representation of the Godhead, the Creator.

In short, this Trinity of previously extraneous creative powers enters into the human personality and is now housed there. This is the source of human creativity.

Having laid down the basic principles for creation and creative power, Neumann turns in his essay to the development of human culture. Having created a space for itself in its own creation, how does this Trinity develop things further on the human level? Neumann is a "stages of development" thinker, and here he draws on his earlier work *The Origins and History of Consciousness* to briefly outline the major stages of humankind's cultural evolution. The stages of development are three major ones and a fourth in process presently.

1. The Primordial Stage. This stage in humanity's history (corresponding more or less to the existence of *Homo Neanderthalensis*) endured over countless millennia—some 300,000 years, according to Neumann[10]—without significant cultural advance or change. It was a kind of slow incubation stage. No creativity, or only minimal creativity in crude toolmaking, is in evidence in this long stretch of (pre- or proto-) human culture. The individuals are still

---

[10] Ibid., p. 343.

largely dominated by species-guided routine adaptations as expressed at the small group (or family) level. This is not far removed from the tightly controlled collectivity that is found in the previous animal ancestors. In the Primordial period, there is no sign of the human psyche "characterized by 'continuous creative formation,' which we regard as characteristic of the human species."[11] The Trinity of creative powers operates largely outside of the individual and has not yet entered into it because there is no suitable home for it; human "personality" is not yet in place to receive it.

2. The Matriarchal Stage. In this stage, which began inexplicably about 40,000 years ago, there is a major breakthrough. (This corresponds to the appearance of Cro-Magnon culture, now preferably called "European early modern human"). Here, individual consciousness begins to emerge quite dramatically, and now we see evidence of symbolic expression and archetypal images in the form of clay figurines, cave paintings and other artworks, and advanced technologies. Humans show evidence of personality on a collective level and are beginning to express creative powers in an entirely unprecedented fashion. But individual consciousness, in the form of the individual ego, remains relatively recessive throughout this stage, and no consistent traditions are established on the collective level. Human experience remains "confined to an inspirational and mantic psychic activity...though this activity was already fully capable of forging morality and producing rituals."[12] Humans in this stage live in a symbolic world and have a "biopsyche," but the nascent ego is passive and observant, according to Neumann, and not active. Elsewhere he calls this a "moon ego."[13] The archetypal images are received (whether from within or without makes no difference because all is symbolic) and recorded but not worked over and developed by an active, engaged, individual ego-consciousness. The Vital Principle and the Ordering Agency are

---

[11] Ibid., p. 344.
[12] Ibid., p. 345.
[13] See E. Neumann, "The Moon and Matriarchal Consciousness."

emerging within the human psyche on a collective level, but conscious intervention and intentionality are minimal. At this stage, humans are symbol-receivers, not symbol-makers.

3. The Patriarchal Stage. This stage inaugurates "the increasingly independent ego and the self-organizing and systematizing conscious mind...man has reached the phase of the actively creative and formative psyche, which involves a completely new kind of takeover of the process of creation from the biopsyche into the psyche of man."[14] It is a leap forward to a new kind of creativity on the part of humankind. Beside this, a creative inwardness appears with "a tendency towards individualization, spearheaded by its outstanding exponent in evolution, the ego-consciousness of man."[15] Now we begin to find "Great Individuals" represented in culture by the King and the Priest. The notion of the individual takes hold, which will generalize from the few to the many over time. Traditions begin to take shape in the form of distinct myths, and there is a deliberate preservation of symbolic material in the form of tablets, temples, and ritual action.

At this stage of development, the human psyche divides: A gap opens, or widens significantly, between ego-consciousness and unconscious processes. The modern psyche begins to emerge. The tension that results between ego and unconscious sets the stage for a special form of creativity unknown previously in the history of the planet, which draws on the unconscious processes on the one hand and is shaped and carried further by the ego on the other. The freedom and independence of the ego to shape and execute, in tension with the unconscious (vital) processes that impinge on ego-consciousness in various ways (visions, intuitions, fantasies, dreams), makes possible the special form of human creativity that we see in this stage and continuing into our own modern times. The Trinity of creation is somewhat divided in this process, however, in accordance with the division of the psyche into conscious and

---

[14] Op. cit., p. 347.
[15] Ibid.

111

unconscious components. The aspects of the Trinity are distributed into different parts of the personality. The Vital Principle is housed basically in the unconscious, while the Ordering Agency takes up its home quite strongly, though not exclusively, in the ego. The Directing Agency continues to do its work in the depths of the collective unconscious, guiding the large-scale evolutionary prospective developments in the history of humankind.

As we see in this section of the essay, Neumann grants tremendous significance to the role of the active (Patriarchy) for human creativity. Its emergence plays a decisive role in how creativity is expressed in the human world, in culture and its evolution. However, he is a Jungian and so does not want to attribute too much value and power to the ego. The development of a strong ego is the contribution of Patriarchy, but it is also only a step on the way to a further psychological development.

4. The Individuation Stage. The Patriarchal stage is superseded by the development of "inwardness," which discovers the ego's source of creative power in the self. In this stage, humans come to recognize the self as the center of creative process and powers in the psyche, and the ego as agent of the self. This is the modern era, and depth psychology enters the picture to radically change consciousness. In this essay and elsewhere, Neumann speaks of this development as the realization of the ego-self axis. This development surpasses the contribution of Patriarchy and takes the evolution of human consciousness a step further. The emergence of the ego-self axis into consciousness brings with it the awareness of the "self field," which overcomes the division between ego-consciousness and the unconscious on a new level. This is not a regression to the earlier stage of minimal differentiation in the psyche, i.e., the matriarchal; it is a new stage of self-realization on a conscious level. Now, from the vantage point of the ego-self axis, the creative process can be apprehended as a product of concerted action between both aspects of the personality.

While Neumann does not spell out the details of a fourth and postpatriarchal stage of cultural evolution in this late essay, he strongly suggests its basic outlines. Much of his late work pertains to overcoming the one-sidedness of patriarchy and the retrieval of the feminine principle, to be integrated into the cultural canon as established by patriarchy. His conceptualization of the ego-self axis is his signature contribution to this vision of a possible cultural future.

Going beyond the patriarchal ego into the next stage requires an intense development of what he calls inwardness. This is not an end in itself but only a tool for the discovery of the true nature of psychic reality. What the patriarchal ego will discover here is that its vaunted ability to utilize the Ordering Principle is not its own but depends on access to the self. The Trinity of creative powers has set up a new dwelling place in the self. This is now separate from its original location in the "extraneous field"—equivalent for Neumann to the *unus mundus*, the unified field that underlies all of reality— but it of course remains connected to it, mirroring it in the human being. In the human personality, the self houses the Trinity of creation, and the developed and conscious ego recognizes that it is, as it were, an agent of the self, carrying out the function of the Ordering Principle. When the ego aligns with the self, forming the ego-self axis, it works alongside the Vital Principle of the self. Out of this combination arises human creativity in its supreme expression.

In Jung's theory, these two aspects in the self (the VP and the OA) could be identified as anima and animus, the syzygy. Anima is the Vital Principle, the source of energy and imagination and fantasy; Animus is the Ordering Principle, executing its will through the ego function. The ego recognizing this and, working with the self, freeing itself of the one-sided commitment to the patriarchal canon and attitudes, gives equal place to the feminine principle. Without the anima, the Ordering Principle becomes sterile and empty of creative potential. Masculine and feminine working in tandem signals the next stage of evolution within human culture.

In the fourth stage, then, the ego is taken up into the Trinity of creation and becomes a participant in its creative activities. When the ego does this, it experiences individual life as destiny. This is the individualization of the Directing Agency, which when lifted into consciousness brings awareness of the meaning of existence, individual and collective, of humankind and nature as a whole. This is what Neumann calls the experience of "inner being," and this goes beyond inwardness, which is merely the means for getting to this level of consciousness. The experience of inner being is equivalent to the conscious experience of the ego-self axis as a unified whole.

Creative Personalities

Looking back now from Neumann's last lecture at Eranos in 1960 to an earlier one given in 1954 titled "Creative Man and Transformation," I will discuss now his analysis of the creative individual. One clearly hears resonances in this earlier essay with the thinking laid out in 1960, as I will draw out. These ideas were already in the background of Neumann's mind as he considered those exceptional human beings that we regard as "creative personalities."

For the creative personality, Neumann writes, "[t]he creative principle is so deeply rooted in the deepest and darkest corner of his unconscious, and in what is best and highest in his consciousness, that we can comprehend it only as the fruit of his whole existence."[16] Thus, creative individuals in their whole being, conscious and unconscious, are given over to the creative process that takes hold of them in often overpowering ways. The Trinity of creation grips them, and the ego-self axis takes over control of their lives, at least for a time. It is a kind of birth-giving process in which the entire personality is involved and seized by the effort.

What is being born in this type of creative process, writes Neumann, is an aspect of the "symbolic world." This invisible world of symbols is being transformed into a specific image or idea that will be brought into consciousness by the creative personality, which

---

[16] E. Neumann, "Creative Man and Transformation," p. 169.

is the place where this transformation takes place. Thus, the creative person is a kind of medium or channel for symbols to come into the light in the world of consciousness. The creative principle, which takes hold of the creative personality like a daimon, is deeply linked to the symbol-making power of psyche, which in his later essay Neumann would call the "Ordering Principle." The creative personality, therefore, is an essential participant in transforming symbols from unconscious to conscious psychic reality. In this essay, Neumann places strong emphasis on the role of the creative personality as symbol-maker and on great value this has for culture. He writes: "It cannot be stressed enough that the key to a fundamental understanding, not only of man, but of the world as well, is to be sought in the relation between creativity and symbolic reality. Only if we recognize that symbols reflect a more complete reality than can be encompassed in the rational concepts of consciousness can we appreciate the full value of man's power to create symbols. To regard symbolism as an early stage in the development of the rational, conceptual consciousness involves a dangerous underestimation of the makers of symbols and of their functions...."[17] The symbol captures unitary reality prior to and beyond the split between "inner" and "outer," and the creative personality is the agent for making this symbolic reality visible.

Creative personalities can perform this function for humankind because of the connection they maintain to the unitary world. Unlike normal personalities, they do not sever the link to the symbolic world as they develop into adults. Again, Neumann uses a developmental schema to explain this special gift, which does not come without a price.

For creative personalities, the stages of development when ego consciousness separates from the unconscious and engages strongly in the challenge to adapt to the cultural canon and its norms are different from that of so-called normal personalities. In the creative personality, the link to the archetypes remains much more intact

---

[17] Ibid., p. 170.

and does not, as it does in the normal case, transfer fully over to the personal complexes and the reality principle, the ego complex. This line of development sets up a particular challenge and tension of its own, different from that of the normal personality: "...the difference between the creative and the normal man...resides in an intensified psychic tension that is present in the creative man from the very start. In him a special animation of the unconscious and an equally strong emphasis on the ego and its development are demonstrable at an early stage."[18] It is not that in the creative personality psychological development is retarded or arrested in the matriarchal stage with its weak ego and its close or even embedded connection to the unconscious. In the creative personality, there is a dual development: Ego development may be similar to that of the patriarchal stage, but it is accompanied by an intensification of the presence of the unconscious rather than a distancing and reduction. This symmetrical development will allow for creativity to take place in this personality.

Neumann marvels at this extraordinary development evident already in childhood: "In this state of alertness the child is open to a world, to an overwhelming unitary reality that surpasses and overpowers him on all sides...this waking sleep...is the unforgettable possession of the creative man...and we...marvel that the creative man should remain fixated in this stage and its experiences.... From childhood onward the creative individual is captivated by his experience of the unitary reality of childhood; he returns over and over again to the great hieroglyphic images of archetypal existence. They were mirrored for the first time in the well of childhood and there they remain until, recollecting, we bend over the rim of the well and rediscover them, forever unchanged."[19]

He wonders how this development can be possible because it seems to defy the normal sequence from the matriarchal stage of embeddedness in the unconscious world to the patriarchal stage

---

[18] Ibid., p. 180.
[19] Ibid., pp. 180-81.

of separation from the unconscious and consequent ego independence. If the conscious personality remains so deeply connected to the invisible unitary world—the "mother"—there must be a lacuna where the "father" should step in and draw the personality out of the maternal background. Certainly a danger lies here. With the father weak or absent, the developing personality risks being arrested or even swallowed up and devoured by the mother. In such a case, the archetypal world would rule, and insufficient ego strength would be constellated to function in the world. A state of possession, even psychosis, would be the net result. Madness surely lies there. Neumann writes: "In the perpetual tension between an animated and menacing archetypal world and an ego reinforced by purposes of compensation, but possessing no support in the conventional father archetype, the ego can lean only upon the self, the center of individual wholeness, which, however, is always infinitely more than individual."[20] This is the challenge handed out to the creative personality. A way to lean on the suprapersonal self and draw support from it must be found.

In fact, many creative personalities have not survived the onslaught of the "menacing archetypal world," and Neumann writes about such an individual in his essay on the young genius poet Georg Trakl,[21] who died in 1914 at the age of 27 from an overdose of cocaine, evidently a suicide, after suffering severe trauma in the early stages of World War I. In the story of Trakl's early life, Neumann finds a powerful activation of the archetypal world combined with childhood trauma and a passive-to-absent father, so minimal ego structure and not enough to survive the brutalities of dire conditions. Under mild circumstances, Trakl could manage, with assistance from friends (Ludwig Wittgenstein, for example, supported him financially for a time), and in this phase of his life, he was able to write his magnificent verse, which was heavily loaded with symbolic imagery. One does not know what might have

---

[20] Ibid., p. 187.
[21] E. Neumann, "Georg Trakl: The Person and the Myth."

become of him had he come through the war years and lived a longer life. The question is: Could he have found a way to "lean upon the self," as Neumann writes? And would this have supplied him with the needed stability to survive subsequent strong activations of the unconscious, to which he was so closely bound? As Neumann analyzes his life and poetry, he finds in Trakl what he calls, quoting his work, "The Moon and Matriarchal Consciousness," a "moon ego"—"It is a 'lunatic' in every sense of the term and its fate is a lunar fate. It is bound to the realm of the nocturnal."[22] This is creative personality with great vulnerability in a patriarchal culture.

The fear of engaging the archetypal world when it threatens to become activated is touchingly described by the now aged doyen of literary criticism in America, Harold Bloom, in his most recent book, *The Daimon Knows*: "I have been rereading *Moby-Dick* since I fell in love with the book in 1940, a boy of ten enthralled with Hart Crane, Whitman, William Blake, Shakespeare…a visionary company that transformed a changeling child into an exegetical enthusiast adept at appreciation rather than into a poet. A superstitious soul, then and now, I feared being devoured by ravenous daimons if I crossed the line into creation."[23] Instead of engaging the daimons directly, Bloom perhaps wisely decided to study the works of the daimon-possessed in the universe of imaginative literature. His all-time favorite poet (perhaps next to Shakespeare, for he is a self-proclaimed Bardolator) is the American Hart Crane, who, like Georg Trakl, wrote magnificently symbolic works and died early (age 32) by suicide. Perhaps Bloom read Hart Crane's fate as a cautionary tale.

The creative personality, writes Neumann, remains receptive and observant, like the ego state of the matriarchal stage of development, but must have the resilience and stamina of an ego grounded in the ego-self axis in order to participate in the creative process unleashed by the activated unconscious, and survive. One

---

[22] Ibid., p. 226.
[23] H. Bloom, *The Daimon Knows*, p. 122.

thinks here of Jung in his crisis at midlife, being severely tested as he decides to follow the "spirit of the depths" in search of his soul and enter into the tumultuous journey to the interior that he has recorded in the Red Book. In the powerful creative process that ensues, he struggles to maintain his identity as he relates to "ravenous daimons" that appear in his imagination and confront him with challenges. Jung was a creative personality who survived the onslaught and lived to transform the experiences into depth psychology. *The Red Book* is his epic poem interwoven with magnificent paintings, and all the clinical, theoretical, and hermeneutical works that followed (CW 6-18) are further products that flowed from the torrent of creativity opened up by his confrontation with the unconscious.

"The creative process is synthetic," writes Neumann, "precisely in that the transpersonal, i.e., the eternal, and the personal, i.e., the ephemeral, merge, and something utterly unique happens: the enduring and eternally creative is actualized in the ephemeral creation."[24] In one of his (to me) most moving essays, written sometime in the late 1950s, titled "A Note on Marc Chagall," Neumann illustrates this union of the temporal and the eternal. Chagall had all the marks of the creative personality—a kind of "moon ego" but a stabile one, an immediate and intense connection to childhood and the mysteries of the symbolic world, a profound dedication to love and the divine feminine—and his paintings reveal "symbolic centers" that are "unquestionably spontaneous products of his unconscious...."[25] Chagall paints out of his childhood—the village of Vitebsk, the animals, the violin player, the bridal couple— but "[i]n this childhood there is as yet no separation between personal and suprapersonal, near and far, inward soul and outward world; the life stream flows undivided, joining godhead and man, animal and world, in the glow and color of the nearby...this is the reality of Chagall's childhood, and the eternal presence of the

---

[24] E. Neumann, "Creative Man and Transformation," p. 189.
[25] E. Neumann, "A Note on Marc Chagall," p. 136.

primordial images lives in his memory of Vitebsk."[26] Chagall was a creative personality who, like Jung, survived the turbulence of youth and an unusual dual psychological development and continued to create into old age. Neumann would attribute this to the constellation and stability of an ego-self axis in the personalities of both men.

Conclusion

I began by recounting the numinous dream of a client in which he witnesses an astonishing creation. The beating heart, which is held at the center of the containing basket, is a totally new and novel being, but neither purely a creation of nature, as our bodies are when they emerge from the maternal womb, nor purely a creation of humans, of the scientists who brought it into reality and put it on display. It is the product of a synthesis of creative forces, natural and human. I believe this is a symbol of what Neumann is expressing in his magnificent metapsychological accounts of the creative process within the human world.

Human creation is an extension of the creative principle at work in all of nature, which has lately (in evolutionary terms) migrated into the psyche of humankind. Human expressions of the creative principle, whether in science, art, philosophy, business, politics, or in any other endeavor, are not purely the products of human intelligence and intention—the patriarchal ego's ingenuity and craft—although these are surely also a part of the story. Genuine human creations are a product of ego-self activities, which draw on both conscious and unconscious agencies, and these agencies have roots in nature and draw sustenance from the world Source, the *unus mundus*. The source of human creative energy lies in the unconscious and ultimately in the Trinity of creation that is active everywhere in nature and has now taken its home in the

---

[26] Ibid., p. 138.

human psyche. The "shaper" that designs this energy and gives it form (Gr. *Gestaltung*), and which keeps it from dissipating or spilling out into excessive and chaotic proliferations of exuberance, is the "Ordering Principle." This too is fundamentally rooted in the unconscious (and ultimately in the cosmic world), whence it forms archetypal images in the psyche from the energies emanating from the Vital Principle.

The creative personality, which is by no means an un-problematic psychological construction and frequently falls into serious states of disintegration and suffering, is situated in relation to the unconscious and the world of consciousness and culture in such a way that it can bring forth the emergent creations of the unconscious and make them available to culture in a particular time and place, using language or artistic methods available and concordant with the culture or scientific techniques and theories of the times. In extroverted types of human activity, such as business or politics, the creative personality also plays the role of midwife, bringing new possibilities into the light and offering them to the relevant culture. Often creative personalities suffer from this birthing drama, either because they are far ahead of their times or because of cultural misinterpretations and misunderstandings or because of fatal flaws and vulnerabilities in their psychological makeup such as seen in the gifted geniuses who die young.

In all of creation as we know it, there is nothing else that participates so fully in the creative process as does humankind. This may beget dangerous hubris and inflation, narcissistic self-importance and thus tragedy, as in the fate of Icarus. Were it not for the Directing Principle, there would be little meaning in all the froth generated by the creativity in nature and humanity. Neumann shows an astonishing degree of faith for such a modern man, as he undoubtedly was, that in the deep and dim recesses of the collective unconscious there is a goal-directed agency moving toward a meaningful destination. We can only look backward, not ahead. If we regard with a kind and forgiving eye the millions of years of evolutionary history that have brought humankind to its present state of consciousness and creative potential, we may retain hope that the future will not be altogether catastrophic.

Mysterium Coniunctionis:
"The Mystery of Individuation"[1]

In 1955, the year of Jung's 80th gala birthday celebration in Zurich and the publication of his book *Mysterium Coniunctionis*, Joseph Campbell published a collection of papers titled *The Mysteries*. This had been the theme of the Eranos Conference held during the Second World War in 1944. The volume consists of 13 lectures by such outstanding figures in Religious Studies as Walter Otto, Karl Kerényi, Walter Wili, Hugo Rahner, and, of course, by the lone psychologist among them, C.G. Jung. "Mystery" seems to have been a topic of general interest in 1955, and it certainly was close to Jung's heart and mind.

Mysterium Coniunctionis grew out of Jung's decades-long study of alchemy, but not only from that source. Other and perhaps more important sources of inspiration were his own personal experiences in active imagination, which resulted in the now published *The Red Book: Liber Novus*, his visions as recorded in *Memories, Dreams, Reflections,* and his work as a psychotherapist, a doctor of souls. If one takes a look at his analytic praxis room, which you enter through a door behind his library, it strikes one as a sacred space (a *temenos*), replete with symbolic objects and stained-glass windows from an old medieval church. One has the distinct feeling that for Jung and his patients it was a quasimagical chamber where the mysteries of

---

[1] Originally published in *The Mystery of Transformation,* 2022. Somewhat changed for this edition.

psychological transformation were practiced. Jung's essay "On the Psychology of the Transference," published in 1944 as a forerunner of *Mysterium Coniunctionis*, is a profound reflection on the mysteries of transformation as they play out in the therapeutic relationship. For good reason, he had earlier called the "fourth stage" of analysis nothing less than "transformation."[2] The mystery of psychological transformation was always "uncanny" and, as he would often point out, "synchronistic," i.e., coming about *Deo concedente* ("God willing"), by seeming coincidence. The entire process of individuation at its deepest level is a "mystery," beyond predictability and rational explanation.

Jung further argued that there was an undeniable resemblance between modern psychotherapeutic treatment and the practices and outcomes of the ancient mystery religions. The practices of mysteries such as those devoted to Demeter and Isis consisted of rites of initiation into the respective cults, which at the same time instigated psychological transformations that would strongly affect the attitude and behavior of initiates for the rest of their lives. They effectively activated and advanced individuation processes in the depths of the unconscious. The rites induced altered states of consciousness in the initiates with the purpose of offering them a numinous experience of "the ineffable." As Jung argues, this was an experience of "the living presence of a numinous archetype."[3]

The most famous of these were the Eleusinian mysteries. In this cult, which was located near Athens and dedicated to the goddesses Demeter and Persephone, the initiates were taken down into the darkness of a cave where they encountered the presence of the goddesses. The experience was *arreton* ("unutterable"[4]) and therefore would necessarily remain secret. The rite's transformative power depended on this ineffable experience. In its 1500 years of existence as an active cult, the rites of the Eleusinian mysteries were

[2] C.G. Jung, "Problems of Modern Psychotherapy," CW 16, paras. 160ff.
[3] C.G. Jung, *Mysterium Coniunctionis*, para. 312.
[4] K. Kerényi, "The Mysteries of the Kabeiroi," p. 37.

never disclosed by the initiates to any outsiders. In part, this is because the initiates were sworn to silence, but another reason was that they *could not* talk about it. It was beyond their powers of articulation. Certain experiences in analysis are like this as well: *arreton*. Clinical reports are normally flat and prosaic, but the experience inside the temenos of analysis may be ineffable.

The mysteries of Isis were of a similar nature. The only even partial testimony to what happened there is found in the picaresque novel *Metamorphoses (The Golden Ass)* by Apuleius, in the concluding chapter, where the author offers a brief glimpse into the secret rites practiced by the priests and experienced there by the initiates.

While Jungian methods of analysis might resemble the mysteries of ancient time in some ways, Jung did not, contrary to rumors, found a cult, meaning by that a closed society with secret rites and rituals of initiation. In their professional societies and institutes, Jungian psychoanalysts do not as a group engage in cultic practices such as the Freemasons, for example, do. Nevertheless, there is an aura of the secret and the sacred in the analytic space. Analysis is committed to strict confidentiality, and it has a powerful transformative effect on the participants due to their strong engagement with the unconscious. At times, they do touch upon "the living presence of a numinous archetype." This is an essential aspect of the experience of the individuation process in analysis. And it does have the emotional quality of "a time filled with sacred events and having a specific atmosphere," which we speak of as a "field." The notion of a psychological field is taken from electromagnetics, and when applied to the interpersonal interactive space between analyst and analysand, it speaks of the conscious and unconscious connections that become activated and generate psychic energy sufficient to induce transformations.

Because of their transformative power, the mysteries of many cultures and religions fascinated Jung. The numerous references to "mysteries," "mysterium," "mysticism," and related topics in the Index of the *Collected Works* testify to his intense interest in this topic. His extensive research into the mystery of transformation was certainly not meant to acquire a token to pass entry into "the spirit of the times," where it would have a negative value for the most part anyway; nor was it undertaken for only purely personal reasons, of which there were plenty, as we shall see. It was rather driven by his discovery of a striking resonance between such spiritual practices and the psychological transformations that he witnessed in himself and in his consulting room as a psychoanalyst. There was something archetypal, i.e., universal, about this process of psychological and spiritual transformation that he named "individuation," and he was intent on exposing it to modern consciousness, which, as he clearly saw, had gone dark on the subject.

For Jung, the word "mystery" would immediately suggest "the unconscious." Phenomena are mysterious because our conscious-ness cannot encompass them or grasp their meaning. Their cause is unknown or opaque and hidden from our view, at least at the moment. As such, they attract projections and become symbolic. The psyche uses its resources to establish a connection to them by projection—of attributes, invisible causes, and imaginative expla-nations. This provides a kind of provisional understanding, but it is not a scientific one based on exact measurement and evidence of causality. In an Editorial Note for the second edition of *Mysterium Coniunctionis*, Jung writes that in the work he is "concerned with psychological facts on the borderline of the knowable."[5] Not only are these psychological facts unknown at the time; they may be largely unknowable in principle because they are not subject to scientific study in the usual sense of the word. Science may never be able to explain them. Some phenomena are beyond the reach of the rational mind to understand even if they can be described in detail. This, Jung states, makes it necessary to use metaphors and images to explore this unconscious territory. His method of interpretation would be amplification, the collection of parallel images from other cultures and times.

---

[5] C.G. Jung, Editorial Note, *Mysterium Coniunctionis*, p. vii.

In fact, the strong use of metaphor and symbol in an explanatory text signals that the subject under discussion is at the "borderline of the knowable" and therefore necessarily carries with it the aura of mystery. Throughout his life, and perhaps most dramatically and personally in *Liber Novus,* Jung was given to exploring the boundaries of the known and the knowable, i.e., the unconscious. His paramount mission in life was to explore the mystery of the psyche.

Alchemy was, for Jung especially in the works of his later years, the most significant of the mystery schools for psychology, but it was far from the only one. Others of major interest were Gnosticism, Kabbalah, Mithraism, the various mystery religions of ancient Greece and Rome, and modern esotericisms. His extensive research into the mysteries of many religions and mythologies amounted to depth psychological research into the unconscious foundations of structures and processes that lie beneath the surface of personal psychological and collective cultural constructions. Jung had from the beginning of his career sought to look beneath and behind the surface of the flux of phenomena, as registered by the senses in conscious life, to perceive the invisible psychological and spiritual forces that shape them. As he understood his mission, the task of depth psychology was to investigate the dynamics and the direction of unconscious processes, in other words the "mysteries," of the psyche. His method was phenomenological: He would study the visible in an attempt to have a look into the invisible background dynamics they all had in common. These he would then call archetypal and take his interpretation from there.

One of the prime archetypal tendencies of the psyche is to instigate unification of "opposites" once they have been constellated and set up in the psyche. This is the *"mysterium coniunctionis"* ("the mystery of union") that Jung is writing about in his final book. It is akin to studying the force of gravity, for gravity, too, is invisible and extremely difficult to pin down theoretically and experimentally. Gravity consists in the action of gravitons, but what are "gravitons"? Are they waves or particles? Or both? Jung's question to the psyche was: How can we understand this type of uniting psychological energy ("libido"), which attracts the opposites and pulls them together? As a psychological force, this mysterious, gravitylike energy is a key to the individuation process. It is an organizing force that produces a unique and whole personality. From his comparative studies, Jung conjectured that this force is archetypal, i.e., universal, and has a critically important role in the inner and mostly quiet and hidden process of psychological transformation by which the scattered and numerous pieces of psyche become united. *Mysterium Coniunctionis* would be his last and greatest attempt to study this process of unification.

A related issue that I will consider in this reflection is the ancient problem of "the many and the one," i.e., the paradox of diversity and unity, as it pertains to individuation, personal and collective. Does the force that presses for unity conflict fatally with the force that presses equally for diversity and plurality? Or are they complementary pressures that balance one another and can both be accommodated in a single design?

The Red Book Experiment—*Liber Novus*

The classic mysteries show a distinct model for achieving the transformation process. They are invariably based on the archetypal pattern of death-and-rebirth. With this in mind, I will recount Jung's story, as told in Jung's Red Book, titled *Liber Novus*. Jung began his "experiment" (as he called it) in active imagination in November 1913, when he was 38 years old. It became a formative psychological transformation experience that shaped the rest of his life, which at the time was just entering its second half. Quite early in this experiment, he encountered two figures who named themselves Elijah and Salome. Both would play a decisive role in his transformation. The account of this encounter begins in Chapter 9 of *Liber Novus,* titled "Mysterium: Encounter," and continues through Chapters 10 ("Instruction") and 11 ("Resolution"). This story marks the climax in *Liber Primus*, the first section of *The Red Book*.

These chapters closely follow the pattern we find in the Eleusinian Mysteries and the Mysteries of Isis: preparation, instruction, initiation. Jung clearly recognized this similarity as acknowledged in a note to the text titled "Guiding Reflections": "This my friend, is a mystery play in which the spirit of the depths cast me. I had recognized the conception, and therefore the spirit of the depths allowed me to participate in the underworld ceremonies, which were supposed to instruct me about the God's intentions and works. Through these rituals I was supposed to be initiated into the mysteries of redemption."[6]

Jung is prepared in various ways by Elijah and Salome for the mystery of transformation. At a critical moment in his encounter with them, he receives a teaching (Chapter 10, "Instruction") that will utterly transform his attitude toward the imaginal figures he is encountering and teach him about what he would later call "the reality of the psyche." Here is the conversation:

> Elijah: "You may call us symbols for the same reason that you can also call your fellow men symbols, if you wish to. But we are just as real as your fellow men. You invalidate nothing and solve nothing by calling us symbols."
> I: "You plunge me into a terrible confusion. Do you wish to be real?"
> Elijah: "We are certainly what you call real. Here we are, and you have to accept us. The choice is yours."[7]

This remarkable declaration by Elijah, which would become bedrock in Jung's theory of the psyche in his later writings, is followed by a dramatic initiation, which is described in Chapter 11, "Resolution." Jung has been carefully prepared for this moment by the prophet and his feminine companion (Jung would, upon reflection, interpret them as Logos and Eros, also as Animus and Anima). At the critical moment, which will mark the climax of this section of *Liber Novus*, he finds himself caught up a vision and

---

[6] C.G. Jung, *The Red Book*, Reader's Edition, p. 178, ftn. 162.
[7] Ibid., p. 187.

involuntarily changed by the mysterious power of transformation. He writes:

> I am seized with fear at what I see.... I see the cross and Christ on it in his last hour and torment—at the foot of the cross the black serpent coils itself—it has wound itself around my feet—I am held fast and I spread my arms wide. Salome draws near. The serpent has wound itself around my whole body, and my countenance is that of a lion.
>
> Salome says, "Mary was the mother of Christ, do you understand?"
>
> I: "I see that a terrible and incomprehensible power forces me to imitate the Lord in his final torment. But how can I presume to call Mary my mother?"
>
> Salome: "You are Christ."
>
> It is as if I stood alone on a high mountain with stiff outstretched arms. The serpent squeezes my body in its terrible coils and the blood streams from my body, spilling down the mountainside. ... The serpent falls from my body and lies languidly on the ground. I stride over it and kneel at the feet of the prophet, whose form shines like a flame.
>
> Elijah: "Your work is fulfilled here. Other things will come. Seek untiringly and above all write exactly what you see."[8]

Years later in a seminar given in 1925 to his students in Zurich, Jung tells them: "The animal face which I felt mine transformed into was the famous [Deus] Leontocephalus of the Mithraic mysteries."[9] Jung goes on in that seminar to compare his experience with the ancient mysteries:

> These images have so much reality that they recommend themselves, and such extraordinary meaning that one is

---

[8] Ibid., pp. 197-98.
[9] C.G. Jung, *Analytical Psychology*, p. 106.

caught. They form part of the ancient mysteries; in fact it is such fantasies that made the mysteries. Compare the mysteries of Isis as told in Apuleius, with the initiation and deification of the initiate.... One gets a peculiar feeling from being put through such an initiation.... In this deification mystery you make yourself into the vessel and are a vessel of creation in which the opposites reconcile.[10]

Clearly, Jung's experience is a modern version of the ancient mysteries of transformation. His experience of "divinization" transformed the anima figure, Salome, and restored her sight, and it took Jung out of temporality and into the realm of the gods, into eternity. The Mithraic god, Aion, presides over time and specifically over the astrological revolutions and is thus beyond temporality and its limitations.

A related issue in *Liber Novus* arises repeatedly around the problem of love. Throughout *Liber Novus*, Jung struggles with the meaning of love. As we know, for Dante the ultimate reality of the universe was Divine Love, and for him this was represented by Christ. In *The Divine Comedy*, the final result of the ultimate revelation in the last Canto is described as follows:

Yet, as I wished, the truth I wished for came
Cleaving my mind in a great flash of light.
But already I feel my being turned —
Instinct and intellect balanced equally
as in a wheel whose motion nothing jars —
by the Love that moves the Sun and the other stars.[11]

Dante becomes one with Love, the divine energy that subsists in the Unus Mundus and is the Prime Mover in the cosmos. In Jung's terminology, this would constitute union with the energies of the Self. In *Liber Novus*, Jung does not reach this level of transformation, but he does get a foretaste of it. Repeatedly and almost

---

[10] Ibid.
[11] Dante, *Divine Comedy*, "Paradiso" XXXIII: 140-146.

compulsively throughout *Liber Novus*, he reflects on the figure of Christ and the Christlike total commitment to love.

It is noteworthy that Jung's calligraphic transcription from the manuscript for *Liber Novus* into the Red Book ends abruptly in midsentence. It is an astonishing rupture in the text, a moment similar to the flash of lightening that concludes Dante's poem. It occurs just as Jung is about to receive a strange gift:

Bird: "Do you hear me? I'm far off now. Heaven is so far away.

Hell is much nearer the earth. I found something for you, a discarded crown.

It lay on a street in the immeasurable space of Heaven, a golden crown."

And now it already lies in...(here the calligraphic text ends)

What Bird deposits in Jung's hand as a gift is "a golden crown, with lettering incised within; what does it say? 'Love never ends.' A gift from Heaven. But what does it mean?"[12] Jung is puzzled by the gift.

From our perspective as contemporary readers of *Liber Novus*, we know that it means Jung is destined to experience a mystery of transformation similar to Dante's. This future is further suggested in the last scene of "Scrutinies," the third section of *Liber Novus*, when Christ makes an appearance in Jung's garden and is recognized by Philemon as "truly a king. Your crimson is blood, your ermine is snow from the eternal cold of the poles, your crown is the heavenly body of the sun, which you bear on your head."[13] A dialogue ensues between Philemon and Christ in which Christ recognizes Philemon as Simon Magus, the ancient magician of biblical notoriety, who has taken this altered form in *Liber Novus*. Philemon tells Christ that he and his wife, Baucis, now play host to the gods, as did the ancient Greek couple. It seems Philemon has extended his identity from the

---

[12] C.G. Jung, *The Red Book*, Reader's Edition, p. 441.
[13] C.G. Jung, *The Black Books*, vol. 6, p. 245.

magician to include that of the humble man who with his wife welcomes divine figures into his home. In *Liber Novus,* he is both characters. Philemon declares that a "prior guest" was received in the garden, and it was "your terrible worm," i.e., Satan, the archetypal Shadow figure whom Jesus rejected and who here is recognized as the brother of Christ. Philemon continues: "Now that I gave the worm a place in my garden, you came to me."[14] The worm brought the gift of "ugliness," Philemon declares, and he asks Christ if he has brought the gift of "beauty." Christ replies: "I bring you the beauty of suffering. That is what is needed by whoever hosts the worm."[15]

Suffering the conflict between this pair of opposites will be the path to the next stages in the mystery of transformation for Jung, and this will be a major theme in his last book, *Mysterium Coniunctionis.*

Some three decades later, in the winter of 1944, Jung takes part in another experience of the union of opposites, this time between the masculine and feminine aspects of the Self, as he is recovering from a heart attack in a hospital bed. In a series of three visions, he witnesses the mystic marriages of Malchuth and Tifereth, Hera and Zeus, and Christ and his Bride. In *Memories, Dreams, Reflections,* he gives full expression to his sense of the numinous nature of these visions in words that echo Dante's descriptions of Heaven in *Paradiso.* Jung says: "These were ineffable states of joy. Angels were present, and light."[16] He will later give a full psychological and theoretical account of the meaning of these visions in his masterpiece, *Mysterium Coniunctionis.*

One curious detail about Jung's *Black Book* entry of the scene in the garden with Philemon and Christ is worth mentioning. *Liber Novus* is based on the entries Jung made into his journals called "the black books" as he was having the experiences. In the now published

---

[14] *Ibid.,* p. 246.
[15] C.G. Jung, *The Red Book,* A Reader's Edition, p. 553.
[16] C.G. Jung, *Memories, Dreams, Reflections,* p. 294.

Black Books, the entry for the garden scene is dated 6.VI.16. The entries into the *Black Books* continue with further entries from later dates, but it is this entry on June 6, 1916, that is the basis for the conclusion of *Scrutinies*, the third and final section of *Liber Novus* as it was composed in the manuscript version. In other words, this entry in which Christ appears in Jung's (Philemon's) garden signifies "The End" of *Liber Novus*. The curious fact is that the end of Jung's life falls on the same day of the same month, June 6. The year of his death in 1961, a number that reverses the last two numbers of the *Black Book* entry date, 1916. Both were Tuesdays, or in German *Dienstag*, meaning a workday (*Dienst* = work; *Tag* = day) of work— or "in service." For Jung, June 6, 1916, was the beginning of his Great Work that would continue until his final day of service, June 6, 1961. The date falls in the astrological month of Gemini, "the twins," a sign that symbolizes the two sides of a single being, symbolic of conscious and unconscious. I present these strange coincidences as a mystery not to be explained. Jung would call it "synchronicity."

Mysterium Coniunctionis—A Study in the Mystery of Individuation

"This book—my last—was begun more than ten years ago," Jung writes in the Foreword to *Mysterium Coniunctionis,* and it is without question his most difficult book to read and comprehend. Densely packed with references and quotations from alchemy, it quickly stops the modern reader from engaging in the usual habit of speed-reading. Unlike most of us, Jung could read alchemy texts in the original languages and assumed (incorrectly) that his readers had an education in the classics similar to his. "Knowledge of both Latin *and* Greek is a prerequisite for understanding alchemy. I read hundreds of manuscripts that had not been translated and that are still not translated today. I also preferred to read the original Latin when these text had been translated. I found them easier to understand."[17] Fortunately for most of us, the English translation of *Mysterium* puts the quotations from alchemy texts into the vernacular. The originals are included in an Appendix for those who have a classics education.

Beyond the problem of navigating among those numerous stumbling blocks, the final destination of *Mysterium* is beset by so many detours and byways, albeit fascinating ones, that the reader is often frustrated and left bewildered and lost. The path to the work's final goal, which is to bring the reader to an understanding of what the union of opposites means psychologically, is not straightforward despite the clarity of the Table of Contents. According to James Heisig, this structure furnished nothing but "a sort of mold into which he could empty his files on alchemical literature."[18] In my view, this would be the opinion of a student who had not spent enough time with the text, but on the surface level, it does have merit. The text is extremely intertwined and subtly woven out of many threads from the alchemical literature. In this sense, it resembles the alchemical works Jung is using. Jung has created, in a way, a mirror image of the alchemical writings he was deciphering.

The basic theme of *Mysterium* is fundamental psychological transformation at several levels, conscious and unconscious. To investigate this, Jung chooses to look at alchemy for models of the transformation process. Alchemy was, after all, an attempt to transform the worthless into the valuable, waste material into spiritual gold. Jung draws on the works of major alchemical figures such as Maria Prophetessa, Senior, Geber, Nicholas Flamel, Gerhard Dorn, Valentinus, Raymond Lully, Thomas Norton, Paracelsus, and Abraham Eleasar as well as alchemical texts from the major collections. His private library of alchemical works, which he assembled over several decades, was one of the most extensive in the world at the time.

---

[17] A. Jaffe, *Reflections on the Life and Dreams of C.G. Jung*, pp. 45-6.
[18] James Heisig, *Imago Dei*, p. 108.

In addition to this formidable obstacle to a modern person's understanding—Greek and Latin quotations in the original, tangled and intricately connected references to obscure alchemical works, a method of exposition that is more circular than straightforward— the reader has to know quite a lot about Jung's earlier writings in order to grasp this one. This book stands at the apex of a pyramid of writings extending from 1900 to 1955. The publication of *The Red Book* in 2009 and *The Black Books* in 2020, moreover, coming more than 50 years after *Mysterium*, add to the complications because they are now also considered to be essential reading in order to understand *Mysterium* adequately. It is a tall order indeed! Many people give up and put the book back on the shelf, saving it "for later." For myself, having lived with this work for nearly 50 years at this point, I still feel like something of a novice explorer poking around in a vast field of hidden gems of psychological wisdom. The word "mysterium" is not out of place! And I confess, it is my favorite of all of Jung's books.

We have to regard this late work in the context of the author's history, personal and intellectual. *Mysterium* is much more than an academic summary of Jung's decades-long intensive studies of Western alchemical writings. It is a profound penetration into the mysterious processes of psychological and spiritual transformation that are inscribed in these obscure, almost undecipherable, texts and demonstrates, albeit indirectly, how they have a bearing on individuation today. Basically, *Mysterium* is Jung's final word on individuation in its furthest reaches of human possibility. It is about the human potential for psychological wholeness and the path to its realization.

Mysterium Coniunctionis is the only volume in the *Collected Works* whose title is not translated into the vernacular language either in the original German or in any of the many translations. Like the Latin language itself, it stands as a monument to the universal and timeless. The title gives this weighty work an archetypal quality; it has a mystical aura about it that is instigated by the title itself.

The Origin of *Mysterium Coniunctionis*: Karl Kerényi and Goethe's *Faust*

In the Introduction, Jung writes that *Mysterium* was initially inspired by Karl Kerényi's monograph, *Das Ägäische Fest* ("The Aegean Festival"). First published in 1941, Kerényi's slim work is characteristically brilliant. It is a poetic reflection on a scene from Goethe's *Faust Part Two* that is set in the mythological territory of ancient Greece, the author's specialty. A renowned scholar of Greek mythology, Kerényi was at the time a regular participant in the Eranos Conferences and an esteemed colleague and friend of Jung's. It was no doubt because this scene in *Faust* is set in the imaginal space of mythological Greece that Kerényi took a special interest in it, and it is because there is a strong alchemical element in it that Jung's interest was so strongly drawn to Kerényi's monograph.

Part II of *Faust* is manifestly symbolic in nature throughout. Unlike Part I, which takes place in the sensible world and is a first-half-of-life story concerning the protagonist, *Faust*, Part II is set entirely in an imaginal realm of archetypal images and symbolic events. Goethe considered the totality of *Faust* to be an account of his own inner life, and Part Two pertains to his experiences and active imaginations in the second half of his life. Like Dante, he completed his *magnum opus* only shortly before his death. Part Two of the work can be read as a poetic summary of Goethe's psychological and spiritual journey in the late stages of individuation, as he delves into the collective unconscious and discovers the source of archetypal transformation and redemption in what he calls "the Eternal Feminine."

What must have especially captured Jung's attention in the episode that Kerényi writes about is the dramatic appearance of the famous alchemical figure Homunculus and the dramatic scene of his *coniunctio* with the beautiful Galatea. In the story, Homunculus was created in Faust's laboratory by the professor's assistant, Wagner, and when we meet the "little man" in this scene set on the Aegean coast, he is eagerly looking for a way to become incarnated as a full human being. He is still enclosed in the womblike alchemical vessel in which he was begotten, and he wants desperately to break out and enter into life fully and materially. When he sees the breathtakingly beautiful Galatea floating offshore on a seashell, he becomes electrified and begins to shine. He enlists the help of a nearby philosopher who throws him into the sea, and off he goes in hot pursuit of his love. As his state of excitement increases in her proximity, he glows more and more brilliantly, and at the climax of their encounter, the intensity of his energy bursts his glass bubble, and the two lustily make the waters boil in the frenzy of their passionate *coniunctio*. Witnessing this incredible scene, the onlooking Sirens sing:

> What fiery wonder transfigures the sea?
> The waves splinter and glitter, what storm can this be?
> All shining and swaying, a progress of light,
> Those bodies aglow as they move through the night,
> And the whirl of the fire all about and around!
> Now let Eros, first cause of all, reign and be crowned!
> Hail to the sea, the shifting tide,
> By sacred fire beautified!
> Hail to the waves, hail to the flame,
> Hail, this event without a name![19]

According to Jung, this scene "is based on *The Chymical Wedding of Christian Rosencreutz*, itself a product of the traditional hierosgamos symbolism of alchemy."[20] The scene from *Faust* is a dramatic example of a *mysterium coniunctionis,* and it impressed itself deeply in Jung's mind. As a result, he set about writing what would become his major work on alchemical symbols and individuation.

Kerényi concludes his commentary on the Aegean Festival by writing pithily: "*Homunculus' Abenteuer ist das Mysterium des Entstehens*" ("Homunculus' adventure is the Mystery of

---

[19] Goethe, *Faust*, Part Two, Act II, lines 8474-8487.
[20] C.G. Jung, *Mysterium Coniunctionis*, p. xiii.

Becoming"—or "Emergence," or "New Beginning").[21] A passionate love affair marks the beginning of the mystery of the transformation that will follow: It plants the seed for the next stage of individuation. In Goethe's poem, this further development will include Faust's imaginal love affair with the divine Helena, the archetypal anima figure of classical Greek culture, with whom he produces a precocious miracle child, the boy Euphorion ("Euphoria"), who flies too high and too far and crashes dead at their feet, whereupon Helena leaves and returns to her life in the realm of the Dead. In the end and at the ripe old age of 100, Faust's soul, upon being released and separated from his body by "the love beyond time" (*"die ewige Liebe"*),[22] is taken up into Heaven, where the Chorus Mysticus sings:

All that is transitory
is precisely [only] a likeness.
What cannot be attained,
Here it takes place.
What cannot be described,
Here it is done.
The Eternal Feminine
Draws us up, on and on.[23]

This is the conclusion of Goethe's *Faust* and not so dissimilar from Dante's in *The Divine Comedy*.

Mysterium Coniunctionis—The Text

Mysterium Coniunctionis is a long, intricately woven, and artfully constructed book. The Table of Contents is useful as a quick initial orientation to this most challenging of Jung's writings. There are six Chapters in *Mysterium*: 1) The Components of the Coniunctio; 2) The Paradoxa; 3) The Personification of the Opposites; 4) Rex and

---

[21] K. Kerényi, *Das Ägäische Fest*, p. 74.
[22] Goethe, *Faust* II, Act V, line 11964.
[23] Ibid., lines 12104-12111. Translation kindly offered by Paul Bishop.

Regina; 5) Adam and Eve; 6) The Conjunction. To summarize them briefly:

Chapter 1 sets the stage. Here Jung names the components in a number of "pairs of opposites" that alchemy deals with: moist-dry, heaven-earth, fire-water, active-passive, spirit-matter, masculine-feminine, etc. There are many images and concepts for this oppositional phenomenon and for their union, and Jung states that the union is often symbolized by a quaternity made up of two pairs of opposites. Most frequently, however, the *mysterium coniunctionis* will feature a cast of two figures, a male-female pair. The story of their union is a drama that includes the archetypal death-and-rebirth event as part of the *coniunctio*. Jung writes that it is "the moral task of alchemy to bring the feminine, maternal background of the masculine psyche, seething with passions, into harmony with the principle of the spirit—truly a labour of Hercules!"[24] For the feminine psyche, it might be considered "truly a labour of Psyche," as in the story of Amour and Psyche told in *The Golden Ass of Apuleius* and interpreted by Erich Neumann.

Chapter 2 introduces the idea of "paradox" as central in alchemy. These are concepts and images, often bizarre, of the union of opposites. An example is the two-headed Rebis. The androgyne is a favoured image. Paradoxes attempt to combine the opposites in such a way as to suggest a hidden, underlying unity, as stated in this alchemical quotation cited by Jung: "Why speak ye of the manifold matter? The substance of natural things is one, and of one nature that which conquers all."[25] Regarding the human personality, this underlying unity is the self. Definitions of the self must therefore be paradoxical because the personality is made up of a number of pairs of opposites: persona/shadow, anima/animus, time-bound/timeless, etc.

Chapters 3, 4 and 5 consist of a detailed discussion of masculine and feminine symbols (Sun and Moon, King and Queen,

---

[24] C.G. Jung, *Mysterium Coniunctionis*, CW 14, para. 35.
[25] Ibid., para. 36.

Adam and Eve) and their separate transformations. The transformations are basically about the processes that effect fundamental changes in consciousness, individual and collective (Sun, King, Adam), and in the unconscious (Moon, Queen, Eve). These transformations are preparatory for the unification possibilities that will follow.

Chapter 6 concludes the book and is the most straightforward section and therefore the easiest to follow. In it, Jung presents a psychological interpretation of the alchemist Gerhard Dorn's formula for a three-stage process that transforms consciousness and takes it to an all-inclusive dimension. I will discuss this in more detail later.

The reason the opposites are such a psychological problem is that they reflect the divided psyche. This splitting apart of the psyche is the result of a normal process of differentiation that takes place in the course of psychological development, individual and collective. It is the result of the birth and growth of ego-consciousness within the original natal self. Ego-consciousness, moreover, is by its nature a separating and differentiating function in the human personality. Without its continuous operation, humans would not be the individual conscious beings they are. The first half of life is largely devoted to this development—separation/differentiation of the ego from the unconscious and also of the individual from physical and social surroundings. This creation of a unique sense of individuality (ego-hood) and identity (persona) is the goal of individuation in the first half of life. From this position, the individual can successfully participate in society as a responsible and self-aware member of the larger collective.

But this development swings a two-edged sword. On the one hand, it offers great benefits; on the other, it creates enormous problems—conflict between oneself and others, neurosis due to repression and one-sidedness, feelings of isolation. The opposites, which are generated out of a preconscious matrix of the original self, introduce conflict. This happens on an individual level and on a cultural level. Original unconscious oneness breaks up into a

COLLECTED WRITINGS OF MURRAY STEIN VOLUME 9

division, which then is driven toward a regained but now more conscious unity.

In *Mysterium,* Jung works with "opposites" derived from alchemy. They are basically masculine/feminine pairs—Sun/Moon, King/Queen, and Adam/Eve (Chapters 3,4,5)—whose union is symbolized in images like the androgenous Rebis. Jung often quotes the axiom of Maria Prophetess as a summary of the process: "One becomes two, two becomes three, and out of the third comes the one as the fourth."

In psychology, we observe this process in the course of development as a portion of the original self breaks away and becomes a personal identity centered by ego-consciousness. The features of the personality that are left out of this identity form a shadow identity made of rejected pieces of the self (the shameful or "bad") and the gender part of the original syzygy (animus/anima unity) that were left out of the conscious identity. Individual identity depends on this development. Then, in later life, the problem becomes how to reunite the separated parts of the self. How this may come about is a fundamental question addressed in *Mysterium.* It is a matter of reuniting the divided self.

Another part of the division that opens in the psyche is between the instinctual body and the idealistic spirit. Freud wrote about this as a conflict between the id and the superego and assigned the civilized person's chronic malaise to this dilemma in his *Civilization and Its Discontents.* Jung takes another and more optimistic view of this conflict between instinct and spirit and sees it as soluble, but he recognizes it as fundamental as well. Both sides of the divide must be transformed before a lasting union can come about. This process of transformation is analyzed in Chapters 3, 4 and 5 of *Mysterium.*

In Chapter 3, the chief actors are Sun and Moon, the former representing the spiritual/cultural structures of the psyche (solar consciousness) and the latter the cycles and rhythms of the somatic unconscious (lunar consciousness). Much of the chapter dwells on the transformations in the lunar realm (anima). Chapter 4 features the figures King and Queen, a social pair of opposites among the archetypal images of the collective unconscious, and here the principle focus is on the transformation of the masculine/patriarchal dominant of consciousness (animus) with the feminine/matriarchal (anima) in a secondary position. In Chapter 5, the argument is that Adam represents the original Anthropos (wholeness of the self) that falls into division, which results in the constellation of the pair Adam (ego-consciousness) and Eve (the unconscious). The feminine/ unconscious aspect (anima, instinct), as represented by Eve and her surrogate, the black Shulamite, is subjected to an intense process of cleansing and transformation whereby she is prepared for union with the similarly transformed male partner, which brings into being Adam Kadmon, a representation of the original self now as reborn.

The Title of *Mysterium Coniunctionis*

The title of the book, *Mysterium Coniunctionis*, should be considered in some detail. The word, *mysterium*, as we saw, refers to secret rites and rituals and to sacramental elements in religious practices. The reference to the religious, therefore, is placed strongly and directly into the title of the book. The title suggests, therefore, that Jung is going to speak about mysteries that invoke the powers of the Divine and draw the presence of the transcendent Being(s) into the human realm. The word *mysterium* implies activities of an invisible power that cannot be fully grasped by human cognition but can be experienced, most obviously in religious contexts. Numinous experiences similar to those described in religious texts may also occur in private moments in the life of the individual and not only in collective settings. *Mysterium* is a word used by Rudolf Otto to speak of the *numinosum* in his famous work of *The Idea of the Holy*: It is, he writes, a *mysterium tremendum et fascinans*.

Because of this network of associations to the word *mysterium*, Jung felt a need to explain his use of religious language in an Editorial Note to the second edition of *Mysterium*:

... if I make use of certain expressions that are reminiscent of the language of theology, this is due solely to the poverty of language, and not because I am of the opinion that the subject-matter of theology is the same as that of psychology. Psychology is very definitely not a theology; it is a natural science that seeks to describe experienceable psychic phenomena. In doing so it takes account of the way in which theology conceives and names them, because this hangs together with the phenomenology of the contents under discussion.[26]

As he explains, Jung looks in this work to the language and concepts of theology for an account of the material that he wishes to discuss scientifically, i.e., psychologically. He does not want to be taken for a theologian, however, but will use theology for his psychological investigations. Psychology will deal with "the mysteries" as experienced phenomena, not as revelations of eternal metaphysical truths. The experience of the *numinosum* means, for Jung, an experience of the archetypal layers of the unconscious. The line between the psychological and the theological is drawn very fine, and Jung will sometimes seem inadvertently to cross over it when he explicates symbolic material in dreams, visions, and alchemical texts.

There is also the important element of secrecy in the connotations around the word *mysterium*. The Latin word is derived from the Greek *mystērion*, meaning secret rite or doctrine (known and practiced by certain initiated persons only), consisting of purifications, sacrificial offerings, processions, songs, etc. This is a reference to such famous ancient mystery cults as the Eleusinian Mysteries and the Mysteries of Isis, where the rites served as the means of initiation into the cult. Secrecy was seen as necessary for the effective transmission to the participants of the spiritual energies invoked in the rites and rituals. The "one who has been initiated" was called a *mystēs*. Initiation implies the transformation

---

[26] Ibid.

of identity that the initiates experience as they move from the status of applicant to graduate. Today we hear a faint echo of this practice in our induction and graduation ceremonies in schools and universities. We might call someone with a Master's degree a *mystés*, an initiated one.

Most interesting and closely associated with the importance of secrecy is that the word *mysterion* derives from the basic Greek word, *myein*—"to close, to shut"—which perhaps refers to closing the lips in secrecy, or to closing the eyes in preparation for the revelation that would take place as a result of the rites. At the base of etymologies, one often comes upon something very simple and, as we say, archetypal. In the Mysteries, we see that silence, secrecy and being closed off from the world in a sacred space, typically in a structure resembling a cave that symbolized the womb, are emphasized.

From the title of Jung's book with that word, *Mysterium,* front and center, we clearly receive notice that what we are about to enter into here is a discussion of something secret, sacred, and touching on the archetypal powers of psychological and spiritual transformation.

Like the first part of the book's title, the second part, *Coniunctionis*, is of critical importance for understanding the work's meaning. In Latin, it means simply "bond" or "union." In chemistry, it would indicate the union of two elements to create a compound. Jung writes at the beginning of the first chapter of *Mysterium*: "The factors which come together in the coniunctio are conceived as opposites, either confronting one another in enmity or attracting one another in love."[27] And in a footnote he quotes from a text by the alchemist Ripley: "The coniuntio is the uniting of separated qualities or an equalizing of principles."[28]

As a predecessor to chemistry, alchemy worked with materials that were considered basic, like the elements in modern chemistry.

---

[27] C.G. Jung, *Mysterium Coniunctionis*, CW 14, para. 1.
[28] Ibid., ftn. 1. From *Theatrum chemicum*, II, p. 128.

The four basic elements were air, fire, water, and earth. There were also the three chemical elements, salt, sulphur, and mercury. The materials for the experiments were collected according to secret recipes, and when placed together, the mixture was called called *prima materia,* which was placed into a suitable container for processing, usually a vessel or flask. The Adept then applied some secret alchemical methods to the *massa confusa* in the vessel in order to sort the mixture into pairs of opposites. These pairs were meant to bond together and join another pair, forming a quaternity, out of which new compounds would be created.

The process would begin with raw materials and pass through a series of operations (*calcinatio, solutio, coagulatio, sublimatio, mortificatio, separatio, coniunctio*), and eventually the result would be something new that could not be found in nature: a new creation. This process was seen as a transformation from the base assembled materials at the outset to the noble product at the conclusion, and it was seen as mysterious because the science was not available to understand the material basis of the process. Into this process the alchemists projected a large variety of images and meanings. It was Jung's genius to apply psychological understanding to the projective processes and to understand the alchemical opus as symbolic of the individuation process.

As Jung interprets the alchemical imagination, the opposites that the alchemists sought to unite on a material level represented features of the psyche—anima, animus, shadow, etc. The union, or integration, of these is the goal of individuation in Jung's theory.

Since the entire opus depends on *coniunctio,* an important question would be: What can motivate the union of the opposites? The magical "transformation factor" in the unification process in alchemy was mercury, symbolized by the figure Mercurius. Mercury was the medium, or bath, in which the conjunction of opposites, as represented by sulfur (the masculine) and salt (the feminine), took place. As an androgynous figure combining the opposites in himself, Mercurius was the catalyst for the process. Without this uniting factor, the opposites would not be brought to the point of interacting with one another. In the alchemical lexicon, Mercurius was defined as the beginning and the end of the process, and indeed as the process itself. Because he was imaged as androgenous, the opposites are both represented in this figure, and this is why he is able to bring them together. He is like a model or template, a symbol of conjunction of the opposites.

Mercurius might be compared to the force of gravity in nature: He is able to pull the separated and oppositional elements toward himself and holds them in place. Mysteriously, too, he dissolves their antagonism, like a diplomat soothing the tempers of oppositional political parties and creating the conditions for dialogue. Without the force of gravity, the universe would simply disperse and disappear into empty space. In psychological terms, Mercurius represents the power of the self to hold the psychic pieces in place as they evolve, to bring them into relation to one another, and to secure their positions in a structure of wholeness. In Kabbalah, the power responsible for the structure of balance among the 10 Sefirot ("emanations" or "opposites") that are represented in the Kabbalistic Tree of Life is Ein Sof, the Infinite. Psychologically interpreted, Ein Sof is the self. Jung discusses Kabbalah and the Sefirot in Chapter 5 of *Mysterium*.

In psychology, the process of reconciliation among the various pairs of opposites—most notably animus and anima, and persona and shadow—is conceived as an extended process of integration whereby ego-consciousness is relieved of its attachment to one side of the opposition, and the unconscious is similarly released from its domination by the other. They can then become a structured totality under the auspices of the self, while still leaving room for the parts to remain discrete and not become melted together into a single homogeneous unit, a kind of "black hole," where gravity is so strong that even photons (light) cannot escape. The goal is to bring the opposites into a delicate and sustained relationship with one another, not to eliminate one in favor of the other. The Tree of Life, like the Rebis, symbolizes this: the two columns on the right and left of the Tree representing Judgment and Mercy, as the two heads of the Rebis figure represent animus and anima in one body.

Mercurius is a mysterious figure in alchemy, a magician. In one of Jung's most fascinating alchemical writings, "The Spirit Mercurius" (CW 13), he interprets Mercurius as "the spirit of the unconscious," which on behalf of the self directs the individuation process on its serpentine path toward the goal of psychological integration and wholeness. It was this mysterious, magnetic, magical "spirit" that Jung detected at work in the background of his own individuation process (as "the spirit of the depths," in *The Red Book*), as well as in his patients' psychological material as it evolved in the analytic process.

In *Mysterium,* Jung writes of Mercurius that "he *is* this marriage on account of his androgynous form."[29] Like the Holy Spirit in Christian theology who binds the Trinitarian Godhead into a stable One-in-Three unity, Mercurius brings into a state of multifaceted unity the many "opposites" of the self. It is the genius of Mercurius that the many do not disappear into a singularity but rather retain their unique qualities and facets, diamondlike, while joining the wholeness structure of the mandala. Thus, room for diversity is preserved while unity is attained.

This is the answer to the dilemma of "the One or the Many." It has often been discussed among Jungian authors: Is the personality multiple and many, or is it one? Polytheism or monotheism? The answer is: "both"—diversity in unity; unity in diversity. This is the only realistic and sustainable goal for individuation given the complexity of the human personality. And this is the net implication of the *Coniunctionis* in the title of the text: It is "unity" but it does not deny or eliminate diversity and differentiation.

---

[29] C.G. Jung, *Mysterium Coniunctionis,* CW 14, para. 12.

The Conjunction

The sixth and final Chapter of *Mysterium Coniunctionis* offers some practical information about the stages of individuation that concern union rather than separation. Jung draws on the work of Gerhardt Dorn, arguably his favorite alchemical author, to describe three stages of coniunctio: 1) the achievement of *unio mentalis*, which consists of a union of soul and spirit; 2) the union of *unio mentalis* with the body, which has been left behind in the preceding stage; and 3) the union with *unus mundus*.

Dorn's model begins with an initial state in which soul and body are fused called *unio naturalis*, which speaks of a natural instinctual life in the body. A change is instigated at some point, and *unio naturalis* undergoes a process of separation (*separatio*) of soul from body. It is kind of awakening. Consciousness takes stock of the situation and introduces a differentiation between the desires of the body and the thoughts of the soul. A period of liminality ensues in which soul moves to spirit and unites with it. A new type of consciousness and identity develops, which is no longer based on ego-body and ego-persona identifications. Thus, the first stage of Dorn's transformation model completes itself. He calls the result *unio mentalis*.

According to Jung, *unio mentalis* describes a psychologically aware state of mind that is no longer dominated by somatic needs and instinctual drives or persona demands for social approval. A new type of individual freedom and inner direction is achieved at this stage of individuation. To reach this state of union of soul and spirit, the "body" has been left behind in a sort of suspended animation state. It continues to exist but in a deathlike sleep. In other words, what the body represents is no longer determinative of state of mind. The cognitive (*mentalis*) outweighs the somatic-emotional at this level of development.

Unio mentalis is then followed by a second stage of conjunction, which consists in a reunion with the body. What was left out as a determinative factor is now taken up, reanimated, and given a new mission. The body is no longer dominant with respect

149

to the ego; rather the ego and the body now stand in service of *unio mentalis*. What develops in this stage is a practical, morally enlightened, engaged attitude toward life in this world. It is not otherworldly but rather grounded in the world of social and material existence. The body has been taken up into the more conscious state of *unio mentalis* and is now included in its purposes and activities.

Finally, there is a third *coniunctio* with what the medieval writers called the *unus mundus*. *Unus mundus* means "the one world." The phrase refers to a commonly shared medieval perception that everything that exists belongs to and within a single unified reality. It is the alpha and omega of existence: the origin and the underlying reality. In Jungian psychology, it would correspond to the collective unconscious whose center and circumference is the self. In scholastic philosophy, it was credited to the spirit of God. In other words, it is the Holy Spirit, i.e., the spirit of Love. To unite personal identity with this ultimate transcendent reality results in a spiritual life that is similarly all-embracing. In this final result of Dorn's three conjunctions, all of the opposites are united in a totality with both immanent (the body) and transcendent (the soul and spirit) dimensions.

The individual's ego-consciousness, moreover, is preserved within this matrix (or "field") of transpersonal wholeness, so diversity (i.e., individuality) and unity (i.e., totality) are both maintained. This is neither an individualistic nor a totalitarian model. It is a *mysterium coniunctionis* of pluralism and unity, the many and the one.

The three stages of individuation represent a progressive movement toward ever greater consciousness. And it moves ego-consciousness toward a state of realization that inner and outer are deeply interconnected. The "whole" includes the individual and all that exists—local and world community, global environment, cosmos. This final development of consciousness presupposes, of course, the deep transformations that have been described in the previous chapters of *Mysterium*. There is no discount ticket to this goal of individuation.

This three-stage description of individuation is a process directed toward ultimate wholeness, and it offers a practical model for thinking about the development toward consciousness that can be observed in analysis. As the subject undergoes a sustained confrontation with the shadow and engages with the figures of the collective unconscious in active imagination, a sense of an inner world emerges that includes the ego but does not make it central. The ego is relativized as the Self comes into view and shows its centrality. Dante's experience as expressed in Paradiso is a beautifully stated religious version of this psychological vision. The final Canto of *The Divine Comedy* is a religious epiphany that results in his most profound transformation:

> already I could feel my being turned—instinct and intellect balanced equally as in a wheel whose motion nothing jars—by the Love that moves the Sun and the other stars.[30]

Conclusion

The distilled message of *Mysterium Coniunctionis* could be stated as a promise:

> Wholeness comes at a high price. But no matter how much you suffer for its sake, you will be rewarded. No suffering for the sake of wholeness will go unrewarded.

The reward is manifold: knowledge of the inner world, personal and collective; a sense of the mystery of the Self in its personal and impersonal dimensions; the establishment of a stable sense of unity within diversity; a vision of purpose and meaning in life; the acquisition of perspective on self and other without judgment and yet with differentiated perception of positives and negatives included in the mandala of wholeness. One could add more features, but the general idea is that the personality that was divided, scattered, and largely unconscious is made whole and is

---

[30] Dante, *Divine Comedy*, "Paradiso" XXXIII: 143-146.

now far more conscious. The union is mysterious, necessarily so, yet tangible in the form of images of the self and a stable state of consciousness that embraces the opposites to the greatest extent possible.

This way does not offer perfection but rather wholeness. I think it can be concluded without the least qualification that this was Jung's ultimate objective in his own life and for those who read his works, engage in analysis, and seriously pursue individuation. *Mysterium Coniunctionis*—his last book—says it all.

Carl Jung and Richard Wilhelm: In Friendship[1]

Carl Jung's friendship with Richard Wilhelm was not incidental. It was decisive for his further development as a thinker and as a personality. In a letter to Wilhelm, Jung speaks of their relationship as fated: "Fate seems to have apportioned to us the role of two piers which support the bridge between East and West."[2] He wrote these words to express the great significance he attached to this friendship. Fate means destiny: The two men shared a common task given to them by Fate, that is, by the Self. The ancient Chinese might say it was given by "the Will of Heaven"; Christians would say this task was "God-given." Jung wrote these lines while he was beginning to work on his "Commentary on 'The Secret of the Golden Flower,'" using Richard Wilhelm's translation of the Chinese alchemy text.

Today, as heirs of their pioneering work, we find it to be our task to extend and strengthen this bridge between East and West. I want specially to mention Professor Shen in this regard, for all the work he has done to contribute to the expansion of this bridge by sponsoring these gatherings of scholars from China and the West. This Conference is one more important contribution to strengthening the vital link between analytical psychology and Chinese culture.

---

[1] First delivered as a lecture for a Conference on Chinese Culture and Jungian Psychology in Quingdau, China in 2023.
[2] G. Adler (ed.), *C.G. Jung Letters,* vol. I, p. 66.

Hexagram 31 and Friendship

Hexagram 31, *Hsien*, as translated into English from the German translation by Richard Wilhelm, is titled "Influence (Wooing)." This Hexagram speaks of friendship. Hexagram 31 looks like this:

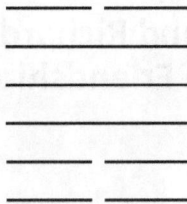

```
____  ____
_____
_____
_____
____  ____
____  ____
```

The upper trigram is *Tui*, the Joyous, Lake; the lower is *Kên*, Keeping Still, Mountain.

Richard Wilhelm writes that this hexagram begins the second part of the *I Ching* and gives us a picture of "the foundations of all social relationship."[3] *Tui* is the youngest daughter, and *Kên* the youngest son. In this constellation, they form a couple, with the feminine above and the masculine below. It is a *puella anima* (the young feminine) joined with a *puer animus* (the young masculine), which means that an abundance of creative feeling and imagination (the anima) unites with youthful creative thinking and discrimination (the animus), and together they create a combination that is highly productive.

One can think of the friendship between Carl Jung and Richard Wilhelm in these terms: It was a happy and creative union of soul (anima) and spirit (animus), which created a lasting bond between them and brought for both of them a further realization of the Self in their individual lives. This is the gift of true friendship. It furthers individuation for both persons in the relationship.

What attracted Carl Jung to Richard Wilhelm and Richard Wilhelm to Carl Jung? Without doubt, it was their shared interest

---

[3] R. Wilhelm, *I Ching*, p. 122.

in Chinese culture. Ancient Chinese culture was the magnet that drew them together and the Mercurial agent that united them. The *I Ching* attracted them to each other in the first place when it appeared in Wilhelm's German translation in 1923, and in their interactions with one another around this shared love of Chinese wisdom they mutually influenced one another. It was Wilhelm's translations that influenced Jung's thinking, and it was Jung's psychological theories that influenced Richard Wilhelm's understanding. Wilhelm's commentary on "The Secret of the Golden Flower," for instance, is guided by references to Jung's thoughts about anima, animus and Self. Jung's writings on synchronicity refer frequently to Wilhelm's translation of the *I Ching*. Between the two of them, they constructed a bridge between Western depth psychology and Chinese culture.

Hexagram 31 belongs to "the House of the Joyous." Certainly the meeting of Carl Jung and Richard Wilhelm was a joyous occasion, and it became a most fruitful relationship.

If we take the two inner trigrams of Hexagram 31 and create with them what is called *Hua Gua*, we get Hexagram 44, *Kou /* Coming to Meet.

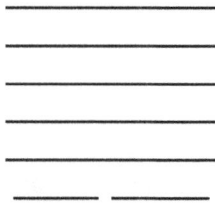

--------------   --------------
--------------   --------------

---------   ---------

Hua Gua gives us further insight into the inner meaning of Hexagram 31. This Hexagram belongs to "the House of the Creative."

This *Hua Gua* configuration of lines expresses the inner direction of Hexagram 31, *Hsien*. This is a cautionary Hexagram and signals the danger of seduction, of meetings and unions that are too easy and turn out to be deceptive. The lower trigram, *Sun*, "the Gentle, Wind," can exert a disruptive force and take control over the relationship. The danger here is that "power" replaces "love" as the ruling principle and thereby threatens the source of true friendship. This is always a danger if relationships are too quickly formed and not carefully enough examined for ulterior shadow motives. The "coming together must be free of dishonest ulterior motives,"[4] as Wilhelm writes in his commentary on this Hexagram. If the relationship is free of such manipulative intentions and hidden shadow motives, as I believe it was in the friendship of Jung and Wilhelm, then the text promises that "all creatures prosper."[5] The friendship between Carl Jung and Richard Wilhelm, although quite brief, shows us that two men with great intellectual gifts and strong personalities can unite in a joint venture without coming into conflict over issues of dominance and power. This gives us hope that such relationships are possible. In their friendship, both men prospered.

It is interesting also to look at the opposite of Hexagram 31. This is called *Zong Gua*, and it is represented by Hexagram 41, *Sun* / Decrease:

This Hexagram shows mountain over lake, the exact reverse of *Hsien,* where lake is over mountain, and it is in "the House of Keeping Still." Here we find energies that are the opposite of *agapé* (love) and creativity. The Hexagram *Sun* signifies decline. In a relationship, this would mean that one partner ascends over and dominates the other. The result would be ever decreasing energy and creativity. Here power rules over love, and the relationship will inevitably collapse.

---

[4] Ibid., p. 171.
[5] Ibid.

The Gifts of Richard Wilhelm

In his friendship with Richard Wilhelm, Carl Jung received two gifts that had a transformative effect on his life's work: the translations of "The Secret of the Golden Flower" and of the *I Ching*. The first confirmed that the individuation process is archetypal, and the second provided what he called an "Archimedean point" from which to move the Western materialistic worldview off its base.

Richard Wilhelm passed away in 1930 at the early age of 57. He was two years older than Carl Jung, so something like an older brother. Wilhelm's health was affected by medical conditions possibly arising from his 25 years in China, but also and perhaps even more critically by the psychological conflict he suffered between his love and memories of China and Chinese culture and the "European man [that] hemmed him in more and more closely, beset him in fact,"[6] as Jung says in his Memorial Address. Jung regarded Wilhelm's illness as a spiritual crisis that resulted in a "sacrificial death."

For Jung, Wilhelm's death was a great loss. In a sense, they had just only begun building the bridge between East and West. After Wilhelm's death, Jung was more or less on his own with regard to this project. He did continue the work of bridge-building between East and West with his commentaries on *The Tibetan Book of the Dead* and *The Tibetan Book of the Great Liberation,* as well as with his exchanges with many famous scholars at the Eranos conferences that began in 1933. But none of his future collaborations with scholars and colleagues had the same quality of friendship that was so clearly and obviously a part of his relationship with Richard Wilhelm. None of them was inspirational in the same way. He speaks in his Memorial Address for Richard Wilhelm of a "spark" that "kindled a light that was to become for me one of the most significant events of my life."[7]

---

[6] C.G. Jung, "Richard Wilhelm: In Memoriam," *Collected Works*, vol. 15, para. 94.
[7] Ibid., para. 74.

In his Memorial Address, Jung spoke movingly about Richard Wilhelm's relationship with Chinese culture and about his relationship with Richard Wilhelm, and through him also with Chinese culture. Jung writes: "Toying only with the surface and externals of the foreign culture, they [foreign scholars] never eat its bread or drink its wine, and so never enter into a real communion of minds, that most intimate transfusion and interpenetration which generates a new birth."[8] The phrases "eat its bread and drink its wine" and "a real communion" echo the most intimate scene in the Christian New Testament between Jesus and his disciples. This shared meal symbolizes the intimate spiritual relationship that has been regarded in Christian tradition as "holy," blessed not only by human intimacy but also with divine presence. This type of relationship is transformative for all who participate in it. From passages like this, we can see how connected Jung felt to Wilhelm spiritually. They related to one another at the level of the Self and not only the ego, and this gave the relationship its inspirational and transformative energy. It became Jung's duty and destiny to continue the work begun with Richard Wilhelm in building the bridge between East and West and using the gifts received from his friend to bring about the transformations promised in their mutual vision of a unified world culture.

Jung observed Wilhelm closely, and he did so with an analyst's eye. He says that Wilhelm "possessed the rare gift of a maternal intellect. To it he owed the unequalled ability to feel his way into the spirit of the East and to make his incomparable translations."[9] Recall Hexagram 31, *Hsien*: the Joyous, Lake, the youngest daughter sits above *Kên*, Keeping Still, Mountain, the youngest son. The feminine is above in the position of consciousness, while the masculine sustains and supports from below. This would be a picture of Wilhelm's intellect. And it would have been this same quality that allowed Jung to come so close to Wilhelm and to enter into his inner

[8] Ibid., para. 75.
[9] Ibid., para. 76.

world and affect him both in his feelings and his thinking. This accounts for Jung's influence on Wilhelm. He found in Jung a master of interpretation whose theories could help him give birth to the project of making the East intelligible to the West.

The Gift of the I Ching: Synchronicity

Jung and Wilhelm first formed their relationship due to a common passion, the *I Ching*. Wilhelm spent years of dedicated effort in translating the ancient text into his native German. Most of Jung's Memorial Address focuses on this great gift that Wilhelm gave to European culture. Beyond that, however, Jung states that it was his personal association with Richard Wilhelm that gave him the opportunity to *experience* "the divinatory power of the I Ching." It was this convincing experience that gave him "an Archimedean point from which our Western attitude of mind could be lifted off it foundations."[10] This is no small claim, for an Archimedean point is a rock solid position that gives one the objectivity (sometimes called a God's eye view) to perceive truth and "a reliable starting point from which one may reason."[11] Archimedes, the pre-Socratic Greek philosopher, argued that if he had a solid point and a long enough lever, he could move the whole world. Jung is claiming he has found this in the *I Ching*. What did he find there?

For the first time in his writings, Jung uses the word "syn-chronicity" in his Memorial Address, and it is in reference to this Archimedean point provided by the *I Ching*. *The Chinese Book of Changes* bases itself on the synchronistic principle, namely on the meaningful chance correspondence between a subject asking a question and a book giving an appropriate response. It is similar to astrology, Jung goes on to say, which is also based on the meaningful chance correspondence between a newborn's innate personality

---

[10] Ibid., para. 78.
[11] https://en.wikipedia.org/wiki/Archimedean_point#:~:text=An%20Archimedean%20point%20(Latin%3A%20Punctum,from%20which%20one%20may%20reason.

and the position of the planets at the moment of birth. Jung saw that synchronicity, if established as a basic principle in addition to causality, would transform science and the Western materialistic worldview. Jung repeatedly and consistently argued that the Western scientific worldview with its exclusive reliance on the principle of causality was not sufficient to account for all the empirical phenomena of experience. He refers to "the hidden qualities of the moment," which the *I Ching* exposes so brilliantly and Western science and philosophy miss entirely. These "hidden qualities" are left out of the rationalistic explanations of science, but they are an important feature of an event. They are what Jung would call "the unconscious aspects" of events, which need to be taken into account for a full explanation. For Jung, the principle of synchronicity is fundamental to the effectiveness of the *I Ching* in describing the quality of the moment in time when a question is asked and the yarrow stalks or coins are thrown. This feature of reality would become the center point of his discussions with Wolfgang Pauli in the years to come and would result in their construction of a new model for describing the totality of reality using the findings of depth psychology and quantum physics.

Jung adds: "What is even more important is that he has inoculated us with the living germ of the Chinese spirit, capable of working a fundamental change in our view of the world."[12] In his Memorial Address, Jung uses two metaphors to describe the profound effect that Wilhelm's translation of the *I Ching* worked in him, the one from ancient Greek philosophy ("an Archimedean point") and one from modern medicine ("an inoculation"). What an inoculation does, as we well know from our recent experience in the COVID pandemic, is to support resistance in the immune system against the effects of a virus. The *I Ching* is a medicine, Jung claims, to prevent an attack of "scientism," the powerful virus that has infected the West, which when allowed full effect in the psyche takes it over and possesses it with its one-sided and deleterious

---

[12] C.G. Jung, "Richard Wilhelm: In Memoriam," para. 78.

ideology of materialism. Materialism is the illness of the West, in Jung's view. It represses the spiritual capacities of the mind and drives them into basement of the unconscious, where they cause severe psychological and cultural problems. Individuation is blocked on all levels of human life by an ideological proscription on the reality of the spirit, the higher dimensions of the Self. In Jung's view, the *I Ching* can open the way once again for Western people to gain access to the invisible powers that rule the psyche and support higher forms of cultural development. Or, better said, the I *Ching* can be used as an inoculation to block the total dominance of the materialistic worldview and to make space for realization of "acts of creation in time," i.e., synchronicity. With this medicine, the Western mind can regain its balance and wholeness.

In retrospect, we can think of the meeting of Carl Jung and Richard Wilhelm as itself being a synchronistic event. At the "right time," which the Greeks called *kairos,* these two men met, and from this meeting there came a relationship that resulted in a line of thought that could transform an established worldview, moving it from scientific rationalist materialism to what is today being called "dual-aspect monism."[13] This is the idea that a unitary neutral field underlies all material and psychic phenomena and houses the potentials for realization exhibited in both, sometimes in relation to time and sometimes not. Synchronicity events are meaningful coincidences that produce transformation and development on both levels. On the human level, synchronicity is essential for individuation; on the material level, it is necessary for evolution. The full conscious realization of this timeless monad, the Self, is the capstone of the individuation process. This new worldview that combines Western science and Chinese wisdom would become the philosophy for our time and for the future.

The *I Ching* was for Jung a decisive confirmation of an intuition he had previously entertained about the psyche as a whole, namely,

---

[13] See H. Atmanspacher and D. Rickles, *Dual-Aspect Monism and the Deep Structure of Meaning*, Routledge, 2022.

that its development is controlled and directed not only by biology but more importantly by an invisible spiritual force that takes it beyond the limits of the material body. This was the same view that he discovered in "The Secret of the Golden Flower." What impressed Jung about using the *I Ching* was that it provided access to this invisible realm. This was a huge breakthrough, because Western thought at the time limited human knowledge to what could be perceived and established by the senses and the rational mind. Consulting the *I Ching* reached beyond this type of knowledge to "the Will of Heaven," and could show its active presence in the phenomenal world, in collective history-making and in the life of an individual. And it was "empirical," that is, not merely speculative but subject to verification. This grounded Jung's intuition in time and space and offered concrete evidence for the pattern-making and change-making powers of the spiritual dimension. Jung would say that it confirmed the theory of the collective unconscious and the archetypal energies. With great excitement, Jung reports in his Memorial Address for Richard Wilhelm an experiment that was carried out in Zurich:

At his first lecture at the Psychological Club in Zurich, Wilhelm, at my request demonstrated for me the *I Ching* and at the same time made a prognosis which, in less than two years was fulfilled to the letter and with the utmost clarity. Predictions of this kind could be further confirmed by numerous parallel experiences.[14]

This satisfied Jung's need for scientific evidence to confirm or reject theoretical hypotheses. With the *I Ching*, there was proof that invisible patterns exist in the spiritual realm and have real effect in the phenomenal world. This would break through Kant's strict line of demarcation between the phenomenal and the nouminal worlds, which argued that humans could not penetrate the nouminal barrier and gain knowledge about or from it. The evidence for synchronicity in the phenomenal world disputes Kantian limits of knowledge.

---

[14] Ibid., para. 84.

Jung's Tribute to Richard Wilhelm

Jung concludes his Memorial Address with a moving statement of gratitude for all that Richard Wilhelm in friendship gave him:

Wilhelm's life-work is of such immense importance to me because it clarified and confirmed so much that I had been seeking, striving for, thinking and doing in my effort to alleviate the psychic sufferings of Europeans. It was a tremendous experience for me to hear through him in clear language things I had dimly divined in the confusion of our European unconscious. I feel myself so very much enriched by him that it seems to me as if I had received more from him than from any other man.[15]

This testimonial to their friendship shows us Carl Jung's deep respect and love for his friend Richard Wilhelm. It was a relationship that changed the direction of his research. Richard Wilhelm's gift of a translation of "The Secret of the Golden Flower" guided Jung's interest directly into alchemy, which occupied him for the rest of his life and served as the source for his most mature writings on the psychology of the unconscious. The translation of the *I Ching* gave him the opportunity to develop the theory of synchronicity and to transform the materialistic worldview of the West.

---

[15] C.G. Jung, "Richard Wilhelm: In Memoriam," CW 15, para. 95.

Red Book Papers

The Red Book[1]

Jung's big, red Liber Novus[2] is a meticulously stylized record of the author's journey through the psyche's Underworld and his consequent psychic transformation at midlife. The gorgeous presentation of this work in the 2009 edition titled *The Red Book: Liber Novus,* constitutes a landmark in Jung's published *oeuvre*. This is not only because for the first time since its inception nearly 100 years ago has Liber Novus now become available to scholars and to the public, but also because of the care and cost that went into this production. It is a gorgeous publication of a unique literary and artistic work by an extraordinary man. Everything about *The Red Book* is bigger than life.

The Red Book comprises more material than is contained in the work that Jung himself created in his private library and called his Liber Novus. There is first of all an exact facsimile of the pages in Jung's Liber Novus, meticulously photographed and presented on

---

[1] Originally published as "Critical Review" in the *Journal of Analytical Psychology* 55:1, 2010. Somewhat modified for this edition.

[2] For clarification: *Liber Novus* is the title of the written text produced by Jung in manuscript, which forms the basis for the calligraphic text in his Red Book plus the pictures painted into Jung's Red Book. The Red Book is his oversized leather bound red book which contains part of the *Liber Novus* manuscript in calligraphic script and additional paintings that extend beyond the date of the conclusion of the manuscript in 1916. *The Red Book: Liber Novus* is the published work, which includes both a facsimile of Jung's Red Book and selections from the manuscript. The Black Books are Jung's journals, the entries in which form the basis for *Liber Novus* and more.

heavy paper pages covered with calligraphic script and paintings. Following this, there is an Introduction by the editor, Sonu Shamdasani, and then comes the transcribed text (in the original German in the German edition, and in translation in the English edition). Finally, there are three appendices containing material that was never a part of the transcript Jung created from his Black Book journals for the purpose of creating Liber Novus. The editor's Introduction and numerous footnotes for the text offer a wealth of information about how Liber Novus was constructed in several phases over the course of some 15 years.

To maintain the distinction between Jung's original handmade work and the published book, I shall refer to the original object as Jung's Red Book or as Liber Novus without italics and to the published work as *The Red Book* with italics. (The spine of Jung's Red Book bears the title Liber Novus, and for the published book this is used as a subtitle.)

Jung Agonistes

At the heart of Jung's Liber Novus is an Agon (from Classical Greek ἀγών meaning "contest"). In his native German, Jung would call it an *Auseinandersetzung*. Jung is wrestling with powers and principalities, light and dark. Like every Agon, this is a struggle that is impossible to undertake without breaking into a sweat, and Jung sweats a lot and breathes hard throughout. In the Agon, there are invariably the prot-agonist and the ant-agonist(s) grappling with one another. It is a wrestling match or a shouting match, a hot debate or a tense collaboration, but in every case, it is a test of wills, and it presses everyone involved, including the audience, to the limits of their stamina and endurance. To read *The Red Book* certainly tests one's stamina. Most people have to put it down after a page or two and take a break.

In the narrative, published here in three parts (Liber Primus, Liber Secundus, and Scrutinies), there are a large number of figures against whom Jung finds himself in the role of Protagonist. Excluding the Protagonist, I count 22 individual figures in the text, plus some others who come in groups (e.g., demons, Kabiroi, Shades, Souls). The figure of Jung, represented in the persona of "I," is the only continuous presence throughout. As such, the author confronts the others in turn, argues with them, discourses with them, struggles for clarity with them or for enlightenment or for satisfaction. Each figure brings something slightly different into play as the Agon unfolds. Several of the figures, such as Elijah and Salome and Soul, return from time to time, while others appear only once and then disappear.

Jung is an Agonist here in a complicated sense, since he himself is what he is confronting. "I" and "Others" are constituents of a single complexity, the psyche of C.G. Jung. The Other(s) appear in the form of imaginal figures who appear to the Protagonist suddenly and spontaneously as he gazes intently into the darkness of his nocturnal psyche, offering a variety of challenges that lead to dramatic moments that test him, often severely and sometimes even to the last breath. In the narrative, the Protagonist is searching, questioning, accepting, discarding, separating, debating, and in the process transforming himself.

What we see is a dramatic representation of a modern man searching desperately for the Way, in order to become oriented to this complexity and what it portends. In the process of searching out and following the Way, the Protagonist experiences extreme anxiety and a perceived high potential for catastrophe. One senses throughout the narrative that he is walking a fine line between sanity and madness as he becomes ever more intensely involved in these inner dialogues and dramas. At one point, he actually finds himself committed to an insane asylum and assigned to a fat little psychiatrist who diagnoses him with religious mania. Being himself a psychiatrist, Jung knew well how he would appear through this lens. The challenge is relentless, at times exhilarating, at times entertaining and even humorous, and at times deeply disturbing.

Who comes out the winner in this struggle between Jung's "I" and his alters? Does the Protagonist find the Way in the midst of all this confusing material and so many voices? All things considered, he does prevail, or at least he survives, and in the midst of it, he goes through a major transformation. He does find the Way, which leads to recovery of contact with his soul. His initial cry, "My soul, where are you?" is answered. Initiation and transformation are the hidden purposes of the whole process, although perhaps not known to be the goal from the outset. As it turns out, this process is governed by an invisible force named "spirit of the depths," which stands opposed to the "spirit of this time." As with all authentic initiations, a positive outcome is not a foregone conclusion at the beginning. At moments in the narrative, the Protagonist is threatened with madness and loss of control of his mental faculties. He (and, by turn, we also as readers entering into the narrative imaginatively and ever more deeply as we proceed) cannot know how this initiation is going to come out until the last page is written.

In fact, however, there is no final page within the covers of Jung's Red Book. Jung's Agon went on longer than indicated in the calligraphic text. The narrative simply stops in midsentence, as though the author had been interrupted and forgotten to come back to this work. When he did finally return to it some 30 years later in 1959 and tried to add a closure, he stopped in midsentence again. Perhaps he was trying to tell us something with these inexplicable and for him uncharacteristic sudden breaks. The editor of *The Red Book* has fixed this problem to an extent by including the pages from the draft that bring Liber Novus to a satisfying conclusion. The third section of *The Red Book*, titled Scrutinies, includes *Septem Sermones ad Mortuos*, the Gnostic cosmology spoken by Philemon, Jung's spiritual teacher.

Even *The Red Book* as now published represents only a fragment of what was for Jung a lifelong struggle between his conscious ego personality and the often oppositional, or at any rate radically different, will of the unconscious. It was this contest, more than his childhood, his marriage and other relationships, his professional career, or any other factors, that would shape and form him into the profound and multifaceted personality he became. As depicted in *The Red Book*, Jung's Agon was the struggle of a solitary man in search of the Way to realize and accept his personal destiny.

Some Relevant Historical Dates and Figures

To many it will come as a surprise that the entire content of the first layer, the basic "quarry" so to say, for Liber Novus as written out in the so-called Black Books, takes place over such a short period of time—only 160 days, beginning with the first entry on 12 November 1913 and concluding with the entry on 19 April 1914. This layer is found in 32 entries in the Black Books. To put this into biographical perspective, one must understand that this was a critical period in Jung's life and one he kept reflecting upon in the following decade and a half.

The paintings in Liber Novus are partly a pictorial representation of what is found in the calligraphic text, but they also, and more importantly, constitute a level of Jung's individuation process that went beyond the text and in many ways surpassed it. It seems that Jung outgrew the process shown in the narrative, which is limited to the period 1913-1916, whereas the pictures extend into the late 1920s. This later process represented in the pictures portrays Jung's arrival at symbols of the Self, which is not achieved in the text itself.

In *Memories, Dreams, Reflections,* Jung states that his "confrontation with the unconscious," which is the Agon that we find detailed in *The Red Book*, began with his break with Freud. Freud is not mentioned directly in Liber Novus, nor are any other persons from Jung's actual life. However, the dramatic narrative of the work does tell the story of Jung's struggle to separate himself from Freud and from his previous intellectual positions. Since the purpose of the inner work was to find his own Way, Jung was certainly fully aware that this was a path that had to take a distance from Freud's influence. Jung's Way would not be based on previous learnings or on the assumptions of the age in which he lived. By going with what in *The Red Book* is called the "spirit of the depths" and leaving behind the "spirit of this time," Jung was venturing beyond the pale of what was permitted to a European intellectual of the time. He knew that he was in danger of forfeiting the reputation for reliable psychological and scientific thinking that had made him famous by the time he was in his 30s. The intellectual positions he was taking leave of had been built up throughout his life to date. They were the basic assumptions of the age he had learned in high school and university and continuing in his psychiatric training at the University of Zurich's Burghölzli Klinik. His scientific research projects there ("Studies in Word Association") and his work under the influence of Freud and the school of psychoanalysis were consistent with the same line of thought prevalent in Enlightenment Europe since the 18th century.

His differences with Freud, at first minor and latent but present from the beginning of their relationship in 1907, become sharper and more significant after their trip to America in 1909. They reached a climax with Jung's publication of the second part of *Wandlungen und Symbole der Libido (Transformations and Symbols of the Libido)* in the *Jahrbuch* in September of 1912. Freud's dismissive reception of this work led to an angry exchange in their personal correspondence, and on 6 January 1913, Jung wrote to Freud that, following Freud's request to break off the personal side of their collaboration, he would burden him with no further letters of the sort he had been sending. He closed his final letter to Freud with a quote from *Hamlet*, "The rest is silence."[3]

Eight months later, on 5 August 1913, Jung gave a lecture in London in which he used the term "analytical psychology" for the first time, thereby opening a public breach between his own views and those of his former mentor. A month later, at the IPA Congress in Munich (7-8 September 1913) and in the midst of a disputatious atmosphere charged with tension between two factions—Freud and his followers on the one side and the "Zurich school" people on the other (Freud fainted in Jung's presence for the second time during

---

[3] W. McGuire (ed.), *The Freud-Jung Letters*, p. 540.

this Congress) —Jung was reelected president of the IPA, but with the whole contingent from Vienna abstaining from voting. Jung won the showdown with the Viennese in Munich, but it was not sustainable. Freud was clearly still the dominant force in psychoanalysis.

On 27 October 1913 after hearing through a mutual acquaintance that Freud was questioning his *"bona fides"* in psychoanalytic circles, Jung sent Freud a formal letter of resignation from his position as editor of the *Jahrbuch*, a post he had held since the journal's inception.

These events formed the backdrop of his "journey to the beyond" (to *"Jenseits"* in Jung's original German). It would be from the adventures undergone in that realm and guided by the Spirit of the Depths that Jung would compose Liber Novus in the years following. On 12 November 1913, just two weeks after sending Freud his letter of resignation from the *Jahrbuch*, Jung made his first entry in the Black Books that would begin the basic narrative as entered later into the Red Book. These entries continued for a period of 160 days and amounted to a total of 32 separately dated notations: four entries in November, nine in December, 14 in January, four in February, none in March, and a final one on 19 April 1914. On the next day, 20 April 1914, Jung submitted his formal resignation as president of the IPA, and 10 days later, on 30 April, he resigned from the medical faculty of the University of Zurich. He was now on his own, a free man.

We should not underestimate the risks this freedom posed for Jung. It is clear that one of Jung's major challenges and accomplishments during this Agon was to confront and to overcome his fear of going it alone. In the active imagination materials published in *The Red Book*, we come again and again upon the image of the Solitary. In the end, the meaning of this figure, variously portrayed in the narrative, would guide all that Jung did and thought throughout the rest of his life. This period of inner work created the basis for a decisive turning point in Jung's orientation toward himself and the world. He had found his Way, that of an individuating man seeking to maintain the right relation to his own soul. The Tower at Bollingen, which he began constructing in 1922 on a remote piece of property on the upper end of the Lake of Zurich, was a logical extension of Liber Novus.

A Note on Jung's Theology in the Red Book

We cannot ignore the religious implications of this journey, since Liber Novus is in many ways a spiritual document that is trying to break through to a new theology. Its title, Liber Novus, suggests that Jung saw it as a new New Testament. Jung's preoccupation with the problem of evil is evident in *The Red Book*. This would culminate some 40 years later in his *Answer to Job*. For Jung, the doctrine of evil as *privatio boni* was a totally unsatisfying solution to the omnipresence of the power of evil in the world.

Jung's theological seriousness on this topic did not come at the expense of his sense of humor. In *The Red Book* there is a quite hilarious passage in Chapter 21 of Liber Secundus, titled "The Magician," wherein Jung conjures the Holy Trinity and tries to afix Satan onto it as it is rising upward toward the heavens, thereby making evil a theological reality equal to the other members of the Trinity. This does not work because Satan objects on the grounds that a Quaternity is too static: Nothing would happen in the world if he joined the Godhead. He must be kept apart from the Trinity because, to have some buzz and creativity going on in the cosmos, he had to be free to cause disruptions. Not tied in too tightly to the pure and the good, he had the freedom to stir things up in the cosmos and to activate change and movement.

Later in *The Red Book*, in *7 Sermons*, Abraxas is presented as a possible solution to what the integration of evil might practically look like, since he displays a combination of polarities. Still, one wonders if Jung was inclined to accept this as a replacement for the Christian Deity or as a final statement. In *Seven Sermons to the Dead*, the Dead who have come back from Jerusalem unsatisfied do not exactly take to Abraxas either, and Jung makes no further references to the Figure. When Martin Buber alluded to Abraxas in their vitriolic exchange and labeled Jung a modern Gnostic, Jung denied it, called Abraxas a "sin of my youth" and not to be taken seriously.[4] In the extensive correspondence with Father Victor White between 1945 and 1960, in which the problem of evil and various doctrines of God were thoroughly discussed, there are no references to Abraxas, although Jung frequently proclaims his disgust with the Christian doctrine of *privatio boni*. Jung may not have found an answer to the problem of evil in Abraxas, but he still wanted to hold out for a new God image that would somehow include archetypal shadow, a.k.a. absolute evil, within the God-image.

Since Abraxas is as close as he ever got to naming such a Deity, we should not dismiss Buber's intuition either that Jung's had a Gnostic shadow informing some of his theology. A quasi-theological version of the ideas contained in *Seven Sermons to the Dead,* and therefore indirectly associated with Abraxas and with the Alexandrian Gnostic teacher Basilides, appeared years later in his book *Aion,* wherein Jung elaborates a version of all-encompassing reality based on a series of Gnostic quaternities and relates this mythological vision closely to his psychological construct of the Self. *Aion,* a late work, could be seen therefore as the translation of a theme from Liber Novus into contemporary psychological theory.

Jung the Magician

A pivotal moment in the adventures recounted in *The Red Book* is Jung's acceptance of a Magician's wand (Chapter 19 of Liber Secundus). When it appears suddenly in his hand, he does not know what it is or what to do with it. He quickly learns that its power can make him strong and impervious to the slings and arrows of others' criticism and jibes. Although he does not say so explicitly, this would serve to protect him from the criticisms he must have been anticipating from Freud and the Viennese as well as from philo-

---

[4] C.G. Jung, "Religion and Psychology: A Reply to Martin Buber," CW 18, para. 1501.

COLLECTED WRITINGS OF MURRAY STEIN VOLUME 9

sophers and churchmen who would not be able to accept the reality of the psyche that he was uncovering. Jung recognized that a sacrifice was required, however, in order to receive the full force of Magic's power—the sacrifice of "solace," the giving or receiving of comfort. In other words, Jung recognized that he had to develop a tougher skin in order to wield the wand of Magic. But what is Magic's value beyond self-protection? And how to use it ethically?

To find out, the Protagonist goes in search of the great Magician, Philemon. What he learns from Philemon in the Chapter titled "The Magician" (Chapter 21 of Liber Secundus) is critical, both for this moment in his life when he was separating his professional identity from the ambitions of Freud and psychoanalysis and for his future work as psychological theorist and thinker. Philemon tells him that science is limited and cannot grasp or ever explain the part of reality that is irrational. The scientific method, he explains, can only understand and grasp the potentially rational, the portion of reality that is founded on or governed by laws and principles, which is subject to expression in mathematical formulas and which therefore rests on logical foundations. The rest is not accessible to science. The role of Magic is to make the other part of reality, the nonrational, intelligible. Most intelligent people can follow the scientific path, and that is enough for them, says Philemon, but for those who have opened the door to chaos, as Jung has in these adventures through *Jenseits*, this is not enough. They realize that they need something beyond science if they are to cope with the irrational portions of the mind and of reality and to explicate this. This is the function of Magic. Magic can make the irrational intelligible.

In *Memories, Dreams, Reflections,* Jung writes that the material he generated as a consequence of his confrontation with the unconscious occupied him for the rest of his life, as he tried to translate the meaning of the images into an acceptable language for the times.[5] The material in Liber Novus and Scrutinies was not

---

[5] C.G. Jung, *Memories, Dreams, Reflections*, p. 199

suitable for publication because it was not congruent with the "spirit of this time," and so he chose not to publish it in this form. Rather, he had to "incorporate this incandescent matter into the contemporary picture of the world."[6] Jung's project was to make the irrational chaos of the inner world intelligible, to create a map for the territory and to name its major features, to give himself and others a way of dealing with the invisible life of the mind, or at least that portion of it that cannot be measured and investigated by the normal scientific methods of psychology and psychiatry. This exploration and mapping constituted the investigation of the unconscious, using the tools of active imagination and dream interpretation and then translating the findings into a language that people could understand and use. This would be the challenge for a true depth psychology. The opus of the years that followed the period when Jung experienced the "stream of lava" that we find in *The Red Book* was dedicated to translating his discoveries into the construction of analytical psychology.

Where *The Red Book* can assist the interested scholar is in tracking the more personal and subjective origins of many of Jung's later ideas and attitudes. Many people have observed the traces of influence left by various philosophers, poets, and other intellectual sources on Jung. A list of the ones mentioned would include Plato, Kant, Schopenhauer, Hegel, C.G. Carus, Goethe, Schelling, the Gnostics, the alchemists, the Eastern religions, and the Western religions. While all of this is no doubt valid and true since Jung was so widely read, we can now see the details of an entirely different source of influence. The images and narrative and the commentary on them, which we can study in *The Red Book,* contributed essential ingredients to Jung's thinking. This source opened up to him precisely in the period when the fundamental ideas that would shape analytical psychology were beginning to take on a particular form in Jung's mind. Coming first as symbols and then putting them through a process of thought and reflection that would transform

---

[6] Ibid.

them into abstractions and psychological theory, Jung created his specific vision for depth psychology. The turmoil, trials of initiation, and transformations they engendered in him changed his worldview indelibly. *The Red Book* gives us the closest glimpse of the Big Bang that created analytical psychology.

The Genre Question

Liber Novus is a kind of book, but of what genre? It can be compared to many other works in Western literature, but it is distinctly unlike almost all of them in many respects. It may be read as a literary work akin to Dante's *The Divine Comedy* or Homer's *Odyssey*, since it uses the metaphor of a journey through uncharted territories, including the Underworld, but it is quite different from these canonical literary masterpieces in that it does not have the consistency and rigor of poetic and artistic style that characterize these works nor the authorial skill and command of the artist's conscious ego. In fact, Jung the author relinquished control in these active imaginations precisely in order to facilitate the emergence of the dialogue and images in their raw form. This can be at times quite shocking.

Liber Novus is also not a scientific work like Darwin's journal *Voyage of the Beagle*, although it takes the form of a journal record of a voyage of discovery. But it does not partake of the rationality of science and in fact rejects scientific principles and values in favor of imagination and what Jung calls "the intuitive method."

Some people have compared it to works of visual-and-poetical art like Blake's *An Island in the Moon* or *The Four Zoas* since it includes so many stunning paintings and illustrations, but the intention in Liber Novus is not really an artistic but rather a psychological one. This is the world of psyche as seen and experienced by Jung, he insists, including the odd way he thought about it at the time. Nietzsche's *Thus Spoke Zarathustra* comes to mind as a possibly comparable work, and many of the footnotes in *The Red Book* allude to it. Although it seems that Liber Novus is partially modeled on this work and displays similar rhetorical flourishes, Jung decisively rejects the role of prophet/avatar and makes himself, not others, the chief subject of analysis and the target of the transformation that is aimed for. Unlike Nietszche, whose own ego standpoint is not to be found in *Thus Spoke Zarathustra*, Jung asks questions of his inner teachers throughout Liber Novus and raises objections to what they are asking him to take aboard. *Liber Novus* also bears comparison to St. Augustine's *Confessions*, a meditative and personal account of the individual's search for God and for a proper relation to Deity, but Jung does not have the same certainty of doctrine and faith as the Saint, and he does not end up in the same place, i.e., as a man of faith in the biblical God, although *Liber Novus* does affirm the centrality of love and the spiritual necessity for making the ego into a vessel to receive the Deity if and when It chooses to arrive and in whatever form.

Liber Novus, therefore, seems to stand quite alone. I see it as a literary and pictorial fragment of a lifelong psychological journey to the Self. In *The Red Book* we are privileged to witness key elements in Jung's individuation process during the critical midlife period, when he completely revamped his conscious attitudes and recovered his lost connections to his own depths and to his life's path, and when he made a rediscovery of his soul, of which he was desperately in need as he sought a new way to go on with his life. I think of it as a modern rendition of a type of work like "The Dialogue of a World-Weary Man with His Ba,"[7] an Egyptian text of four millennia ago. If *Liber Novus* can be assigned to a genre, it would to the group that might be called *Timeless Documents of the Soul*.

---

[7] See H. Jacobsohn, "The Dialogue of a World-Weary Man with His Ba."

What Is *The Red Book* for Analytical Psychology?[1]

Although the field of analytical psychology shows many diverse influences from a wide variety of theoretical perspectives and is deeply multicultural, it must nevertheless be recognized that the major ancestor of all who participate in its life is C.G. Jung. His published work remains the common baseline for theorizing and praxis. Some of Jung's writings are essential and central, however, while others may be seen as peripheral. People have their favorites among the many books and papers that Jung left as his heritage, and they will also have their most disliked pieces. We all make selections based on interests and background, as well as on personal complexes. Which of them should be selected as primary and essential by the field and which are to be considered secondary has thus far not been definitively established.

In 2009, a long withheld and controversial work, *The Red Book*, was published, and the question is: What does this mean for analytical psychology? How does it fit into the legacy? For more than 70 years, this medieval-like illuminated calligraphic text with many paintings lay first on the shelves of Jung's private library and then in a bank vault. It is quite evident that Jung was ambivalent about its place in his official *oeuvre* since he kept it private in his lifetime and left no instructions concerning its publication posthumously.

---

[1] Originally published in *Journal of Analytical Psychology* 56:5, 2011. Published here with some modifications.

Moreover, it is an unfinished work. It came to the Jungian family of analysts and scholars like a long-concealed illegitimate child, and one who may have quite exceptional information to offer about an obscure period in Jung's creative life. With its publication, it, too, must be considered as part and parcel of the heritage, whether one likes it or not. Such long-lost children are a challenge to integrate into established families.

So, what is *The Red Book* for analytical psychology now that it has arrived and after so many of Jung's writings have by now been already published? Does it belong in the canon? Is it a seminal work for analytical psychology to be placed beside Jung's other major works, or is it to be taken as the equivalent of a writer's diary and sketchbook, akin to Leonardo's *Notebooks*, which shows the early workings of a brilliant mind as the creator prepares for his more serious scientific contributions to the world? Conversely, one can ask: Are Jung's later writings no more than an explication of this monumental symbolic work to make it more accessible for modern readers and thinkers? Perhaps it is both.

As a commercial publishing venture, *The Red Book* was phenomenally successful, with sales figures soaring far beyond expectations. Whether the people who purchase it have read it or not, this surprising popular reception shows that there is an appeal to general audiences. The astonishing wave of attention generated by this colorful work, moreover, has had the consequence of increasing the visibility of Jung and Jungian analysts in public awareness worldwide. Some people have celebrated this, others have found it threatening or distasteful.

Here I will consider the question of *The Red Book's* place and possible significance in the field of analytical psychology. Jungian psychoanalysts are, after all, heirs of C.G. Jung, and this newly published work is now a part of the inherited package. I am speaking, therefore, not from a popular culture viewpoint but from the perspective of what *The Red Book* might contribute (plus or minus) to those who carry on the work of psychoanalysis in the spirit of C.G. Jung.

Analytical Psychology, a Tradition

The professional members of the field of analytical psychology belong to a tradition that was begun in Zurich, Switzerland, by Jung and a group of others who were leaving Freud's school. By using the term "tradition" (from the Latin *trader,* hand over, deliver), I mean a historical culture that contains a more or less well-defined set of values, perspectives, ideas, and attitudes that is delivered (handed over) from one generation to the next for an indefinite period of time. There are long and venerable traditions, and there are new ones that have yet to prove their endurance in time. In modern history, one speaks of the "scientific tradition," for example, which is made up of a culture of like-minded people who employ a method of investigation with generally accepted rules of verification, who subscribe to such values as objectivity and integrity, and who pass these methods and values from teachers to students in schools and laboratories through the generations. The scientific tradition is relatively new compared with other traditions such as humanism and the religious ones.

If one searches for how traditions are transmitted, one finds a variety of channels. Traditions are often borne along importantly by texts (a literary canon and sacred books). Some are handed on primarily through oral transmission and ritual. And for some (as for our tradition of depth psychology and praxis), it is by a combination of texts, oral transmissions from teachers and supervisors to students, and rituals of initiation (passing exams, receiving diplomas, advancing from analyst to training analyst to supervising analyst, etc.).

Contemporary Jungian psychoanalysts are in the third, fourth, fifth and sixth generation of a family of clinicians who work in and with the perspectives offered by the progenitor, C.G. Jung. The first and founding generation was made up of Jung himself and a few other figures who were close to him, such as Emma Jung and Toni Wolff; the second generation was composed of those who worked directly with Jung (e.g., H.G. Baynes, Gerhard Adler, James Kirsch, Esther Harding, C.A. Meier, Erich Neumann, Marie-Louis von Franz,

Barbara Hannah, and Joseph Henderson, among others); in the third generation were those who studied and analyzed with the members of the second generation (importantly, Michael Fordham, Elie Humbert, Hans Dieckmann, Mario Jacoby, Adolf Guggenbühl-Craig, James Hillman, Helmut Barz, June Singer). Every Jungian psycho-analyst can establish his or her own specific generation by tracing the lineage back to Jung. In my case, I am of the fourth generation, and those who have worked with me in analysis and supervision would be the fifth generation.

Many of our teachers had a more direct link to Jung himself than we do, and our students have a yet more distant one. What difference does this make? Does Jung's centrality and the influence of his ideas fade and diminish through the generations? Does the tradition change and gain new features due to introjections from other sources?

Here I would like to consider how a tradition maintains itself *spiritually,* that is, in the "spirit of the founding figure," and how it retains a living sense of the symbolic presence of its founder(s), and in addition what this means and what its importance may be for the tradition. Into this reflection, I will then fold the discussion of a potential role for *The Red Book* in analytical psychology.

The Transmission of Spirit in Tradition

One of Jung's earliest published writings, his fifth and last Zofingia Lecture, given in January 1899, is titled "Thoughts on the Interpretation of Christianity, with reference to the Theory of Albrecht Ritschl." In that early talk delivered to his fraternity brothers at the University of Basel, Jung shows his interest in theology and boldly criticizes a view expressed by the famous Protestant theologian of his day, Albrecht Ritschl (1822-89). Ritschl held that the spiritual influence of Christ is passed on from generation to generation more or less mechanically through a process of teaching and learning within the community of believers. This is a strictly causal, material account of the process of historical transmission of a narrative content. The presence of Christ is kept alive in the minds and hearts of Christians by virtue of their membership in the community of believers and by their education in this community's values, ideas, and teachings. The community transmits Christ from one generation to the next by a process of teaching and learning. A text like the Bible is important as an object of study and a sourcebook for orientation, but a deep understanding and personal integration of its vision are seen to be dependent upon the effectiveness of the teaching of the community in which one participates as a Christian. The Bible's inspirational power and effect on the minds and hearts of believers do not depend upon the Holy Spirit or any other supernatural agency. In his view, the reality of Christ is transmitted through the ages by the means of communities of faith passing down the teachings and memories from earliest generations to later ones. There is nothing metaphysical or mystical about this process of transmission. It is pure cognitive-behavioral psychology, and spiritual transmission has nothing to do with archetypal images and energies or with something magical like synchronicity.

As a 24-year-old medical student with only an amateur's understanding of theology, for which he apologizes in the introduction, Jung objects vehemently to this mechanical theory of transmission of spiritual reality.[2] His objection is precisely that it leaves out the mystical element: "The mystery of a metaphysical world, a metaphysical order, of the kind that Christ taught and embodied in his own person, must be placed in center stage of the Christian religion," Jung argues. "No religion has survived, or ever will, without mystery, to which the devotee is most intimately

---

[2] In *Memories, Dreams, Reflections,* Jung says: "Ritschl's theology was much in fashion in those days. Its historicism irritated me, especially the comparison with a railway train." Aniela Jaffe adds the footnote: "Albrecht Ritschl compared Christ's coming to the shunting of a railroad train. The engine gives a push from behind, the motion passes through the entire train, and the foremost car begins to move. Thus the impulse given by Christ is transmitted down the centuries." C.G. Jung, *Memories, Dreams, Reflections,* p. 97.

bound."[3] Here Jung identified a basic problem in 19th-century liberal Protestant theology: It had become too rational. In this early essay, Jung sees experience of the Divine Other as foundational for a living spiritual tradition, without which it becomes sterile and nothing more than the routine repetition of received doctrine. This had been his own experience of the Swiss Reformed Church, as he reports in *Memories, Dreams, Reflections*.[4]

What is surprising as we read this essay is Jung's explicitly positive regard for the term "metaphysical." In all of his later psychological writings, he would eschew anything having to do with "metaphysical" terminology, saying repeatedly that he is speaking only as a psychologist and not as a theologian. However, what he actually did, subtly, with his later psychological theory was to find a way around speaking about transcendence as "metaphysical" while retaining much of the sense of what this term conveys. For "metaphysical" he substituted the term "archetypal," and for "the supernatural world of ghosts, gods and angels" he used the concept of "the unconscious." In this way, he discovered a channel of communication whereby numinous figures and powers can be transmitted from one generation to another without metaphysical or supernatural agency. This is similar to what science has done by explaining the creation of the universe, electromagnetic force, gravity, the nature of light, and so forth without reference to a supernatural God. What was previously attributed to divine powers and sources has been explained by natural ones. Jung did the same with respect to the forces of the mental world. Visions and mystical experiences are not a manifestation of supernatural beings and energies in human consciousness but rather the appearance of the autonomous archetypes of the collective unconscious. Later, the theory of synchronicity would be added, which introduces the notion of objective meaning due to the manifestation of "creative acts...the continuous creation of a pattern that exists from all

---

[3] C.G. Jung, *The Zofingia Lectures*, p. 109.
[4] See *Memories, Dreams, Reflections*, pp. 91-98.

eternity."[5] Synchronistic events are neither the eternally predestined actions of God (John Calvin) nor the products of a subtle chain of causality in the physical world (Albert Einstein), but rather the regular discontinuities in the psycho-physical cosmos that are not predictable except as statistically probable and convey an objective source of meaning through "meaningful coincidences."

Later, Jung could therefore speak of the power of numinous archetypal images, energies, and processes emerging within the space-and-time-limited world as the consequence of synchronistic concatenations in the depths of the collective unconscious where psyche and matter are one and constitute two sides of a single whole. These occur at moments of significance in the lives of individuals and communities, and they have the effect of enlivening and energizing them with a sense of transcendent meaning. It is these acausal meaningful events that most deeply keep a spiritual tradition alive and vital, and not the rational teachings of texts and techniques that go on within the communities of the committed. They are, in theological terms, signs of the working of the Holy Spirit and the continuous presence of God within the historical process. In other words, Jung concludes that it takes spirit to keep spirit alive.

Transmission of "Jung" in Analytical Psychology

What about the transmission of "Jung" in our tradition of analytical psychology? I put quotation marks around the name of the founding figure because by asking how "Jung" is transmitted in our tradition, I do not mean to ask how veneration for C.G. Jung the man is fostered through the generations. Rather, I am asking how the spirit that he embodied is kept alive, a spirit that has nourished the hearts and minds of his students and has inspired them to form a tradition that continues to thrive today around the world as analytical psychology. Does what Jung said in that early Zoffingia Lecture have relevance for this question? Does transmission of symbolic and

---

[5] C.G. Jung, "Synchronicity: An Acausal Principle," CW 8, para. 967.

numinous images that convey transcendence and meaning take place in the tradition of analytical psychology? Does synchronicity play a role in this?

In purely practical and mundane terms, the tradition of analytical psychology is today passed down, though only in part, by means of the training programs that have been created by professional Jungian institutions worldwide, all of which are housed within the International Association for Analytical Psychology. In addition to these recognized institutional channels, there are many others that pass through academic circles, study groups, Friends of Jung societies, readers of Jungian books, and nowadays denizens of the internet. In the training programs of the professional institutes, candidates are required to study the texts of the discipline and to master the methods and techniques needed to practice Jungian psychoanalysis competently, legally, and with some measure of confidence. But as the Swiss Reformed tradition did for Jung, our psychological tradition can lose its aliveness and deeper qualities of significance and meaning if there is no archetypal and synchronistic support. If people read Jung's works and are not moved within their own souls, in other words if symbolic resonance is absent, the spirit is not transmitted. The words are mere marks on a page and carry only superficial cognitive significance. When new figures arrive on the scene, they capture their interest, and the "ancestor" becomes a portrait of a fine old gentleman hanging on the wall. As time goes by, the picture fades, and newer and more exciting images beckon the later generations, who go off in other directions and build new houses of their own, occasionally lifting a toast to the old Swiss ancestor with a funny moustache who was a bit cranky and eccentric but "thank God" left them some money to do their own thing. In this way, the tradition fades away and passes into history. In time, it becomes a footnote in the history of depth psychology, which is itself a footnote in the history of psychology, which is a footnote in the history of philosophy, and so forth.

On the other hand, if the transmission of "Jung" is augmented by numinous experience, including synchronicities, by dreams and life-transforming "moments of meeting" with the spirit that Jung the man embodied and voiced in his writings, the tradition will continue to be revitalized over long stretches of time. The fading that many movements suffer for want of transcendent grounding will not be characteristic of this one.

Does this mean that we should look upon Jung as a sort of god, a Christ figure to be worshipped and mystically united with in ecstatic visions? Is this cult? Personally, I find this idea distasteful and off the mark, because it leads to obscurantism and defensive distortions of history. However, one does need to discover and experience an archetypal ground in, around, or beneath the ancestor figure, one that can emanate transcendence and constellate symbolic resonance. There must be synchronicities involved in "meeting Jung," whether in dream or text. If this numinous figure cannot be the biographical Jung himself, then what is this image in our tradition? What or who symbolizes "Jung" for us?

The Red Book

The belated publication of Jung's *The Red Book: Liber Novus* in 2009 landed in the middle of the field of analytical psychology with a big splash. For some, it was an embarrassment ("We have not become psychologists in order to listen to revelations and to adopt a pseudo-religious ideology of 'the self' (or each develop our own one),"[6] while for others it is an awesome and inspiring addition to the Jungian heritage ("Now, for me, this material is some of the most exquisite you will find in any religious or spiritual tradition: Beauty in the Dark. Jung grapples with human embodiment on its own terms, graphically sacrificing body and soul for the sake of Soul. This book is a literary masterpiece because it embodies Jung's deepest personal, spiritual transformation, taking the reader on that perilous journey along with him."[7] There has been considerable uncertainty

---

[6] W. Giegerich, 2010. "Liber Novus, that is, the New Bible," in Spring, Vol 83, p. 380.
[7] K.L. Evans, 2011. Personal communication.

among Jungians about how to receive this astonishing and complex gift from our common ancestor. Is it a curse or a blessing?

As with all such anomalous inheritances from founding figures in intellectual or religious traditions, there are a variety of possible interpretations of its meaning. For example, Martin Luther discounted the importance of several books of the Bible and considered the last book, The Revelation to John, without evidence of inspiration by the Holy Spirit. For other serious readers of the Bible, Revelation lies at the very center of what the Holy Scriptures mean to communicate. It is hard to be neutral about texts like this. It seems to me that it does matter how one comes down on the value of *The Red Book*, but whatever the judgment of individuals may be, the tradition itself must from now on include this work as a major item in its inventory of received texts. For some, it will be a book of inspiration, for others a work to be avoided except perhaps for historical and biographical interest or regarded as a preparation diary or notebook for the scientific works to follow.

For myself, I consider *The Red Book* as a potentially powerful instrument for transmission of the numinous images that underlie and ground our tradition and link it to older historical traditions. It can also serve as a text that offers people useful guidance for how to deal with experiences of the numinous images of the collective unconscious when they befall them. I would therefore locate it in the center, albeit somewhat uneasily as I will explain later, rather than on the periphery of our inheritance as Jungians. *The Red Book* is "precious," as one friend who prefers to remain anonymous said and meant that in the genuine sense of the word, not ironically.

As a potentially active transmitter of the numinous ground underlying analytical psychology, *The Red Book* can play the role of a foundational text with a symbolic value beyond the literal meaning of the words inscribed in it. Such texts inspire later work and thought and are returned to again and again by later generations because they transmit the genius for a cultural domain. I use "genius" here in the Latin sense of the word as the guiding spirit or tutelary deity of a person, family, or place. *The Red Book* contains such a genius in the figure of Philemon and makes it available for transmission to the tradition.

Philemon, Genius of *The Red Book*

What we find in *The Red Book* is the story of a very time-bound and human-all-too-human narrator/protagonist (i.e., Jung) setting out at midlife on a journey with "the spirit of the depths" to rediscover his lost soul. In the course of his wanderings, he passes through a number of gripping inner experiences that we can view as profound initiations into archetypal mysteries. Moreover, in passing from passive witness to active participant in these visions and dialogues, the protagonist also becomes an actor in the transformation of the figures he encounters. In the course of the narrative, he gives birth to a new god image, Phanes, who unites the opposites. Finally, the protagonist discovers that the "genius," who is the "spirit of the depths" and responsible for all the images and experiences in this realm, is "Philemon."

Who is Philemon? What is his symbolical value and meaning? It is important to become acquainted with him, since Philemon is the primary symbol for the authorial spirit that shapes *The Red Book*, and this is what will be transmitted by this work to later generations of the tradition in which this work is housed.

In *The Red Book*, Philemon appears as a figure of importance primarily in the third section, Scrutinies. However, he is introduced to the reader in the last chapter of *Liber Secundus*, titled "The Magician." Jung, the Protagonist in the story, has had to work hard to get to Philemon. A prefiguration of Philemon earlier in the book is Elijah. By the time he approaches Philemon, Jung has undergone major initiations and encounters with other figures. He goes in search of Philemon because, having been given the "wand of magic," he has to find out what it means. So, he sets out to find "the Magician." This is Philemon.

He finds him in retirement, working quietly in his garden tending tulips. Philemon's wife, Baucis, is present in the background but does not play a role. The old man initially ignores Jung and his persistent questioning, saying he is now retired and no longer interested in teaching anyone about magic. Philemon's reticence does not augur well, but in the end he relents and instructs Jung in the paradox of magic. Magic, he teaches, is the complement of reason. Reason can comprehend the part of the world that is rational but no more than that. It cannot understand or grasp "unreason."[8] Much of reality is not susceptible to reason, and this other part can only be comprehended by another type of thinking. This is "magic." Magic proceeds by way of imagination and denotes intuitive understanding of the nonrational. Magic can comprehend the portion of reality that reason misses. Magic is the intuitive understanding of unconscious processes that purely rational methods cannot grasp, a kind of mythopoetic approach to knowledge. The magician is an intuitive whose mind reaches into spaces that science cannot approach directly with its methods and tools.

This is Philemon's first teaching. He makes no further appearances in Liber Novus.

It is at first surprising that Philemon should be the figure selected to be Jung's teacher about magic. In Greek myth,[9] he is a simple farmer whose only claim to fame is his hospitality to the gods, Hermes and Zeus, as they wander the roads of the earth and look for a place to stay the night. His attitude of pious receptivity to the divine strangers is the key to Philemon's good fortune and immortality as a figure in myth. This virtue is also precisely what Jung, the protagonist of *The Red Book*, must develop in himself. The task that is set before him throughout the text again and again is to get over his egoistic ambition and narcissistic pride and to transform his conscious attitude into a receptive womb for the seeds of the future. For this, Philemon would be a model. It is Philemon's receptivity precisely to the divine that is essential. He represents a religious attitude.

---

[8] C.G. Jung, *The Red Book*, p. 314.
[9] Ovid, *Metamorphosis,* Bk. VIII.

In Scrutinies, Philemon's role becomes much more prominent. Here he is the dominant figure and assumes the persona of sage. In his most significant extended appearance in *The Red Book*, he delivers "the Seven Sermons to the Dead." It is particularly the Seventh Sermon, where Philemon teaches the dead about their eternal destiny and directs them to their transcendent home as symbolized by a star, that finally puts to rest the souls of the dead who had been unsatisfied after returning from their trip to Jerusalem.

Throughout *The Red Book*, the protagonist is confronted with the problem of restless ghosts who are desperately searching for an answer that will show them the Way to they know not what. This theme of disturbance and dissatisfaction in the ghostly realm culminates in a visitation that Jung describes both in *The Red Book* and in *Memories, Dreams, Reflections*. Here is the version in *The Red Book*:

> But one night a dark crowd knocked at my door, and I trembled with fear. Then my soul appeared and said in haste, "They are here and will tear open your door."
> "So that the wicked herd can break into my garden? Should I be plundered and thrown out onto the street? You make me into an ape and a child's plaything. When, Oh my God, shall I be saved from this Hell of fools? But I want to hack to pieces your cursed webs, go to Hell, you fools. What do you want with me?"
> But she interrupted me and said, "What are you talking about? Let the dark ones speak."
> I retorted, "How can I trust you? You work for yourself not for me. What good are you, if you can't even protect me from the devil's confusion?"
> "Be quiet," she replied, "or else you'll disturb the work." And as she spoke these words, behold, Philemon came up to me, dressed in the white robe of a priest, and lay his hand on my shoulder.
> Then I said to the dark ones, "So speak, you dead."

And immediately they cried in many voices "We have come back from Jerusalem, where we did not find what we sought. We implore you to let us in. You have what we desire. Not your blood, but your light. That is it."

Then Philemon lifted his voice and taught them, saying (and this is the first sermon to the dead):

"Now hear: I begin with nothingness ..."[10]

During the following several nights, Philemon delivers seven sermons in the style of a Hellenistic Gnostic teacher, whom Jung named Basilides after the historical Gnostic of the second century in the privately published version of *Septem Sermones ad Mortuos.*[11] In *Liber Novus*, it is Philemon who in the Seventh Sermon teaches them of their destiny and their eternal home:

This star is the God and the goal of man.

This is his lone guiding God,

in him man goes to his rest,

toward him goes the long journey of the soul after death,

in him everything that man withdraws from the greater world.[12]

This teaching finally satisfies the grateful dead, as is reported in one of its most poetic passages in *The Red Book*:

But when Philemon had finished, the dead remained silent. Heaviness fell from them, and they ascended like smoke above the shepherd's fire, who watches over his flock by night.[13]

They can now move on to their resting place in eternity.

Who are these ghosts, and what do they mean? In *Memories, Dreams, Reflections*, Jung vividly recalls the experience of their visitation and says of them: "From that time on, the dead have

---

[10] C.G. Jung, *The Red Book*, p. 346.
[11] This can be found in *Memories, Dreams, Reflections*, Appendix v.
[12] C.G. Jung, *The Red Book*, p. 354.
[13] Ibid.

become ever more distinct to me as the voices of the Unanswered, Unresolved, and Unredeemed."[14] In *The Red Book*, they are the ghosts of Anabaptists who appear to Jung earlier in the text and announce that they are going to Jerusalem. Jung says about them that their problem is that they did not "live the animal" part of themselves enough in their lifetime. But in modernity, they are representatives of the unhoused souls of people who have died without a sense of meaning, conflicted and ungrounded. These restless and disoriented dead are the spirits of modernity who die without mythic symbols that would contain their souls and give them guidance. Being without a guiding myth, they search for a solution to a problem they cannot fathom. They travel fruitlessly to ancient places where faith is supposed to have its home, but they come away empty. This was Jung's predicament, too, as a "modern man."

The comforting image of the star as a symbol of transcendence would return to Jung much later in life in a dream and give him solace. He recounts this in a letter to Victor White, which he wrote while recovering from a serious illness in 1946:

The aspectus mortis is a mighty lonely thing, when you are stripped of everything in the presence of God.... Yesterday I had a marvelous dream: One bluish diamondlike star high in heaven, reflected in a round, quiet pool—heaven above, heaven below. The imago Dei in the darkness of the Earth, this is myself. The dream meant a great consolation. I am no more a black and endless sea of misery and suffering but a certain amount thereof contained in a divine vessel.[15]

It was precisely the realization of a link between the human and the Divine, as symbolized by the star, that had settled the disquiet of the unsatisfied dead and given them peace. Now it provides the same solace for Jung in his later years. In *The Red Book*,

---

[14] C.G. Jung, *Memories, Dreams, Reflections*, p. 191.
[15] A. Lammers and C. Cunningham (eds.), *The Jung-White Letters*, pp. 59-60.

Philemon is the mediator of this knowledge. From his own testimony, it is clear that Jung struggled to hold on to this piece of *gnosis.*

In Philemon's final appearance, which takes place in the last pages of *The Red Book*, he welcomes Jung into his garden. Then, a figure dressed in blue and identified as Christ enters the scene, and they converse with him. Surprisingly, Christ identifies Philemon as Simon Magus, the originator of a Gnostic sect in Egypt. Christ wonders whose garden this is, his own or Philemon's. In this decisive moment of encounter, recognition, and questioning, Philemon informs Christ that this is his, Philemon's, garden and not Christ's. Thus, the scales are rebalanced between an image of human wholeness (Philemon as Anthropos) and a God-image (Christ), putting them into a more evenly calibrated relation, a result that Jung has been struggling to achieve in earlier pages. This is the thematic culmination of the whole narrative of *Liber Novus*, and it leads directly into Jung's late reflections on the reciprocal relation between God and man in *Answer to Job.*

Philemon is a figure who can pass between worlds—time and eternity—and who speaks from personal knowledge and experience and not from received doctrine, theory, or belief. He also links depth psychology to ancient Gnosticism because of his association with Simon Magus. He is a mediator, an image for what Jung would call "the transcendent function." But he is not final or ultimate. He is a symbol for an archetypal power and a mystery beyond himself, which can never be exhaustively described or imagined.

What Does the Jungian Tradition Receive from *The Red Book*?

Overall, my conclusion is that *The Red Book* can come to function within the field of analytical psychology as a transmission instrument for the "genius" that lies beyond Jung the man and inscriber of the stories, reflections, and images found in it. This genius, moreover, as symbolized in *The Red Book* by Philemon, exists beyond this work and has its roots in the "metaphysical" (or, as we say, in the metapsychological) world of the archetypes of the collective unconscious. It can enliven and sustain the tradition.

The danger is that we absolutize any particular symbol of this genius and turn it into an idol or some sort of archetypal fundamentalism. The genius responsible for our dreams and visions, we must remember, is compensatory to our conscious world; it does not offer absolute guidance but rather balance and wholeness when brought into relation with consciousness. It can also produce states of possession (or "intoxication," as Jung says of his exposure to Philemon in *The Red Book*), from which consciousness must again be released. Jung does not succumb to religious mania with *The Red Book*, but rather he comes to earth and concludes his adventure with a crucial scene in his garden in Kusnacht where archetypal images and humans converse on a common level. In an important sense, Jung is struggling throughout *The Red Book* to get beyond the power of the archetypal images he meets, including Soul, to dictate their wishes and ambitions to a servile mortal who must obey. The effort brings them into the human world where they can be integrated and made useful for humanity's consciousness as symbols that map the unconscious psyche. On the other hand, Jung knows that the psyche's deepest mystery can never be completely known but must forever be allowed to show itself in new symbols, which in turn must again be integrated and relativized. This is the story of *The Red Book* — an encounter and disidentification with the archetypal images of the collective unconscious. The work functions, therefore, as a model for how the human ego can meet and interact with the numinous archetypal powers of the collective unconscious and can work creatively and modestly with them.

In the final analysis, Jung's *The Red Book* offers a ground plan for an enlarged anthropology and humanism, which receives and embraces the divine with its awesome powers but does not fall on its face before Deity and become enslaved to the superior wisdom and power of the symbol. The human maintains its dignity before the Divine, respectfully, and helps the Divine to become conscious by letting it pass through the doorway of human consciousness and enter into relationship with the human world.

Where I will put *The Red Book* in my arrangement of Jung's literary legacy is beside *Memories, Dream, Reflections*. Neither is a scientific work, both are autobiographical, and both can inspire, fascinate, and offer a touchstone. They are "timeless documents of the soul."

How to Read The Red Book, and Why: The Story of a Modern Man's Search for His Soul[1]

Arisleus tells of his adventure with the *Rex marinus*, in whose kingdom nothing prospers and nothing is begotten. … [The alchemist projects and hears] the King's cry for help from the depths of his unconscious, dissociated state. The conscious mind should respond to this call: One should *operare regime regi*, render service to the King, for this would be not only wisdom but salvation as well. Yet this brings with it the necessity of a descent into the dark world of the unconscious, the ritual *κατάβασης εις αντρών* ["descent to the cave"], whose end and aim is the restoration of life, resurrection, and the triumph over death.[2]

This passage from Jung's Eranos lecture of 1935[3] is a reflection on own *κατάβασης*, his descent into the dark world of the unconscious as recorded in *The Red Book: Liber Novus*. He undertakes this journey in response to a call from "the spirit of the depths," and in the course of it, he discovers Philemon, a Spirit who becomes his guide.[4] In this lecture, he is declaring to the audience

---

[1] Originally published in *The Journal of Analytical Psychology*, 57:3, 2012.

[2] C.G. Jung, *Psychology and Alchemy,* CW 12, paras. 435-6.

[3] For this quotation in the original, see *Eranos Jahrbuch* 1936, p. 64.

[4] In the third part of *The Red Book*, "Scrutinies," Jung realizes an essential truth: "Probably the most part of what I have written in the earlier part of this book was given to me by Philemon [and spoken through me — see ftn. 42]. Consequently I

at Eranos his mission in life, which is to unite the opposites in himself and thereby conceive a new God-image for modern postreligious people. *Liber Novus* should be read with this in mind: It represents Jung's response to "the King's cry for help," the King being the Self, which lies in the depths of the collective unconscious.

Several Contexts to Consider When Reading The Red Book

A supremely strange work like *The Red Book* cannot be intelligently approached and read without consideration of its contexts. I use the plural here deliberately: The work needs to be placed at the center of concentric circles designating ever wider contexts. Seeing it like this will provide an indication of its dimensionality, from narrowly personal to broadly cultural and collective. *The Red Book* is a highly personal work, without question; but it reaches out much further and beyond the strictly personal issues confronting the man Carl Gustav Jung at the time of its composition. Indeed, it addresses us even today, some hundred years after its composition. We are included among the contexts it addresses.

1. The literary context

I will begin by describing several of the closer-in contexts first and then go out from there to what I consider to be the widest and most embracing.

"When reading the literature," Jung writes of alchemy, "one must not be content with just one book but must possess many books, for 'one book opens another.' Moreover, one must read carefully, paragraph by paragraph; then one will make discoveries."[5] This is useful advice also for approaching *The Red Book* as a serious

---

was as if intoxicated. But now I noticed that Philemon assumed a form distinct from me" (p. 339). In a strong sense, Philemon's is the authorial voice heard in *The Red Book*, not C.G. Jung's. In the confrontation with Philemon's productions, Jung finds his own separate, personal voice.

[5] C.G. Jung, *Psychology and Alchemy*, CW 12, para. 423.

reader. To understand this work, one needs to consider Jung's preceding works, especially the immediate predecessor, *Symbols and Transformations of the Libido*, and the subsequent ones (especially the works on alchemy[6]). From the preceding, we can take in many of the author's sources, the multitude of references to world religions and mythologies. In *Liber Novus*, we get a glimpse into his library at the time when he was creating it. From the subsequent works, we gather whence *The Red Book* leads—to an exploration of individual spiritual and psychological development; to the humanization of the divine and the divination of the human; to broad cultural issues and the evolution of human consciousness. This is one crucial context—Jung's own writings.

Broader is the textual context consisting of Jung's literary predecessors, such as the towering Nietzsche, whose presence is ubiquitous in *Liber Novus*. This has already been widely commented upon and is made evident as well in numerous footnotes contributed by the editor. One also hears echoes of Dante's *Divine Comedy*, of Virgil's *Aeneid*, and of Homer's *Odyssey* in the motifs of descent and entry into the underworld and there making contact with the spirits of the dead. The severe self-confrontation with his own shortcomings as told in Scrutinies reminds one of St. Augustine's *Confessions*. Goethe's *Faust* must always be kept in mind since Jung so often used this as a touchstone. Strong tones sound, too, from many biblical passages and from numerous other texts of the world's religions, ortho- and heterodox. The universe of reference points in *The Red Book* is extraordinarily broad and eclectic. All are important to hear when reading the work because

---

[6] "Through Paracelsus I was finally led to discuss the nature of alchemy in relation to religion and psychology – or, to put it another way, of alchemy as a form of religious philosophy. This I did in Psychology and Alchemy (1944). Thus I had at last reached the ground which underlay my own experiences of the years 1913 to 1917; for the process through which I had passed at that time corresponded to the process of alchemical transformation discussed in that book." *Memories, Dreams, Reflections*, p. 209.

they link this modern text to so many antecedents and predecessors and deepen it.

2. The Personal Context

There is also the important context of Jung's personal life at the time of composition of *Liber Novus* and what this work meant for his own individuation process.

"My soul, where are you?"[7] the author cries out at the beginning of the narrative. What, or who, is he looking for, and why? What is the personal context of this radical departure from a world governed by "the spirit of this time" and venture into the unknown with "the spirit of the depths"?

One factor was his break with Sigmund Freud and with Freud's methods for practicing psychoanalysis. Somewhere along the way and in the midst of his intense collaboration and personal involvement with Freud between 1907 and 1912, he had lost track of his soul, and now he needed to restore this relationship to himself and his own inner world. He had gotten drawn into a foreign climate, namely Freud's. And this went far deeper than a mere professional matter. Nearly exactly one year before he turned inward and vocalized this call to his soul, and during the time he was in the most critical phase of his rupture with Freud, Jung had an important dream:

> ... around Christmas of 1912, I had a dream. In the dream
> I found myself in a magnificent Italian loggia with pillars,
> a marble floor, and a marble balustrade. I was sitting on a
> gold Renaissance chair; in from of me was a table of rare
> beauty. ... Suddenly a white bird descended, a small sea
> gull or a dove. Gracefully, it came to rest on the table, and
> I signed to the children to be still so that they would not
> frighten away the pretty white bird. Immediately, the

---

[7] C.G. Jung, *The Red Book*, p. 232.

dove was transformed into a little girl, about eight years of age, with golden blond hair.[8]

This dream of a delightful image of a vibrant young figure, part dove and part maiden, took a sinister turn, however, when she disclosed her commission:

"Only in the first hours of the night can I transform myself into a human being, while the male dove is busy with the twelve dead." Then she flew off into the blue air, and I awoke.

I was greatly stirred. What business would a male dove be having with twelve dead people?[9]

This ominous message was a harbinger of what was to follow a year later when Jung set out to discover for himself what was going on in the underworld, where the male dove was tending 12 dead and how the young girl/dove could be involved in this mystery. When he calls out to his soul, he is calling to this figure. She is mostly absent, hidden in the beyond, and linked to a male counterpart who tends to the spirits of the departed.

The personal context of the creation of *Liber Novus* is an existential crisis that came upon Jung in his 37th year and extended, though with diminished severity after his 42nd year (1917), until he felt it was resolved in his 53rd year (1928) in the famous "Liverpool dream."[10] This culminating dream was set in a place at the end of a small street like the *Totengässchen* ("Alley of the Dead") in Basel and featured a light-emitting magnolia tree which was rooted on an island in the center of a pool in the center of a city square where many streets converged—that is, in a center of a mandala. The 16-year interval between these dreams constitutes the period of the creation of the material in *The Red Book*. This was the period when Jung discovered his voice: "The years when I was pursuing my inner images were the most important in my life—in them everything

[8] C.G. Jung, *Memories, Dreams, Reflections*, p. 171.
[9] Ibid., p. 172.
[10] Ibid., pp. 197-98.

essential was decided,"[11] as he says in *Memories, Dreams, Reflections.*

3. The Religious/Cultural Context

Besides the personal context of *The Red Book*'s creation, we must also consider the wider religious and cultural context of the times. Jung was acutely aware of his historical context in early 20th-century Europe. When he states that before beginning his journey to find his soul he realized that the Christian myth was not the myth he lived by and that it no longer worked for him as a religious framework, he was not speaking for himself alone but for his generation and for several previous generations. Nietzsche's cry that "God is dead" was the culmination of a cultural evolution that had begun in the Protestant Reformation and was later carried further in the Enlightenment. Jung was born into an age of religious crisis and anxiety. The tradition that had formed and supported European culture was giving way, and Jung, along with his whole generation, felt the void opening beneath them.

> ... in what myth does man live nowadays? In the Christian myth, the answer might be, "Do *you* live in it?" I asked myself. To be honest, the answer was no. "For me, it is not what I live by." "Then do we no longer have any myth?" "No, evidently we no longer have any myth." "But then what is your myth — the myth in which you do live?" At this point the dialogue with myself became uncomfortable, and I stopped thinking. I had reached a dead end.[12]

This states the general religious tone of the times: "No, evidently we no longer have a myth." This is a restatement of Nietzsche's more dramatic pronouncement, "God is dead." The cultural context, as was well known and much commented upon by

---

[11] Ibid., p. 199.
[12] *Memories, Dreams, Reflections*, p. 171.

a host of cultural critics of the day, had turned positivistic, materialistic, and secular. Jung saw Freud as representative of this cultural attitude, and so his departure from Freud and his search for his soul stood for a venture in search of something different. It was a spiritual quest. When Jung calls out, "My soul, where are you?" he is speaking for many, not only for himself. "Soul," a word freighted with spiritual and religious overtones, has been lost. Translated, this says that the sense of the spiritual has disappeared from the culture; the land is dry and desolate. T.S. Eliot's poem, "The Waste Land," published in 1922, became emblematic of this state of affairs in modern culture.

Is God Really Dead?

"God is dead," shouted Nietzsche. "Not so fast," cried Jung. "Maybe there is a chance for rebirth." *Liber Novus* can be read as a response to Nietzsche's challenging declaration.

The quest to give "God" a new lease on life, understanding by this a possibility for spirituality in the secular world of rationalistic modernity, is taken up in *The Red Book* a number of times and in various ways. One dramatic instance of this endeavor occurs in the encounter with the mythical figure, Izdubar, who is journeying to the West in search of the land where the sun goes down. The East is a land of spirituality, the West of modern science and materialism. Izdubar has some questions that he thinks can be answered by science and so has headed westward, but when he speaks with Jung, who represents Western culture, this encounter weakens him dreadfully and threatens even to kill him. This meeting constellates the lethal conflict between myth-and-religion on the one hand and scientific rationalism on the other, and Izdubar has no chance of survival in this confrontation. Western science in its positivistic form kills the religious and mythopoetic imagination. They are dismissed as superstition.

Out of compassion for Izdubar, Jung intervenes. He will endeavor to heal him of his wounds and to restore him to vigor, first by declaring him to be a fantasy and putting him into an egg and then by chanting incantations over the egg. The poetic incantations are theurgical. The symbolism and ritual action hark back to ancient times, specifically to Orphism, which Jung had studied in his work, *Wandlungen*,[13] and which he now incorporates into his own ritualistic labors. *The Red Book* picks up on Jung's previous studies of ancient religious practices, and this is important to note as it indicates the deep historical context of this work and hints at its purpose and value for the modern person.

According to Orphic theology, as explained by the Swiss scholar Walter Wili, creation took place as follows:

In the beginning, time created the silver egg of the cosmos. Out of this egg burst Phanes-Dionysus. His name of Phanes unmistakably reveals the root φαν (φαίνειν, "to bring light"; Φαίνεσθαι, "to shine"), and later the Orphics disputed as to whether the god should be considered in the middle voice, as "the Glittering One," or in the active voice, as "the bringer of light"; he was in any case a god of light. For them he was the first god to appear, the firstborn, whence he early became known as Protogonos. He was bisexual and bore within him the seeds of all gods and men. He was also the creator of heaven and earth, of the sun, the stars, and the dwelling of the gods. The sixth Orphic hymn, dated to be sure in the Christian era but preserving old elements, represented him in epic hexameters:

O mighty first-begotten, hear my prayer,
Twofold, egg-born, and wandering through the air;
Bull-roarer, glorying in thy golden wings,
From whom the race of Gods and mortals springs.
Ericapaeus, celebrated power,
Ineffable, occult, all-shining flower.
'Tis thine from darksome mists to purge the sight,

---

[13] See C.G. Jung, *Psychology of the Unconscious*, p. 131.

All-spreading splendor, pure and holy light;
Hence, Phanes, called the glory of the sky,
On waving pinions through the world you fly.[14]

Listen to the resonances with this ancient hymn in Jung's incantations on behalf of Izdubar:

Christmas has come. The God is in the egg.
I have prepared a rug for my God, an expensive red rug
    from the land of morning.
He shall be surrounded by the shimmer of magnificence
    of his Eastern land.
I am the mother, the simple maiden, who gave birth and
    did not know how.
I am the careful father, who protected the maiden.
I am the shepherd, who received the message as he
    guarded his herd at night on the dark fields.[15]

In this first incantation, we hear also echoes of Luke's account of Jesus's birth. The Narrator is preparing for a new birth. This is the core message of *Liber Novus*. The fourth incantation underlines the Orphic connection:

Oh
light of the middle way,
enclosed in the egg,
embryonic,
full of ardor, oppressed.
Fully expectant,
dreamlike, awaiting lost memories.
As heavy as stone, hardened.
Molten, transparent,
streaming bright, coiled on itself.

The Sun, the Gleaming One, is awaiting birth from the egg. And then gloriously he appears as flames blazing upward from the tiny egg:

---

[14] W. Wili, "The Orphic Mysteries and the Greek Spirit," p. 71.
[15] C.G. Jung, *The Red Book*, p. 284.

"Where am I? How narrow it is here, how dark, how cool — am I in the grave? Where was I? It seemed to me as if I had been outside in the universe — over and under me was an endlessly dark star-glittering sky — and I was in a passion of unspeakable yearning. Streams of fire broke from my radiating body — I surged through blazing flames — I swam in a sea that wrapped me in living fires — Full of light, full of longing, full of eternity — I was ancient and perpetually renewing myself — Falling from the heights to the depths, and whirled glowing from the depths to the heights — hovering around myself amidst glowing clouds — as raining embers beating down like the foam of the surf, engulfing myself in stifling heat —Embracing and rejecting myself in a boundless game — Where was I? I was completely sun."[16]

And Jung:

An inexpressible light breaks from his body, a light that my eyes cannot grasp. I must cover my face and cast my gaze to the ground.

I: "You are the sun, the eternal light—most powerful one, forgive me for carrying you."[17]

This is a re-creation story, the rebirth of an ancient God image—the God of light, the Sun. Later in *The Red Book* he will appear as Phanes. The Orphic mysteries offered Jung a model for his efforts to revive the God image and to give birth to a new lease on spirituality outside of religious institutions for modern people who had become alienated.

Another strong echo of the Orphic mysteries occurs in the chapter titled "The Sacrificial Murder." In this dramatic episode, Jung descends to the Netherworld and there comes upon the horrible scene of a dismembered little girl. He is instructed by a shrouded

---

[16] Ibid, p. 286.
[17] Ibid.

female figure, designated as "Soul" in the text, to cut out the girl's liver and to eat it. Revolted, he screams his refusal, but he relents and follows Soul's direction. The following commentary then ensues:

The sacrifice has been accomplished: the divine child, the image of the God's formation, is slain, and I have eaten from the sacrificial flesh. The child, that is, the image of the God's formation, not only bore my human craving, but also enclosed all the primordial and elemental powers that the sons of the sun possess as unalienable inheritance. The God needs all this for his genesis. But when he has been created and hastens away into unending space, we need the gold of the sun. We must regenerate ourselves. But, as the creation of a God is a creative act of highest love, the restoration of our human life signifies an act of the Below. This is a great and dark mystery...through the sacrificial murder, I redeemed the primordial powers and added them to my soul. Since they became part of a living pattern, they are no longer dormant, but awake and active and irradiate my soul with their divine working. Through this it receives a divine attribute. Hence the eating of the sacrificial flesh aided its healing. The ancients have also indicated this to us, in that they taught us to drink the blook and eat the flesh of the savior. The ancients believed that this brought healing to the soul."[18]

In this reflection on sacrificial murder, we hear both Christian and Orphic elements. In Orphic religion, writes Walter Wili, "Zeus could enter into his domination of the world only by devouring the primal god Phanes. By this act he assimilated and embodied the whole previous world. The world of Zeus was thus a rebirth. It was the world of Phanes enriched by the action of Zeus himself; it was the presence of all souls and all things, as the profound Neoplatonist

[18] Ibid, p. 291.

Proclus recognized, saying: 'After he had devoured Phanes, the essential forms of the universe became manifest in Zeus.'"[19]

What Jung has done is to bring the mysteries forward from ancient mythological and theological enactments into the human, the personal, the individual, and the psychological domain, describing essentially the same mystery within the consciousness of modern sensibility. It is a reenactment of ancient mysteries but in a modern context and moves the action from a metaphysical to a metapsychological realm, from "out there" (or "up there," or "back then" or "the beyond") to the "in here." *The Red Book* as an account of a process of divinization of the human.

The New God Image

About Phanes, the original and most all-encompassing Deity of Orphism, Jung says in the Legend above painting 113:

> This is the image of the divine child. It means the completion of a long path. Just as the image was finished in April 1919, and work on the next image had already begun, the one who brought the [sun] came, as Philemon had predicted to me. I called him Phanes, because he is the newly appearing God.[20]

The Red Book's editor, Sonu Shamdasani, names Phanes "Jung's God" in a footnote,[21] and in reference to this painting, he directs the reader to several important passages in *The Black Books,* Jung's private diaries. The Phanes painting as shown in *The Red Book* was completed in April 1919. However, a year and a half earlier, on September 28, 1916, Phanes is described as a golden bird.[22] This links the figure to the dream of 1912, when the soul first appeared as a white bird that then turned into a girl of 8 years with golden hair.[23] On February 20, 1917, Jung links Phanes to Abraxas as his

---

[19] W. Wili, "The Orphic Mysteries and the Greek Spirit," p. 73.
[20] C.G. Jung, *The Red Book*, p. 301, ftn. 211.
[21] Ibid.
[22] C.G. Jung, *The Black Books*, vol. 6, p. 260.
[23] C.G. Jung, *Memories, Dreams, Reflections*, p. 171.

messenger,[24] and on May 20, 1917, Philemon says that he will become Phanes "when this man dies. ... I do not die. I am already Phanes."[25] So here we see a thread running from the soul image of 1912, to Phanes of 1916, to Abraxas and Philemon of *Septem Sermones* of 1916, to these later reflections in 1917 and paintings of Phanes also in 1917,[26] to the Red Book painting of 1919, an important continuity of images stretching over seven years. On September 11, 1917, Philemon delivers a glorious paeon to Phanes that sounds like something straight out of the cult of Orphism:

Phanes is the God who rises agleam from the waters.

Phanes is the smile of dawn.

Phanes is the resplendent day.

He is the immortal present.

He is the gushing streams.

He is the soughing wind.

He is hunger and satiation.

He is love and lust.

He is mourning and consolation.

He is promise and fulfillment.

He is the light that illuminates every darkness.

He is the eternal day.

He is the silver light of the moon...

He is the flickering stars.

He is the shooting star that flashes and falls and lapses.

He is the stream of shooting stars that returns every year.

He is the returning sun and moon....

He is the friend of man, the light emanating from man,
the bright glow that
man beholds on his path.

He is the greatness of man, his worth, and his force."[27]

---

[24] C.G. Jung, *The Black Books*, vol. 6, p. 280.

[25] Ibid., p. 297.

[26] See U. Hoerni, T. Fischer, B. Kaufmann (eds.), *The Art of C.G. Jung*, pp. 122-25.

[27] C.G. Jung, *The Black Books*, vol. 7, pp. 158-59.

On July 31, 1918, or about 18 months later, Phanes himself speaks:

The mystery of the summer morning, the happy day, the completion of the moment, the fullness of the possible, born from suffering and joy, the treasure of eternal beauty, the goal of the four paths, the spring and the ocean of the four streams, the fulfillment of the four sufferings and of the four joys, father and mother of the Gods of the four winds, crucifixion, burial, resurrect, and man's divine enhancement, highest effect and nonbeing, world and grain, eternity and instance, poverty and abundance, evolution, death and the rebirth of God, borne by eternally creative power, resplendent in eternal effect, loved by the two mothers and sisterly wives, ineffable pain-ridden bliss, unknowable, unrecognizable.... Completion is poverty. But poverty means gratitude. Gratitude is love.[28]

And on August 2 of the same year:

"I am the eternal light.... I am the bliss beyond joy and suffering.... I am the height beyond high and low.... I am the love beyond embrace and mourning.... I am the center beyond dawn and dusk.... I am the One...."[29]

On January 4, 1920, Jung painted picture 123, which features Phanes watering plants and has the inscription: "This is the caster of holy water. The Cabiri grow out of the flowers which spring from the body of the dragon. Above is the temple."[30] So we see the process continuing and now stretching onward as Jung gives agency to the God image. In the following painting, Jung shows Phanes sitting on a cushion between the mundane world of everyday life and business below and a fiery wheel, ablaze like the sun, eight flames emanating from the wheel's circumference, above. Below,

---

[28] Ibid., pp. 192-93.
[29] Ibid.
[30] C.G. Jung, *The Red Book*, p. 306, ftn. 233.

there lies an orderly Swiss landscape that is scarcely aware of what is shining so brilliantly in the heavens above. From the text surrounding this image, we gather it indicates a prophecy of things to come:

> What will come lies within yourself. But what lies there! I would like to avert my eyes, close my ears and deny all my senses. I would like to be someone among you, who knows nothing and who never saw anything. It is too much, and too unexpected. But I saw it and my memory will not leave me alone.[31]

To this the editor appends two sentences from the *Draft* that were deleted in the calligraphic text: "How can I fathom what will happen during the next eight hundred years, up to the time when the One begins his rule? I am speaking only of what is to come."[32] The light above indicates the future, and its glory is too much to take in, too bright for the human eye.

In Jung's later theoretical writings, the figure of Phanes would be folded into the meaning of the term Self, the transcendent wholeness of the psyche. In the discussions of the Self in *Aion*, we have the final result of the project that began with placing Izdubar in an egg, declaring him a fantasy, and locating God in the psychic rather than the metaphysical realm. What was lost from the metaphysical world through the effect of modern consciousness is recovered in the psychic world. The new age would be characterized by the psychological rather than the metaphysical.

What we read in *The Red Book* is the mythopoetic account of this new emergence of spirituality in modernity. In no way did Jung advocate turning the course of history back to a mythological state of mind. He knew the cultural evolution of the past several centuries was irreversible. The question was, and is: how to go forward?

How to read *The Red Book*? I suggest reading it as a personal experience of "the mysteries" that underlie many religions, but on

---

[31] Ibid., p. 306.
[32] Ibid. ftn. 236.

213

a more conscious level—that does not become fused and identified with the figures that imagination produces—that observes them, interacts with them, and lets them go their way—but that is at the same time transformed by the experience. Jung's ego-consciousness is a strong protagonist on location throughout the Red Book experience and never loses its grounding. This sets *The Red Book* distinctly apart from Nietzsche's *Zarathustra* yet places it strangely close to ancient mystery religions such as we find described in *The Golden Ass of Apuleius,* where the protagonist is transformed in a series of initiations.

Jung titled his work *Liber Novus.* With this astonishing title, the book asserts its priority over the biblical predecessor. It is displacing (usurping?) the authority of the two biblical Testaments, Old and New, and replacing them with a Testament for the new era of human consciousness to come. The work is offered as a text for the beginning of a new Aeon, the Age of Aquarius. It could be called the Age of Phanes if we follow Jung's lead. In this respect, it stands beside, or surpasses, Nietzsche's *Thus Spoke Zarathustra* as a book for the future of the human spirit.

The relation of *Liber Novus* to the New Testament is the key issue, however. In several passages, the Protagonist dismisses Christ as the dominant religious figure of the new age, telling him that he has suffered enough and is now entitled to a decent retirement. The day has come in the evolution of human consciousness for individuals to take responsibility for their own sins and not keep heaping them upon the Divine Savior and asking him to bear the sins of the world for us. It is incumbent upon modern persons to take over the job of finding redemption for themselves, individually and in their own way, through the inner process of reconciliation and atonement that Jung would call individuation, a psychospiritual path to wholeness and personal divinization. This message would reverberate through his later writings and comes to clear expression in his late work, *Answer to Job,* where he calls for the "Christification of many." *Liber Novus* is the dramatic account of Jung's personal achievement in this regard. It can also be a guidebook for those who would do likewise. *Liber Novus* announces the end of religion as the West has known it and the beginning of a new age of individual spirituality.

This is the broad cultural and religious context of *The Red Book*. In the first centuries of the Common Era, as the Christian consensus was evolving but had not yet received its final dogmatic expression, syncretism in religious belief and practice was the rule of the day. Near Eastern, Egyptian, Greek (Hellenistic), Roman, and a variety of mystery religions melded into a *massa confussa* that eventually clarified into the Creeds of Christianity. Standing at the beginning of a New Era in the cultural evolution of the West, as Jung saw himself to be in the days of his creation of *Liber Novus*, syncretism again was a characteristic feature of the religious and spiritual ferment. In *The Red Book* this is taken up and colors every page. Underlying the syncretism is the process of initiation into the mysteries and the birth of a new God image. Phanes appears eventually, but he is interchangeable with Izdubar, Elijah, and Philemon. All are manifestations of the same core of primordial energy and light. All are fiery harbingers of new consciousness and a deep source of spiritual energy. Any one of them could qualify as the central idol of a new religious dispensation, a new cult. Instead, in Jung's later *opus* all are subsumed under the rubric of psychology—they are images of psyche, archetypal forces to be contended with, capable of unleashing nuclear energies within the psychic matrix and carrying it onward or destroying it and the planet as well. The mind of the psychologist rules in the New Age and displaces the mind of the theologian with his metaphysical hubris.

The central figure of the *Liber Novus* is not the God figure but the human ego figure struggling to understand, becoming transformed, suffering, and prevailing. What Yahweh is for the Hebrew Bible and Jesus for the New Testament, the humble, bewildered, courageous Narrator is for *Liber Novus*—the central fulcrum around whom all else revolves. Not to say that he is in control of the narrative, but he is a continuous and constant presence throughout, the others making their entries and exits and eventually leaving him

215

to his solitude. Individuation, not salvation, is the theme of *Liber Novus*. The New Heaven and New Earth now reside within the human psyche. As the text declares: "The way is within us, ... not in Gods, nor in teachings, nor in laws. Within us is the way, the truth and the life."[33]

Why Read *The Red Book*?

There are many good reasons to read this astonishing record of Jung's inner journey. Let me list some of them.

Perhaps most important for Jungians is that *The Red Book* gives heretofore unsurpassed expression to so many of the deeply embedded views and attitudes in his later work. It opens a window to the experiential and visionary presuppositions underlying his psychological theory—for example, the (to many very strange) notions of an objective psyche and a nonegoic center of the personality, the Self. *The Red Book* reveals the *mundus imaginalis* behind the psychological theories of analytical psychology. Its figures and narrative claim psychic reality, not only metaphorical status, and so represent forces beyond the control of conscious ego and on a par with the gods of old who controlled the lives and individual destinies of premodern humankind. From *The Red Book*, we learn about Jung's ontological premises and epistemology. His theories were rooted in his experience, and *The Red Book* shows us this, not only tells us about it as do the many other texts published thereafter. One can also read *The Red Book* for its literary merit, especially in the original German. There is an aesthetic motive here. There are many beautiful and moving passages in *The Red Book* and some that will, I am sure, become a part of Jungian culture in the future. Also, its many awesome and impressive works of art, as well as the meticulous calligraphic detailing of the text, bring pleasure to the eye and mind. For this reason, the work has been exhibited as "a work of art" in museums.

---

[33] Ibid., p. 231.

One can read it as well for inspiration. Insights derived from the narrative can have a highly stimulating effect on one's own psychological and spiritual development. Jungian analysts worldwide have reported this result among their patients. *Liber Novus* carries our thoughts in new directions and opens our minds to subtle differentiations within the spiritual landscape. In this sense, it may function as a text akin to the Bible, for so many people a source of spiritual insight and "lift." Readers of *Liber Novus* might be inspired to go on a similar imaginal journey for themselves, and in this endeavor they can read it for guidance.

Ultimately, *Liber Novus* represents a modern form of theology and can be profitably read for this feature. It can be seen as an early contribution to what is now called "Theo-poetics." This type of theological reflection begins with a personal account of a spiritual journey and perhaps an awakening to something "beyond," to a numinous center of authority and destiny, and it is therefore rooted in the experience of the individual author rather than in received text or doctrine. Upon this platform of experience, a poetic discourse and reflection is elaborated about the nature of ultimate reality, the "ground of Being." If one is given to undertaking a project such as this, *The Red Book* can serve as a foundational sourcebook.

Personally, as the mountain climber said when asked why he sought to scale those impossible heights in the Alps, I read *The Red Book* because it is there! It is indeed a magnificent challenge.

Systema munditotius: A Psychogram[1]

Introduction

I think we can state without too much hesitation that a primary and universal function of the human mind is to create, or to discover, order. The depiction of order in the world is found in all cultures and all times. The impulse is archetypal. Levi-Strauss states it with wit and elegance: "This necessity for order is at the foundation of the thought that we call primitive, but only inasmuch as it is at the foundation of all thought."[2] Humans are order-creating and order-perceiving creatures.

One important way of expressing such created or perceived order is to make a map. A map is a depiction of order in a specified domain—geographical (land masses), astronomical (stars and planets), spiritual (invisible worlds) or mental (psychic objects). The order depicted in a map may be true to its object or not, so maps must be checked out by experience and further refinement of data as they become available.

A map of the known elements within a given terrain also depicts the relationship of the various objects within that domain to one another. Each individual object is thus contained within a larger structure and has a relationship to all the other objects in that domain. Thus, in a map of a geographical area, "my city" is shown

---

[1] Originally given as a lecture at a conference on Psychology and Art in Syracusa, Sicily in 2011.

[2] C. Levi-Strauss, *La Pensee Sauvage*, p. 17, quoted by Dubuisson, p. 19.

in relation to all the other cities in the area depicted and is therefore contained within that specific territory; or in a map of the mind, the "ego" is shown in relation to the complexes, the archetypes, and the self, and so it is shown as contained within the psyche as a whole. Maps show contexts that hold and contain specific items.

Maps thus provide, in addition to order, two essential elements that assist with conscious functioning: orientation and containment.

Cosmograms and Psychograms

Cosmograms are geometric figures that depict a cosmology. They are maps of the entire known, perceived, and believed-in elements of reality (cosmologies). They appear throughout recorded history and depict the relation between the earth, the stars, and the planets, as well as among humans and gods or other spiritual entities, and they typically show humankind's place within an ordered structure. Traditional cosmologies are made up of a combination of astronomy, geography, anthropology, and theology—all of them "-logies" or derivatives of "logos," i.e., order, structure. They reflect the structuring activity of the mind as it seeks to find order in the cosmos and to locate the human within the larger picture. As the scholar Daniel Dubuisson defines cosmologies, they are "'systems,' 'productions,' or 'creations' to designate…universes conceived of by human beings wholly in order to inscribe their persons and existence therein and thereby give them meaning."[3]

In ancient times and through the Middle Ages, the place of humans was fixed more or less in the center of the cosmogram, between the realm of the gods above and the animals, plants and minerals below. This has been called "the great chain of being," and it was assumed in many writings well into the Renaissance, as in the plays of Shakespeare. In the arrangement made on such "maps" or cosmograms, the order between various levels of being is clearly established. From these maps, one can find one's place, one's

---

[3] D. Dubuisson, *The Western Construction of Religion,* p. 216, n. 8.

"home," and in this way one finds also meaning in relation to the whole and a proper attitude toward others, such as gods, angels, animals, men, women, rulers, ruled, etc. A political and social system is evident in such maps.

When we come to Jung's time, that is, the late 19th and early 20th centuries, we confront an entirely new understanding of the cosmos, of the earth's history, and of humanity's place in it. Geology had transformed the understanding of the planet's history; biology and evolutionary science had radically altered the perception of where humans belong in "the chain of being"; and psychology and psychoanalysis were remapping the interior world of the human psyche. I will focus here on the maps Jung made of the inner world of the psyche. We can call these maps "psychograms." Like cosmograms, they show the relation of individual objects to one another, and they depict a "whole," a space that offers the user of the map a means of orientation and a container. Such a psychogram puts together disperate experiences of the inner world, of its figures and dynamic internal relationships, and arranges them into an orderly whole. In the creation of such maps we see the ordering mind at work, creating system and meaning by arranging the pieces of experience into a coherent pattern. Maps also help us to think in a more orderly way. Images of art can assist understanding and serve thinking, a function of art not much noted in most art history courses nowadays but certainly a familiar function of art in the Middle Ages.

Systema Munditotius

We know from *Memories, Dreams, Reflections* and now also after the publication of *The Red Book* and *The Black Books* that Jung was plunged into a state of disorientation and inner confusion during and after his break with Freud in 1912-13. Courageously, he entered into the realm of inner turmoil and chaos, and using his powers of introspection, his intelligence, and the tool he developed for inner exploration, "active imagination," he attempted to find his way. The results were brilliantly recorded and worked out in his private Red Book. The basic contents that form the bedrock narrative of the now meticulously edited and beautifully presented publication, *The Red Book: Liber Novus,* were recorded between November 1913 and June 1916. The paintings were placed into the pages of Jung's Red Book between 1915 and 1929. In the early years of this period, Jung worked out a secondary level with his reflections, interpretations, and additions to the primary material. From this manuscript he selected the text that we now find written out in calligraphic script in *The Red Book.*

In the early years of this creative period, a great wave of material flooded into Jung's consciousness in the form of visions, dreams, and images from his active imaginations. After that, he went to work on this material—reflecting, interpreting, painting, and putting into order what he had experienced. An early result of this ordering process was the famous mandala titled *Systema munditotius,*[4] painted in 1916, which he constructed in close temporal proximity to the reception of the *Septem Sermones ad Mortuous.*[5] This colorful and carefully balanced mandala, which I will refer to as a *psychogram,* is a constructed depiction of the contents of the "inner world" that Jung had explored in the previous two years through the use of active imagination. It shows the relation of the parts to one another and to a whole. It serves as Jung's map of the deep psyche as he experienced it at this time in his life. This is what he says about it some years later: "It portrays the antinomies of the microcosm within the macrocosmic world and its antinomies."[6]

At the top of this psychogram, we find a group of four images: 1) Erikapaios or Phanes (the boy, in a winged egg); 2) a candelabra with seven flames, beside which stand the words "fire" and "eros";

---

[4] See C.G. Jung, *The Red Book,* p. 364.
[5] See B. Jeromson, "Systema Munditotius and Seven Sermons: Symbolic Collaborations with the Dead."
[6] A. Jaffe, *C.G. Jung—Word and Image,* p. 75.

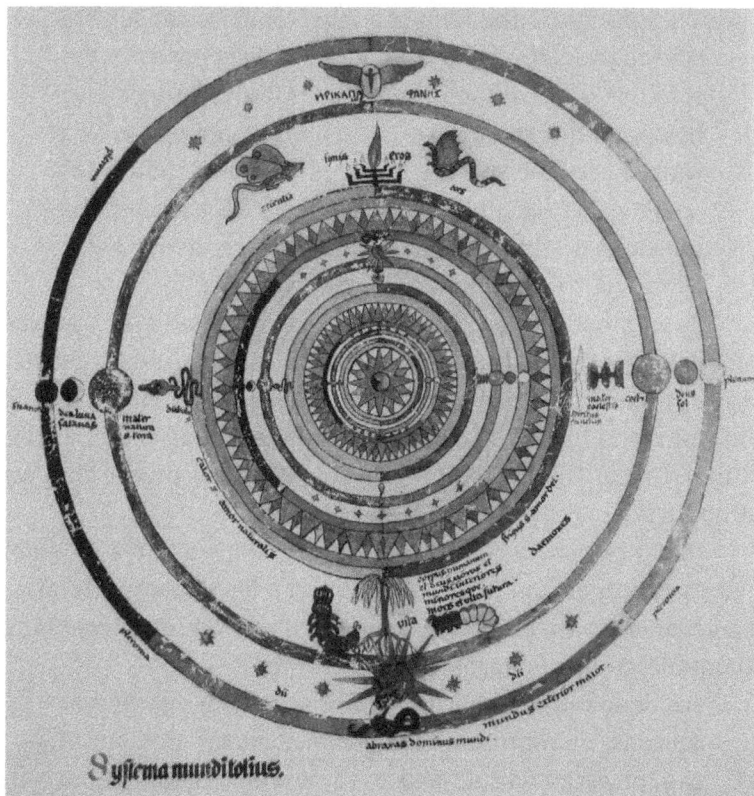

3) *ars*, a winged serpent or worm; and 4) *scientia,* humorously shown as a winged mouse. About Phanes, Jung says (retrospectively, in 1955): "At the very top, the figure of the young boy in the winged egg, called Erikaoaios or Phanes and thus reminiscent as a spiritual figure of the Orphic Gods."[7] In his Red Book, Jung paints this figure of Phanes brilliantly (Image 113). He is one of the key images, a foreshadowing of the new religion about which Jung speaks several times in reference to the Age of Aquarius.

About the other three figures in this section of the mandala, Jung writes:

---

[7] C.G. Jung, *The Red Book. Reader's Edition*, p. 560.

... a light-tree in the form of a seven-brached candelabra labeled *ignis* ('fire') und *Eros* ('love'). Its light points to the spiritual world of the divine child. Art and Science also belong to this spiritual realm, the first represented as a winged serpent and the other as a winged mouse (as hole-digging activity!). — The candelabra is based on the principle of the spiritual number three (twice-three flames with the great flame in the middle)...."[8]

In summary, this upper section of the mandala contains aspects of the psyche that represent its spiritual nature, the higher strivings and asperations, the intellectual and meaning-creating functions, and the potential for enlightenment. One could call this "the higher self." It would be to this level of the psyche that we attribute the making of art and maps.

In the bottom region of the psychogram, we find a group of figures corresponding to the ones above: a figure named Abraxas; a tree of life; a "monster" (*Ungeheuer*); and a grub (*Engerling*). About this group of images Jung writes:

His dark antithesis in the depths is here designated as Abraxas. He represents the *dominus mundi*, the lord of the physical world, and is a world creator of an ambivalent nature. Sprouting from him is the tree of life, labeled *vita* ('life')...the lower world of Abraxas is characterized by five, the number of the natural man (the twice-five rays of his star). The accompanying animals of the natural world are a devilish monster and a larva. This signifies death and rebirth.[9]

This is the psyche's lower world, the realm of instinct and material existence, of death and rebirth. Its dominant symbol (god or ruler) is Abraxas, and this figure stands in tension to its counterpart above, Erikapaios/Phanes. This one could call "the lower self." It is not spiritual but material, not heavenly bound or

---

[8] Ibid.
[9] Ibid.

upward-striving but earthy and rooted in physical existence. The vertical axis consists, therefore, of a tension between spirit above and nature or instinct below.

The horizontal axis is equally tension-laden. On the left side, we see several images arranged in what look like orbits: a phallus; a serpent wound around it; the moon; and Satanas. Of this region, Jung comments:

A further dimension of the mandala is horizontal. To the left we see a circle indicating the body or the blood, and from it rears the serpent, which winds itself around the phallus, as the generative principle. The serpent is light and dark, signifying the dark realm of the earth, the moon, and the void (therefore called Satanas).[10]

Jung identifies this phallic, or masculine, side of the mandala as morally ambiguous (both black and white and named "Satanas"), creative, and tending toward the lower region of the mandala. There is an affinity between this region on the left side of the *Systema* and Abraxas, Lord of the material and instinctual regions of the psyche. The left side pulls downward toward the instinctual roots of life, so toward literal sexuality and direct engagement with the material world.

This stands in tension with the right side of the mandala, where one sees the contrary tendency in the images of a dove, a chalice and the sun, all tending upward toward "fullness." Of this Jung writes:

The light realm of rich fullness lies to the right, where from the bright circle *frigus sive amor dei* [cold, or the love of God] the dove of the Holy Ghost takes wing, and wisdom (Sophia) pours from a double beaker to left and right.—This feminine sphere is that of heaven.[11]

The right side strives toward the upper region, toward the light, toward the spiritual dimension symbolized by Phanes. This is feminine sexuality as opposed to the masculine phallic sexuality of

---

[10] Ibid., p. 561.
[11] Ibid.

225

the left region, which, as Jung is taught by Philemon in the Fifth of the *Septem Sermones*, moves toward the spiritual and is of the heavens, while masculine sexuality is of the earth. In this horizontal axis, then, we find the tension between between masculine and feminine. Here Jung is sorting out the energies and tendencies of the various figures he has confronted in his active imaginations, as recorded in *The Red Book*—Elijah and Solome, the bird-soul and the serpent-soul, the Red One and Ammonius, and so forth.

At the center of the mandala, there is a series of concentric circles that should be imagined as going ever further inward, moving toward an infinitely tiny centerpoint. Of this, Jung writes:

> The large sphere characterized by zigzag lines or rays represents an inner sun; within this sphere the macro-cosm is repeated, but with the upper and lower regions reversed as in a mirror. These repetitions should be conceived of as endless in number, growing smaller until the innermost core, the actual microcosm is reached.[12]

The mandala as a whole is anchored in this center as by gravity. Jung uses the terms "macrocosm" and "microcosm" to describe the relation between the outer spheres of the mandala and its center. However, as we know, the whole mandala is of the "inner world," of the psyche. So what does it mean that he speaks of a "macrocosm"? Perhaps it could mean that the features on the outer parts of the mandala belong to "the objective psyche," as Jung would speak of it in his later writings, that is, to the collective unconscious, to the realm of archetypes. They would be images of the archetypal world and therefore could also reflect extrapsychic structures and dynamics that extend into the material and spiritual worlds which lie outside of and beyond the human psyche, which belong to the *anima mundi* or the soul of the world. The microcosmic aspect of the mandala, on the other hand, has to do with our subjectivity as we experience it directly in our own psyches, in our lived experience, as well as in nightly dreams and active imagination. Thus, the mandala would be

---

12 Ibid.

an attempt to chart the relations between the human and the nonhuman dimensions of reality and ultimately to link the individual psyche to the ultimate structures of Being. This is the meaning of "as above, so below." The microcosm mirrors the macrocosm, and the psychogram is therefore also a cosmogram. It is the *systema* of the *munditotius* (the total world, the cosmos).

Background: A Sketch for *Systema munditotius*

In preparation for creating *Systema munditotius*, Jung made a Sketch, which is recorded in Volume 5 of *The Black Books*.[13] With this sketch, we can trace Jung's thinking as he sought to put his experiences in active imagination in an orderly framework and to create a psychogram, namely the finished mandala titled *Systema munditotius*..

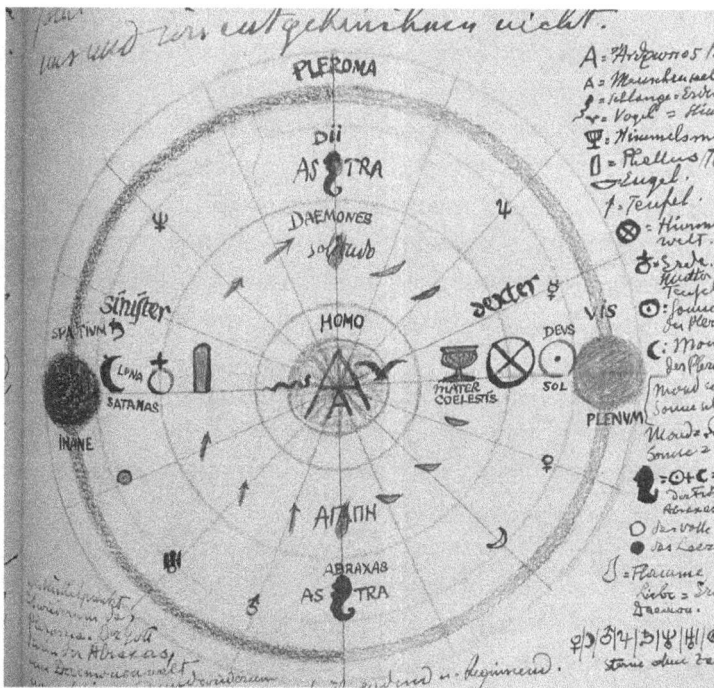

---

[13] C.G. Jung, *The Black Books*, vol. 5, p. 175.

At the center, he places two A's, which in the Legend provided he names: "A = Anthropos, Man" and "a = human soul." From the Sketch, we have an indication of what he intended to place at the center of *Systema munditotius*. "Anthropos" refers to the archetypal Self with a capital "S"; "human soul" is a lesser image of it, the personal self, i.e., ego-consciousness and the personal complexes. "Homo" surrounds them at the Center of the psychogram, just as the Earth appeared at the center in cosmograms from Ptolemy through the Middle Ages. The center of the Sketch also includes the idea of a union of opposites, as we see in the images of serpent (body, instinct) to the left and bird (spirit) to the right.

In the Sketch, the images at the ends of the horizontal axis are quite similar to those in the *Systema munditotius*: the Moon; the Phallus and Satanas on the left; and Mother, Sun and Fullness on the right. However, the upper and lower regions are much less worked out and defined in the Sketch than in the finished image. In the Sketch, upper and lower are almost identical, featuring Abraxas above and Daimones below as the dominant figures. The vertical axis shows very little tension or difference in the Sketch, whereas in the *Systema* this tension is pushed to a high degree of intensity and in fact defines the fundamental pair of opposites in the psychogram as a whole, that between spirit and matter/instinct. In the Sketch, the tension of opposites is carried more strongly by the horizontal axis, while in the *Systema* it is shared by both horizontal and vertical axes.

In this development from Sketch to finished image, we can see Jung's ordering, thinking, mapmaking function at work—he is seeking symmetry and a more balanced statement of the tensions within the psyche. As with his formulation of psychological types where he begins with a single pair of opposites (thinking and feeling) and then completes this with a second pair (sensation and intuition), here is the same process at work of finding an instrument that will bring order out of a *massa confusa* of material.

Other Mandalas in *The Red Book*

The *Systema munditotius* of 1916 formed a ground plan for Jung's later thinking and theorizing about the psyche and also for further mandalas that he would paint in years following the construction of the *Systema*. In 1919, he entered a brilliantly colored mandala into the Red Book (Image 105). The painting style is very different from the *Systema* mandala, but the basic structure is the same. This, too, is a map of the psyche. At the top is the figure of a "wise old man" in the seated position of meditation. This figure corresponds to Erikapaios/Phanes of the *Systema* and represents the spiritual dimension of the psyche. Here the young Phanes has been replaced by a more wizened figure, perhaps representing Philemon, who had assumed a key role in *"Prufungen"* ("Scrutinies"), the third part of *The Red Book* narrative. At the bottom of this mandala is a rather severe-looking, dark, upright figure with hair of fire and holding a temple in his arms. In the *Systema*, this was the position of Abraxas, the tree of life and the monster and the grub. The figure in this later mandala represents, according to Jung's own commentary in 1950, "Loki or Hephaistos.... The old man corresponds to the archetype of meaning, or of the spirit, and the dark chthonic figure to the opposite of the Wise Old Man namely the magical (and sometimes destructive) Luciferian element."[14] This seems to be perhaps a darker energy than Abraxas represented in the earlier mandala. In the intervening years, Jung had witnessed the mad destructiveness of a World War driven by a "Luciferian element." He also records that he had seen "the blond beast" in the dreams of his German patients, which would reveal its passion for destruction in the following decades.

On the left, we see a female figure with long hair, dressed in red and with arms crossed. In the *Systema*, this position is occupied by the Phallus and Satanas. On the right stands a second female figure with hands held out in a receptive gesture, dressed in the cool

---

[14] C.G. Jung, "Concerning Mandala Symbolism," CW 9i, para. 682.

color of blue. In the *Systema*, this position is occupied by feminine figures that tended upward toward the spiritual. Here she seems similarly inclined. Of these figures Jung says: "The two female figures can be recognized without difficulty as the two aspects of the anima."[15] As in the *Systema*, the affinities of these figures with the chthonic and instinctual on the left and with the spiritual on the right are evident and reflected in the choice of colors.

The center of this mandala is occupied by a brilliant blue and white star. This position corresponds to the center of the microcosm in the *Systema*, which was also occupied by a star and a round object but less detailed and brilliantly colored. In this mandala of 1919, the center is highlighted and calls attention to itself. The star is a significant symbol of the Self as stated in the Seventh Sermon to the Dead as Philemon concludes his teachings with this moving passage:

At immeasurable distance a lonely star stands in the zenith.

This is the one God of this one man, this is his world, his Pleroma, his divinity.

In this world, man is Abraxas, the creator and destroyer of his own world.

This star is the God and the goal of man.

This is his guiding God,

In him man goes to his rest,

Toward him goes the long journey of the soul after death, in him everything that man withdraws from the greater world shines resplendently.

To this one God man shall pray.

Prayer increases the light of the star, it throws a bridge across death.

It prepares life for the smaller world, and assuages the hopeless desires of the greater.

When the greater world turns cold, the star shines.

---

[15] Ibid.

Nothing stands between man and his one God, so long
as man can turn away his eyes from the flaming
spectacle of Abraxas.

Man here, God there.

Weakness and nothingness here, eternally creative
power there.

There total sun.[16]

In this mandala of 1919, we see that Jung places the
transcendent star at the center. He has prioritized the Self and given
it centrality. This would have huge implications for his future
psychological reflections and writings.

Later Maps of the Psyche

Jung's mapmaking did not cease with these mandalas from the Red
Book period. As I argued in my book *Jung's Map of the Soul*, Jung's
whole psychological theory, which was developed and articulated
after the working out of the psychogrammatic images of the Red
Book in its mandalas, is an expression of his mind's ordering and
mapping tendencies. In the late 1940s, Jung was again busy with
diagrams to describe his conceptualization of the psyche.[17]
Ostensibly these were derived from his studies of Gnosticism, as
he indicates in *Aion*, but we can see clearly that they have strong
similarities to his psychographs from the Red Book period. In "the
Moses Quaternio," for example, the Higher Adam at the apex
corresponds to Erikapaios/Phanes from the *Systema*; the Lower
Adam corresponds to Abraxas at the bottom of the *Systema*. In the
inner axes of the horizontal dimension, we find the same tension
between masculine and feminine that we see in *Systema*, although
with a further complication that there are four figures now instead

---

[16]C.G Jung, *The Red Book, Readers Edition*, pp. 534-35.
[17] C.G. Jung, *Aion, CW* 9ii, paras. 347-421.

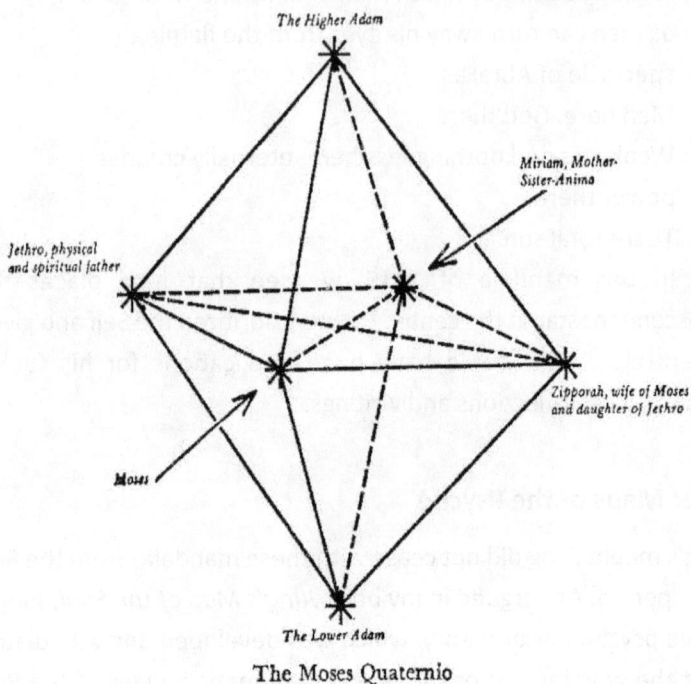

The Moses Quaternio

Figure 1

of only two, and these comprise two pairs, one a father-daughter pair and the other a brother-sister pair.[18]

Following this and descending into the unconscious and then into the subregions of the self, Jung constructs three further hexagrams (The Shadow Quaternio,[19] The Paradise Quaternio,[20] and The Lapis Quaternio[21]) and stacks them one on top of the other.

If we look at the two Quaternios above the line that runs sharply across the diagram, we see a map that resembles the Sketch for *Systema*: Homo is at the center, and above is the higher spiritual

---

[18] Ibid., para. 359.
[19] Ibid., para. 367.
[20] Ibid., para. 374.
[21] Ibid., para. 377.

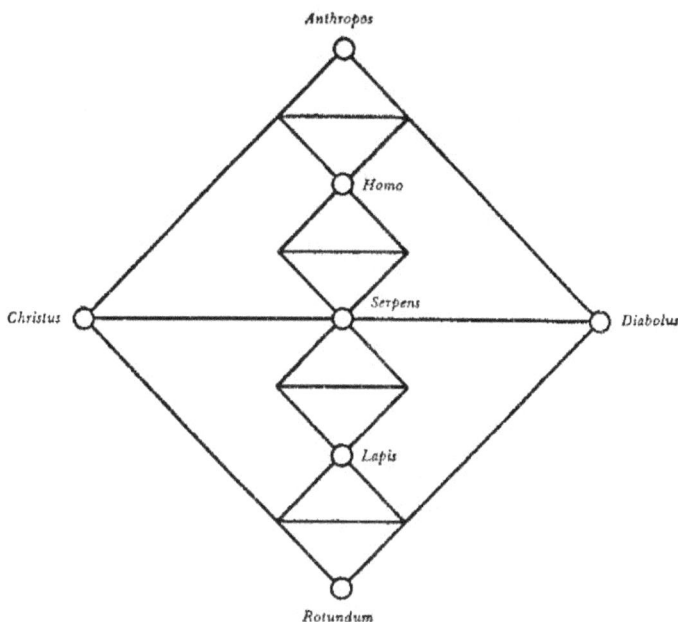

Figure 2 Four Quaternities

realm (here called "Anthropos") and below is the lower material region of *Serpens* (Abraxas in *Systema*). The two Quaternios below the line extend the vertical axis downward into the vegetative dimension of the material world (in the Paradise Quaternio with a tree at the center) and into the essential components of matter itself (earth, water, fire, and air in the Lapis Quaternio), until the diagram reaches down into the subatomic world itself and dissolves into pure energy, which is akin to the spiritual regions at the top of the diagram. In this, we see Jung's extension of the psychogram into territories not explored in the Red Book phase but later in his study of alchemy.

In a letter to Victor White,[22] Jung sketches this same map of the self, but with an interesting difference.

---

[22] Lammers, A. (ed.) (2007). *The Jung-White Letters* (London: Routledge), p. 122.

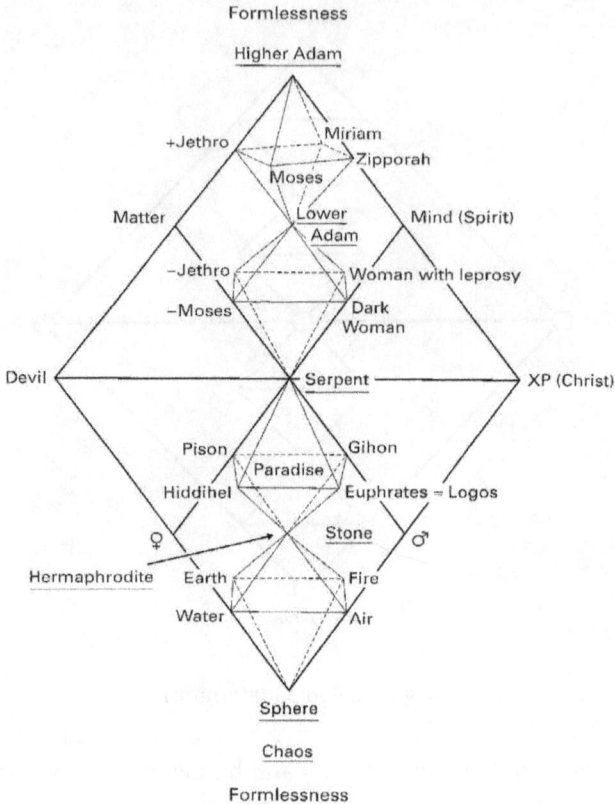

Figure 4 Quaternities in Jung's letter

In the figure published in *Aion*, the horizontal axis shows Christus on the left side and Diabolos on the right; in the sketch, this is reversed, with Christ on the right side and the Devil on the left. The sketch corresponds more closely to the *Systema*, where Satanas is on the left and Sophia is on the right (now replaced by Christus). I assume Jung reversed this in *Aion* in order to get a clockwise movement into the diagram he then presents,[23] which shows the top and bottom of the construction of four hexagrams united and whole construction in motion.

---

[23] Op. cit., p. 248.

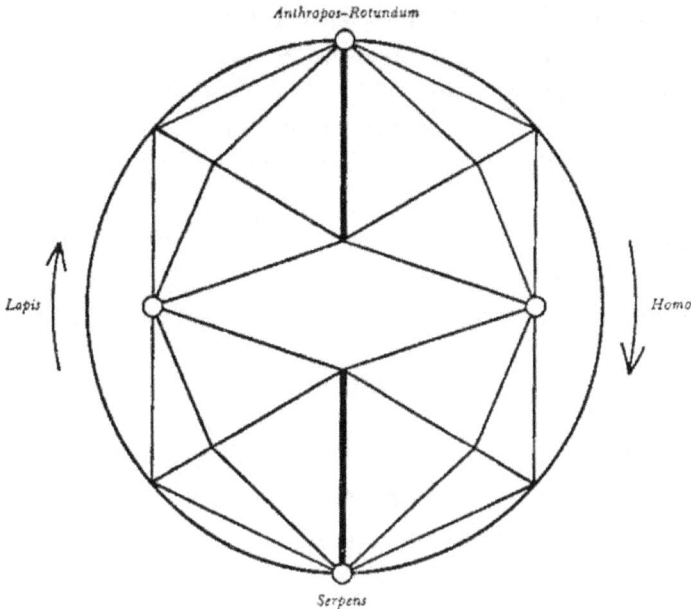

Figure 3 Uroboros Quaternities

In this drawing, Jung has added a dynamic, energic element to the psychogram in order to capture the individuation process that unfolds as the human being develops in time on four different levels, extending from spiritual and mental to emotional and instinctual to purely physical.

One question I have asked myself about these later diagrams is: What has happened to the *star at the center*, so important to those earlier mandalas from the Red Book period? My conclusion is that it is present but tucked away out of sight. I have the thought that it is embedded in Anthropos-Rotundum circle at the top of the cycle, because this is where spirit and matter come together and unite and from where synchronicity—the creation of meaning in time—originates. When Jung writes about synchronicity, he insists on using the word "meaningful" in discussing these types of coincidences, and by this he has in mind something radically transcendent, like the star: "Synchronicity postulates a meaning which is a priori in relation to human consciousness and apparently exists outside man."[24] In another passage, he uses the remarkable phrase, "acts of creation in time,"[25] indicating by this an active factor that generates the "new," and with it "meaning," without reference to cause-and-effect chains of events. That would be the "star" in action as it begins new cycles at the top of the orbit. Thus, the transcendent element, the star, is concealed within this upper "point" of the rotating mandala and provides the cycles with new direction and meaning, not just endless repetition of the same patterns.

Conclusion

What can we make of all this mapmaking on Jung's part? Maps serve practical purposes—guidance, orientation, containment. So, with reference to Jung's psychograms, I think there are a number of points to consider.

1. The *Systema munditotius* and later mandalas and psychograms provided Jung himself with a means to orient himself within a vast array of obervations and experiences and to direct his thinking. This was of great value to him, especially during his midlife "confrontaton with the unconscious," but also later in his psychological theorizing. They provided models to assist his hypothosizing.

2. They also played a powerful role in his thinking about psychotherapy, in that the mandala presents a picture of opposites held in tension without splitting, repression, projection, or other defensive operations. They underline the possibility of gaining and maintaining conscious wholeness despite the pressures from within and without to disown parts of the self for the sake of adaptation and adjustment to social and narcissistic pressures. The

---

[24] C.G. Jung, "Synchronicity: An Acausal Connecting Principle," CW 8, para. 942.
[25] Ibid., para. 965.

psychograms portray and encourage a movement toward conscious wholeness and are therefore in themselves of therapeutic value. They also help practicing psychotherapists to orient their thinking and approach.

3. Jung's psychograms can help to orient other contributors to psychotherapy and depth psychological theory by holding up a template that shows all the factors that must be considered and included within a theory of the human psyche as a totality, both for practice and for research.

4. A cautionary word, however: Models, maps, and graphs may be misleading and cause us to overlook or to underplay certain factors. They draw our attention to certain features of the "landscape" but may miss others. They can slant and prejudice our thinking. The church's commitment to the Ptolemaic model of the universe, for example, retarded creative thinking and fresh observation and made scientific discovery much more difficult. One can fall in love with a cosmograph or a psychgraph and thereby stumble into bland repetitions of old formulas when the times are ready for a new approach and a fresh vision. Jungians must also be careful of this hazard if we mean to continue to develop the field of analytical psychology.

The point is that maps prove their usefulness if they help guide people into and through the territory they claim to describe. When they lead people astray, they should be put aside in favor of something better.

The Red Book as a Journey to Individuation[1]

It is quite strange to be lecturing on *The Red Book: Liber Novus* to lands so far away from its home on the shores of Lake Zurich in Switzerland. And yet, one must recognize that the book does not belong only to that place. It is a book for all the peoples of the earth, although it is located in a particular mentality, that of the psychologist C.G. Jung.

Jung himself did not travel to the Far East in his lifetime. His closest contact with Chinese culture, for instance, was through his readings and his friendship with Richard Wilhelm, the Protestant missionary to China, who translated many of the Chinese classics into German. Nevertheless, Jung felt a deep kinship with Chinese culture and philosophy, which is so evident in his writings, such as in his "Commentary on 'The Secret of the Golden Flower'" and his Foreword to the English translation of the *I Ching*. In *Liber Novus* itself, there is an important image that Jung thought of as Chinese in style and tone.[2] Jung painted this into the Red Book shortly before receiving the translation of *The Secret of the Golden Flower* from Richard Wilhelm. It was a meaningful coincidence, which he carefully noted at the bottom of the picture in *Liber Novus*

Today the world is much smaller than it was in 1913 when Jung began the entries in his diary that would become the text for the

---

[1] Previously unpublished. Delivered as an online lecture to a Chinese audience in 2020.
[2] See C.G. Jung, *The Red Book*, image 163.

Red Book. At that time, China was very far from Europe, and Chinese culture was known by Europeans only through a few books by travelers and scholars. There was practically no bridge between West and East. Jung and Richard Wilhelm played an important role in constructing that bridge, Wilhelm as a translator and Jung as a psychological interpreter. Between them, they brought Chinese culture to the attention of Europeans in the West and set out to create the foundations for a new world culture that would combine religious and philosophical traditions from all parts of the world.

In composing *Liber Novus*, Jung was building another kind of bridge, this one between the day and night sides of the psyche, conscious and unconscious. We can speak of solar and lunar consciousness, two types of cognition and two types of perception. A parallel is what Jung called two types of thinking, directed thinking and fantasy thinking. This would be another way to speak of this difference. As Jung read the Chinese texts translated by Richard Wilhelm, he concluded that the type of thinking shown in the *I Ching* and *The Secret of the Golden Flower* would be much closer to fantasy thinking, or associative thinking, while directed thinking was characteristic of modern science as it has been developed over the centuries in the West. In *Liber Novus*, we find a combination of the two types of thinking, fantasy thinking in the active imagination dialogues and the dreams, directed thinking in the commentaries written subsequently about them. Tying them together and adding a further dimension are the artistic works, the paintings.

What did Jung really accomplish in *The Red Book*, and how can that have some significance for us? These are the questions I would like to consider with you in what follows.

To answer the first question I will make a quick reference to a text that is familiar to you who are from the cultures of the East and also to us in the West, thanks to the work of translators and interpreters like Daisetz Suzuki, "The Ten Ox-Herding Pictures." The series of Zen images begins with a man looking for his lost ox. He is confused and disoriented. Then he spots a trace, a footprint, and then catches a glimpse of the ox. Next, he ropes the ox and struggles with him, then tames him, and finally rides him home. Success! But the series does not stop here, even though in some texts it does and logically very well could stop here, for this indicates a completion of the initial mission. However, this is a text about enlightenment and not only about finding and taming our archaic self and nature. The seventh image shows the man without his ox and kneeling in meditation, gazing at the full moon, and then the series reaches a climax with this Zen Buddhist Ensō image. The text associated with the eighth picture reads:

Whip, rope, Ox and man alike belong to Emptiness.

So vast and infinite the azure sky

that no concept of any sort can reach it.

Over a blazing fire a snowflake cannot survive.

When this state of mind is realized

comes at last comprehension

of the spirit of the ancient patriarchs.[3]

This leads in the next-to-last picture to an image with the title "Return to the Source" and finally to the 10th picture, "Entering the Market with Arms Hanging Loose." These final three images in the series show initiation into transcendence and enlightenment. The last picture brings the enlightened sage back into the community of his fellows as a savant and teacher.

This is a very brief summary of this profound psychological and spiritual text. I will not discuss the images or the sequence in detail as I have done elsewhere,[4] but will focus on the eighth picture of the Ensō in particular and make some reference also to the ninth and 10th with respect to Jung. What Jung achieved with the tool of active imagination, which he more or less invented for his own purposes though drawing on other traditions of imaging and meditation, was to come into contact with "the spirit of the ancient

---

[3] Roshi Philip Kapleau, *The Three Pillars of Zen*, New York; Anchor Books, 1980, p. 321.

[4] M. Stein, "Psychological Individuation and Spiritual Enlightenment," in *Collected Writings*, vol. 1.

patriarchs." This we see most powerfully depicted in his conversations with Elijah and Philemon. These are ancient patriarchs of the biblical and Gnostic traditions, and they are identical in spirit with the sages and patriarchs of all wisdom traditions. In China, you would identify them with the ancient Ch'an masters and Taoist sages.

What Jung was doing by engaging in this exercise in active imagination was to contact the spirit of the ancestors directly, not through the study of books and intellectual avenues of learning. This engagement took place in stages and over a period of time.

One can readily see what an enormous amount of time and effort went into creating *Liber Novus*. What did Jung bring away with him from this contact with all these figures and with the "spirit of the ancient patriarchs?" Above all, he had an experience of the "source," the psychic powers that create us and give us our identity and our destiny. Along the way, he also found the Ox (his archaic self) and established a good relationship with it. He could ride it home, as shown in the sixth ox-herding picture. But beyond that, he got the gift of magic and the Seven Sermons to the Dead, a precious teaching akin to Gnostic wisdom and wisdom traditions worldwide. We could say, he had an experience of living in Tao.

In his "Commentary on 'The Secret of the Golden Flower,'" Jung writes about Tao as follows: "If we take the Tao to be the method or conscious way by which to unite what is separated, we have probably come close to the psychological meaning of the concept."[5] For Jung, this reunion of what has been separated means reunion of conscious and unconscious. When this is done, it puts consciousness in contact with the self: "...the realization of the opposite hidden in the unconscious...signifies reunion with the unconscious laws of our being, and the purpose of this reunion is the attainment of conscious life or, expressed in Chinese terms, the realization of the Tao."[6] This connection with "the unconscious laws

---

[5] C.G. Jung, "Commentary on the Secret of the Golden Flower," CW 13, para. 30.
[6] Ibid.

of our being" is what Jung finds in his inner journey as described in *The Red Book*. The return to lunar consciousness is a return to the source, as we see also in the seventh picture of the ox-herding series.

What we learn from *The Red Book* is that this return and reunion—this healing of the division within—is accomplished by Tao, that is, by the way of active imagination and the intensive interpretation of dreams and the images that appear in active imagination.

The narrative of *The Red Book* follows the pattern of a journey. It begins with a call to the soul—"My soul, where are you?"—and proceeds into darkness and chaos and into the desert where the protagonist remains for 25 nights. It is in the desert that the soul comes fully alive and reveals herself as an independent being, free of the ego's wishes and intentions and having a mind of her own. This is Jung's first great discovery in the Red Book experience: The soul is an autonomous factor in the psyche that has to be dealt with on her own terms. In fact, he discovers, he is dependent on her rather than she on him: "I did not know that I am your vessel, empty without you but brimming over with you."[7]

As the narrative proceeds, Jung comes upon images and figures who also demonstrate a remarkable amount of autonomy. They all seem to have a will of their own, and it is all he can do to keep himself from fleeing out of this underworld and dismissing it all as mere fantasy. Two important figures he confronts after his encounter with the soul are Elijah and Salome. He is a prophet, and she is his daughter. They disclose their own reality as timeless figures of the psyche who have been together eternally. In a critical dialogue with them, the protagonist tries to dismiss them as mere symbols, and they insist on their reality: "We are real and not symbols," Elijah tells him. Again, the message is that the psyche has an autonomy and integrity of its own, beyond the beliefs and prejudices of the

---

[7] C.G. Jung, *The Red Book, A Reader's Edition*, p. 145.

ego. These lessons force Jung to take the psyche seriously as a living reality.

In the text of *Liber Novus*, we see that Jung, the Narrator, is trying to understand the meaning of the active imagination that is unfolding with such astonishing force and reality in his lunar world. Thus, he interprets Elijah as "logos" and Salome as "eros." These are conscious categories of interpretation inherited from Greek philosophy, which help Jung's solar consciousness to make a bridge to the discourse that is taking place within his imaginative world. The commentaries are as important as the experiences because both solar and lunar sides of the mind are important, and the goal is to form a bridge between them. It is not enough to have dreams, practice active imagination and paint pictures. The conscious mind must also grapple with the meaning of this material and attempt to bring itself into a dynamic and meaningful relationship with the images.

Jung powerfully states this point in a comment he made to students in 1925, some 12 years after the active imagination took place that he is referring to in this seminar. He describes to his students a scene, which we now can read for ourselves in *Liber Novus*, in which he, as the protagonist in the drama, actually takes the form of Christ on the cross and experiences the suffering of the crucifixion. He explained this experience to his students as a "deification mystery" and said: "Anyone could be caught by these things and lost in them—some throw the experience away saying it is all nonsense, and thereby losing their best value, for these are the creative images. Another may identify himself with the images and become a crank or a fool."[8] For years following experiences such as this one and others recorded in *The Red Book*, he struggled to find their meaning for his own life. This was the work of integration, of bridge-building between conscious and unconscious, of letting the Tao perform its healing function.

---

[8] C.G. Jung, *Analytical Psychology*, p. 99.

Acts of Imagination and the Creation of the (Inner) World[1]

The Setting

Liber Novus, which I read here as a Mystery Play akin to those of the Middle Ages, begins on November 12, 1913.[2] The setting is Kusnacht, a small village on the lake eight kilometers south of Zurich, the bustling business center of Switzerland, a city of banks, captains of industry, two universities of international reputation, a grand opera house, and the famous Burghölzli Psychiatric Klinik. The Spirit of the Times rules supreme in the city where it rules imperiously and proudly according to the highest standards of modern European culture. For the German-speaking Swiss, this Zeitgeist is inspired by the nation to the north, Deutschland, famed for its positivistic scientific methodologies, its philosophers (Kant, Schopenhauer, Nietzsche), its classical music geniuses (lately, Richard Wagner), and its skeptical and subversive attitude toward religious beliefs and experience (Goethe, Feuerbach, Marx). The bitter conflict between science and religion is at a boiling point in these times, a conflict that destroyed, as Jung witnessed, his pastor father's vocational life. This Spirit of the Times bears the name, Modernity.

---

[1] Originally published in *Jung's Red Book for Our Time*, M. Stein (ed.), vol. 5, 2022.
[2] C.G. Jung, *The Black Books*, vol. 2, p. 149.

Curtain Up

C.G. Jung, a 38-year-old "alienist" (as psychiatrists were then called) and until recently the designated crown prince of Freud's still fledgling psychoanalytic movement, is not satisfied by what he has found in psychiatry and Freud's psychoanalysis. Both are under the control of the Spirit of the Times. Having given himself to this spirit quite thoroughly for the past decade, he now realizes something essential is lacking. At this moment in his life, he finds himself like Dante, lost in a dark wood, and like the Ox-Herder of Zen Buddhist fame who suddenly becomes aware that his beloved Ox has gone missing.

On this night in November, Jung sits down at the desk in the private study tucked away behind the library on the first floor of his home, whose windows face out to the garden and to the lake beyond, and calls out into the darkness: "My soul, my soul, where are you? I call you—are you there? I have returned, here I am again."[3] He knows what's missing: it's soul. Jung's need for soul is answered initially by a spirit whose name is the Spirit of the Depths, which invites him to follow a different path from the one offered by the Spirit of the Times. This Spirit's instruction will be quite other than what he has been receiving previously from his teachers and mentors. This Spirit calls for imagination first, rational thinking second, the reverse of the methodologies used in modern scientific research and more akin to poets, artists, and alchemical adepts. The thinking mind will take second place in this experiment to the imagining mind. A record will be kept in his private journals, the Black Books.

Jung's imagination takes him (and us) on a journey into a mysterious inner world that will frighten, surprise, and enlighten him over the course of the next several years. His first encounter with a personality is a feminine figure named Soul. This is the one he has called for out of his window. After many days of empty

---

[3] Ibid.

frustration in the desert, his cry is finally answered when she speaks to him softly and says simply: "Wait."[4] Not a welcome message.

Jung offers a commentary on this critical initial moment of encounter with the anima in an essay he wrote some 30 years later titled, "Paracelsus as a Spiritual Phenomenon":

> The anima belongs to those borderline phenomena which chiefly occur in special psychic situations. They are characterized by the more or less sudden collapse of a form or style of life which till then seemed the in-dispensable foundation of the individual's whole career. When such a catastrophe occurs, not only are all bridges back into the past broken, but there seems to be no way forward into the future. One is confronted with a hopeless and impenetrable darkness, an abysmal void that is now suddenly filled with an alluring vision, the palpably real presence of a strange yet helpful being, in the same way that, when one lives for a long time in great solitude the silence of the darkness becomes visibly, audibly and tangibly alive, and the unknown in oneself steps up in an unknown guise.[5]

To the knowledgeable reader, it is clear that this is an autobiographical statement referring back to his encounter with Soul in 1913.

Following the appearance of Soul, Jung's continuing acts of imagination reveal the persons and narratives that he will use for the creation of *Liber Novus*, his dramatic and pictorial portrayal of an inner world. It resembles a medieval mystery play with com-mentary: a series of scenes offering spiritual instruction and the Protagonist's reactions. *Liber Novus* was obviously conceived to look like an illuminated manuscript of the Middle Ages. This "new book" will in turn serve as a foundation for Jung's psychological thinking and practice for the rest of his life. The Spirit of the Depths is Jung's

---

[4] C.G. Jung, *The Red Book, A Reader's Edition*, p. 141.
[5] C.G. Jung, "Paracelsus as a Spiritual Phenomenon," *CW* 13, para. 216.

guide, his Virgil, as he makes his way Dante-like through the opaque underworld that he will later call the collective unconscious.

The dialogue between *imagination* and *cognition* constitutes this work's methodology, and it will continue later in Jung's work both for theorizing and for clinical practice. He imagines, and then he thinks interpretively. This reversal of mental faculties amounted to a critique of Enlightenment and modern scientific thinking for Jung, but clearly it did not mean the elimination of rational thinking. A bust of the emblematic savant of the French Enlightenment, Voltaire, remained prominently displayed on the tile stove in his library, but he was joined in the room by the works of the alchemists on the shelves to his left and the imaginal Philemon.

Our Times: the 21st Century

Turning now to our present moment in history a century later from these first scenes in *Liber Novus*, we have to ask: What is our Spirit of the Times? And do we, like Jung, need also to go in search of soul in our now postmodern age? We live in a world of incredible interconnectedness, yet without a spiritual center or a meaningful collective narrative that offers people guidance for their lives. Our time has been designated by the Polish philosopher Zygmund Bauman "liquid modernity." Everything is fluid, nothing quite stable. The ego is untethered—we live without the sacred presence of numinous religious figures among us. The temples are museums. This induces anxiety and emotional regression to paranoid splitting. People have had to learn to swim in this fluidity, but mostly they are swimming in tight circles and without a sense of coherence of the whole. The guidance of a transcendent North Star is invisible to the naked eye. Where is our Virgil? Who or what will be our guide? Soul, where are you?

Our existential crisis is not only about the individual. It is also much more general. It is an issue for the entire human world. "Anima mundi, where are you?" would be our collective cry. Pandemic, genocidal wars, increasingly dire effects of climate change, economic insecurity, hunger, migration—these conditions affect everyone on the planet today. Is there a Spirit of the Depths around that can guide us through this Inferno, perhaps to the emergence of a meaningful narrative that can stabilize the global community and provide a sense of meaning?

Liber Novus and the Red Book: Acts of Imagination

While taking a walk with Michael Fordham during a break at a conference at Ghost Ranch, New Mexico, in August 1985, I was surprised when he stopped and musingly, as if almost to himself, said:

"You know what was Jung's most important discovery?"

"No, what?" I asked.

"The inner world," he answered.

I've never forgotten his words, nor my surprise at hearing him say that. It was a Ghost Ranch Conference on the topic, "Abandonment," and his lecture was titled "Abandonment in Infancy." For all his attention to the mother-infant dyad and its close observation, he saw Jung's contribution to depth psychology clearly: It was the discovery of the "inner world." Had he been privy to Jung's Red Book? Did he know what it contained long before it was published?

It's much easier today for us to agree with Fordham's opinion because we have *The Red Book* available. Its publication in 2009 revealed Jung's inner world for all to see. And with the further publication of his Black Books in 2020, we can now study in greater detail how this inner world was discovered and created. It is important to recognize that Jung's inner world as portrayed in *The Red Book* was not only a discovery but also a creation. Through a series of acts of imagination, Jung discovered the figures and the narratives that would constitute the *prima materia* for the creation of an inner world. The diary notes written into the Black Books show us the basic elements of the multilayered work that would be constructed over the course of 16 years. The opus was one of revising, expanding, subtilizing, refining, commenting, painting and thereby creating what we now have available in *The Red Book* as edited by Sonu Shamdasani.

Although the Red Book was left unfinished, it nevertheless amounts to a magnificent work of imagination, art, and reflection. Like the mysterious *lapis philosophorum* of the alchemists, which reputedly had the uncanny ability to transmute into gold whatever metal it touched, this book has a powerful transformative effect on people who come into close contact with it.

The quasi-magical aura surrounding the Red Book, which Jung kept carefully private in his lifetime, is due to its psychological source, a "faculty"[6] that Jung, referencing an author of the *Rosarium Philosophorum*, calls "true imagination."[7] "True imagination," as opposed to "fantastic imagination," taps into the deepest levels of the archetypal psyche, which makes possible the creation of an inner world. This creation is to be compared to the material creation of the stars and the planets that are the result of Divine acts of imagination. When God imagines, the alchemists taught, the images take material form and become reality. When humans, who are beings created in the image of God (*imago Dei),* imagine truly, the images take psychic form as an inner world, which may oscillate between psyche and matter and thus constellate synchronistic events that combine psychic and material elements.[8]

We should note that the word "magic" is embedded in "imagination," implying something mysterious and inexplicable about acts of true imagination. When Jung writes about this magical element, he is cautious and somewhat indirect, but he does suggest that the material objects that symbolize true imagination (paintings, drawings, sculptures, and works like his Red Book) may have so-called magical effects on their surroundings by constellating

---

[6] C.G. Jung, *Psychology and Alchemy*, CW 12, para. 396. Jung quotes Sendivogius's expression, "imaginative faculty."

[7] Ibid., para. 360.

[8] Ibid., para. 396.

synchronicity.[9] He based this speculation on his experiences, which he records in *Liber Novus* and *Memories, Dreams, Reflections*.[10]

For instance, in January 1916, after he began copying his narrative in calligraphic script into the big red book with blank pages that he had purchased for the purpose in Zurich, he was confronted with uncanny manifestations. The house seemed filled with spirits, he writes. His son has a peculiar dream, and his daughter saw a ghost in the room. It was a Sunday afternoon, and the doorbell of his residence in Kusnacht began ringing wildly but no one was at the door. Then suddenly, a crowd of "spirits of the dead" arrived, loudly demanding answers to their questions. The result was "Septem Sermones ad Mortuos." This uncanny falling together of intensive work with his inner world and manifestations in his material environment took place in early 1916, around the same time he was sketching the outlines for "Systema munditotius," his first and arguably most significant mandala, in his Black Books. I cite the ringing of the doorbell as the kind of strange happening when a powerful unconscious content ("the spirits of the dead") is about to emerge and in conjunction with the creation of that symbol of the Self, the "Systema munditotius." The *Septem Sermones* is a product of true imagination on a prophetic level, and its delivery (by Basilides in the published version, or by Philemon in *Liber Novus*) had the effect of resolving the urgent questions of the spirits of the dead and releasing them to their eternal rest. The whole incident as Jung describes it in *Memories, Dreams, Reflections* is magical, and so it must also have struck him when it took place in early 1916.

Magic is something Jung learns about from Philemon, as depicted in a comically dizzy-making scene at the end of Liber Secundus of *The Red Book*, in the Chapter titled "The Magician." To Jung's entreaty to teach him how to do magic, Philemon responds reluctantly by giving him some mind-bending instructions, which understandably confuse Jung. Finally, Jung cries out in despair:

---

[9] C.G. Jung, *Mysterium Coniunctionis*, CW 14, para. 758.
[10]

Jung: "I conclude that it is an inescapable condition for
the adept that he
completely unlearns his reason."
Philemon: "I'm afraid that is what it amounts to."
Jung: "Ye Gods, this is serious"[11]

It is not until the last scene in *The Red Book*, at the end of the
section titled "Scrutinies," that Jung discovers the true identity of
Philemon. He is Simon Magus, the ancient magician of New
Testament notoriety who tried to bribe the apostles into showing
him how to use the Holy Spirit for his own purposes as magician.
According to legend, Simon Magus, who was always accompanied
by a beautiful young courtesan named Helena, was the founder of
a Simonian Gnostic sect in Egypt. In Jung's active imagination, he
takes the form of Philemon, still a magician but now coupled with
Baucis. This character was famous in Greek myth for welcoming the
wandering gods, Zeus and Hermes, into the home he shared with
his wife, Baucis, who for their hospitality to the gods were blessed
with abundance in this life and continued union afterwards. Jung's
Philemon is a complex and ambiguous figure, to say the least:
several historical personalities combined; human and temporal but
more than that; a trickster magician and a Gnostic sage, for Jung an
archetypal image of the Self.

At one point, Jung suspects that Philemon is behind the whole
linguistic elaboration of this experiment in true imagination, a subtle
creator daimon like the alchemical Mercurius, who has taken possession of his consciousness while engaged in acts of imagination. Jung
is highly suspicious of magic; nevertheless he finds himself fascinated
by it. What is he to make of it? Will he become a magician like Simon
Magus and the founder of a new Gnostic sect? Maybe. He wonders
what he is to make of this inner world experience he is having.

And what are *we* to make of it? In one sense, it is delusional,
as Jung the psychiatrist well knew as well. In another sense, it is
revelatory of a counterreality, a psychological domain that com-

---

[11] Jung, *The Red Book, A Reader's Edition*, p. 401.

pensates the naturalistic worldview that dominates consciousness for "modern man" and excludes anything to do with the spiritual as superstitious nonsense. The search for soul and the Spirit of the Depths have taken Jung to this imaginal world, and now he will have to figure out what to make of it.

Final Scene in *Liber Novus*: "In the Garden"

We come now to the closing scene of this Mystery Play, *Liber Novus*. This constitutes the play's climax and lysis. In Volume 6 of the Black Book, the entry dated June 6, 1916 (note the date),[12] shows that Jung took a break from his practice at noon that day and walked into his garden. There he came upon a spectral visitor and spoke to this figure as follows:

> I met you in the garden, beloved. The sins of the world
>   have conferred beauty upon your countenance.
> The suffering of the world has straightened your shape.
> You are truly a king. Your crimson is blood, your ermine
>   is snow from the eternal cold of the poles, your crown
>   is the heavenly body of the sun, which you bear on
>   your head.
> Speak to me, my master and beloved![13]

This is a direct address from C.G. Jung to the mystery figure. In *The Red Book*, however, the personae have been altered. There, Jung first meets Philemon in his garden, then a "blue shade" approaches, and the above address is put into the mouth of Philemon. In making this change, Jung distances his persona from the mystery figure.

The text in *The Black Books* continues with Christ now addressing Philemon, who has suddenly appeared on the scene:

---

[12] In *The Red Book*, the date is mistakenly given as June 1. In *The Black Books*, vol. 6, p. 245, however, it is clearly June 6.

[13] C.G. Jung, *The Black Books*, vol. 6, p. 245.

X: Oh Simon Magus, who hides in Philemon, are you in
   my garden or am I in yours?

Ph-Ø: You are, Oh master, in my garden. Helena and I are
   your servants. You can find accommodation with us,
   because Philemon and Baucis have become what
   Simon and Helena were. We are the hosts of the Gods.
   We granted hospitality to the terrible worm. And
   since you came forward, we took you in. It is our
   garden that surrounds you.[14]

The conversation is taking place in this world, namely in Jung's
garden in Küsnacht. Philemon represents humanity and stands in
for the Protagonist (Jung). On the other hand, Christ is God,
transcendent and eternal. The two are trying to work out the
relationship between their two worlds. In Jung-the-psychologist's
work, this topic is taken up as "The relation between the ego and
the unconscious,"[15] which is the title of a lecture he gave on exactly
the same date at the Zurich School for Analytical Psychology. This
lecture would be revised in 1928 and later published in Volume 7 of
the *Collected Works*, *Two Essays on Analytical Psychology*. The
relation between ego and unconscious was a theme that would
occupy Jung for the rest of his life, finally culminating in the
magisterial *Mysterium Coniunctionis* in 1955/56.

Christ is surprised at Philemon's claim to the garden and
responds to him as follows:

X: Am I not the master? Is this garden not mine? Is
   not the world of the heavens and of the spirits
   my own?

Philemon explains:

Ph-Ø: You are, Oh master, here in the world of men.
   Men have changed. They are no longer the

[14] Ibid.
[15] See Jung, *Two Essays in Analytical Psychology*, Pt. 1, CW 7.

> servants and no longer the swindlers of the
> Gods, but they grant hospitality to the Gods.[16]

Over the course of history, he argues, human beings have taken control of their world. The relationship between human beings and the gods, i.e., the ego and the unconscious archetypal powers, has changed. The modern attitude is no longer one of service to the gods or cheating the gods out of their just deserts. Human beings no longer live with a mythological worldview; this is now godless modernity. However, Philemon represents a new development, a postmodern attitude of hospitality to the mythological, i.e., the images of the collective unconscious. This is what Jung describes as a fifth level of consciousness in his 1942 Eranos lecture, "The Spirit Mercurius."[17] It goes beyond the modernist rejection of myth as fake news and misguided superstition.

Philemon continues his explanation:

> Your brother came before you. Oh master, the
> terrible worm, whom you dismissed, when he gave
> you clever counsel in the desert with a tempting
> voice. You took the counsel, but dismissed the
> worm. He found a place with us.[18]

This could be a subtle reference to Goethe's *Faust*, where Mephistopheles is welcomed into Faust's library and then proceeds to guide him Into the world of power and pleasure and through all its heights and depths. In other words, Satan has been welcomed into the sociopolitical world of humankind (including, of course, the religious institutions), whereas Christ rejected him.

> But where he is, you will be also, since he is your immortal
> brother. When I was Simon, I sought to escape him with

---

16 Ibid., p. 246.
17 C.G. Jung, "The Spirit Mercurius," *CW* 13, para. 249.
18 C.G. Jung, The Black Books, vol. 6, p. 246.

the ploy of magic and thus I escaped you. Now that I gave the worm a place in my garden, you come to me.[19]

This statement of the brotherhood of Christ and Satan would become a signature feature of Jung's concept of the Self as a *unio oppositorum*, a paradoxical union of good and evil. You can't have one without the other, in his view. The implication for psychology is that entering into a relationship with the unconscious will necessarily bring both sides of the Self into play. It is a cautionary note for analysts to keep in mind when working with the unconscious. However, as this text expresses, when shadow is welcomed, the opposite will also be called forth. They are the closest of kin.

In the conversation, Christ admits the truth of Philemon's observation but then asks:

X: "Even so, do you know what I bring you?"

To which Philemon replies:

Ph-Ø: This I know not. I know only one thing, that whoever hosts the worm also needs his brother.

What do you bring me, my beautiful guest? The worm brought me ugliness. Do you bring me beauty?[20]

Philemon is thinking, if the worm brings ugliness, Christ must be bringing its opposite. But Christ surprises him when he replies:

X: I bring you the beauty of suffering. That is what is needed by whoever hosts the worm.[21]

It is an astonishing answer to the problem of evil and one that many people will find unsatisfactory, even distasteful. It certainly does not correspond to the Buddhist goal of liberation from all suffering. It does correspond, however, to Jung's view, as often restated in his correspondence and writings, that evil cannot be deleted by religious practices, meditation, dogmatic formulas, or wishful thinking. It is woven into the fabric of human life, a factor

---

[19] Ibid.
[20] Ibid., pp. 246-47.
[21] Ibid.

that is unavoidable and ineradicable. The worm is here to stay. And the God who is the Father of both Christ and Satan, therefore the author of good and evil, is beyond our understanding.

This dialogue in the garden took place, as I noted earlier, on June 6, 1916. When I looked at that date for the first time, a bell rang in my mind. Jung died on June 6, 1961, the same date except with two numbers reversed, the 1 and the 6. Both dates fell on a Tuesday. The one spells the conclusion of *Liber Novus*, the other the conclusion of Jung's life. Jung died in his home in Kusnacht in a room near his library and private study and overlooking the garden where the conversation with Christ had taken place 45 years earlier to the day. It's a strange coincidence. It's a piece of the magic that surrounds *Liber Novus* and Jung's Red Book.

The Mystery Play Extended: Paintings in the Red Book and a Dream

As we know, this is not the end of the story of Jung's search for a personal myth. That would not be complete for another dozen years or so when Jung had his famous Liverpool dream. In the meantime, there was much further work on the Red Book, which we see in the astonishing paintings inscribed there. His dream of the light in the darkness in the center of a fountain at an intersection in Liverpool (1927) is represented in the painting titled "a window opening on to eternity."[22] It's a painting Jung dedicated to his recently deceased friend, Herman Sigg. According to his reflections in a seminar in 1932, however, this painting represents the message in the Liverpool dream.[23]

The penultimate painting in Jung's Red Book is associated with a synchronicity. Jung tells the story in *Memories, Dreams, Reflections,* that when he painted this in his Red Book, he saw that

---

[22] *Black Books*, v. 1, p. 158.
[23] Ibid.

it had a Chinese character. At that same time, he received in the mail Richard Wilhelm's translation of the Chinese alchemy text "The Secret of the Golden Flower" with a request that he write a commentary on it. This meaningful coincidence set Jung off on a completely different path in his life's journey, namely the investigation of alchemy as symbolic of the individuation process. This turn would occupy him for the rest of life and lead to the culminating work, *Mysterium Coniunctionis*.

Does this suggest that acts of true imagination can have an influence on history? Does the work with symbols using *imaginatio* constellate not only personal psychological meaning by making the unconscious conscious, but actually move the levers of historical developments in ways that we cannot comprehend but continually observe? Sounds a bit like magic. In *Mysterium Coniunctionis*, Jung writes about a stage of individuation that links the individual to *unus mundus*. This would be a way of thinking about the relation of a person's private individuation journey to the course of history. They are mutually interactive.

Curtain Down

Thomas Arzt, for whom this Symposium is also a posthumous tribute, was a man of big ideas. From private conversations with him, I gathered that he was looking for the birth of a new Axial Age, to use the phrase coined by Karl Jaspers for the age that saw the appearance of Buddha, Socrates, Plato, Lao-Tse, and the biblical prophets, etc., and led to the transformation of human culture worldwide. In our time, it would lead to the birth of a new collective narrative and *Weltanschauung* that would move consciousness to another level, perhaps to include importantly the fifth dimension within the constructs of modernity and postmodernity, thereby transforming the whole. Thomas Arzt saw *The Red Book* as a pivot point for this transition, and he considered its publication in 2009 synchronistic, coming as it did at the inflection point in human history that we are witnessing dramatically today. Were he here today, he would tell us how he sees the potential of *The Red Book* as a major contributor to this enormous cultural transformation.

References

Adler, G. (ed.). (1973). *C.G. Jung Letters*. Vol. 1: 1906-1950. Princeton, NJ: Princeton University Press.

_____. (1975). *C.G. Jung Letters*. Vol. 2: 1951-1961. Princeton, NJ: Princeton University Press.

Atmanspacher, H. and Rickles, D. (2022). *Dual-Aspect Monism and the Deep Structure of Meaning*. New York and London: Routledge.

Bair, D. (2003). *Jung. A Biography*. Boston, New York, London: Little, Brown.

Bennet, E.A. (2006). *C.G. Jung*. Wilmette, IL.: Chiron Publications.

Bernadini, R. (2016). "Neumann at Eranos." In *Turbulent Times, Brilliant Minds*. (Eds.) E. Shalit and M. Stein. Asheville, N.C.: Chiron Publications.

Bishop, P. (2002). *Jung's Answer to Job: A Commentary*. Hove, UK, and New York: Brunner-Routledge.

Bloom, H. (2015). *The Daimon Knows*. New York: Spiegel and Grau.

Buber, M. (1923/1937/1970). *I and Thou*. New York: Charles Scribner's Sons.

_____. (1952/1988). "Religion and Modern Thinking." In *Eclipse of God*. Atlantic Highlands, NJ: Humanities Press International.

Cambray, J. (2004). "Synchronicity as Emergence." In Cambray, J. and Carter, L. (eds), *Analytical Psychology: Contemporary Perspectives in Jungian Analysis*. Hove, UK, and New York: Brunner-Routledge.

Campbell, J. (1955). *The Mysteries*. New York: Pantheon Books.

Dante, A. (2003). *The Divine Comedy*. Translated by John Ciardi. New York: New American Library.

Dieckmann, H. (1991). *Methods in Analytical Psychology*. Asheville, NC: Chiron Publications.

Donati, M. (2004). "Beyond Synchronicity: The Worldview of Carl Gustav Jung and Wolfgang Pauli." *Journal of Analytical Psychology* 49:5.

Dourley, J. (1992). *A Strategy for a Loss of Faith: Jung's Proposal*. Toronto: Inner City Books.

_____. (2007). "The Jung-White Dialogue and Why It Couldn't Work and Won't Go Away." *The Journal of Analytical Psychology*, 53:3, 275-295.

Dubuisson, D. (2007). *The Western Construction of Religion*. Baltimore: Johns Hopkins University Press.

Edinger, E. (1984). *The Creation of Consciousness: Jung's Myth for Modern Man*. Toronto: Inner City Books.

Ellenberger, H. (1970). *The Discovery of the Unconscious*. New York: Basic Books.

Euler, W. (2004). "Christ and the Knowledge of God." In *Nicholas of Cusa: A Guide to a Renaissance Man*, edited by Christopher Bellitto, Thomas Izbicki, and Gerald Christianson. New York/Mahwah, N.J.: Paulist Press.

Evans, K.L. (2011). Personal communication on List of International Association for Jungian Studies.

Fordham, M. (1957). *New Developments in Analytical Psychology.* London: Routledge.

Frey-Rohn, L. (1974). *From Freud to Jung.* New York: Putnam.

Gaillard, C. (1998). *Le Musée Imaginaire de Carl Gustav Jung.* Paris: Éditions Stock.

Galimberti, U. (1989). "Analytical Psychology in an Age of Technology." In *Zeitschrift fur Analytische Psychologie und ihre Grenzgebiete* 20.

Giegerich, W. (2010). "Liber Novus, that is the new Bible." *Spring Journal,* 83.

Goethe, W. (1994). *Faust,* Part Two. Translated by David Luke. Oxford: Oxford University Press.

Hakl, H.T. (2013). *Eranos: An Alternative Intellectual History of the Twentieth Century.* Sheffield, UK and Bristol, CT: Equinox Publishing.

Heisig, J. W. (1979). *Imago Dei. A Study of C.G. Jung's Psychology of Religion.* Lewisburg, PA: Bucknell University Press.

Hoerni, U., Fischer, T., Kaufmann, B. (eds.). (2018). *The Art of C.G. Jung.* New York and London: W.W. Norton & Co.

Hogenson, G. (1994). *Jung's Struggle with Freud.* Asheville, NC: Chiron Publications.

_____. (2006). "The Self, the Symbolic, and Synchronicity: Virtual Realities and the Emergence of the Psyche." In L. Cowan (ed.) *Edges of Experience: Memory and Emergence.* Proceedings of the 16th International IAAP Congress for Analytical Psychology. Einsiedeln: Daimon Verlag, pp. 155-167.

_____. (2010). "Emergence of the Self." In M. Stein (ed.), *Jungian Psychoanalysis,* Chicago: Open Court.

Jacobsohn, H. (1968). "The Dialogue of a World-Weary Man with His Ba." In *Timeless Documents of the Soul*. Evanston, IL: Northwestern University Press.

Jaffé, A. (ed.) (1979). *C.G. Jung – Word and Image* Princeton, N.J.: Princeton University Press.

_____. (1989). "The Creative Phases in Jung's Life," in *From the Life and Work of C.G. Jung*. Einsiedeln, Switzerland: Daimon Verlag.

_____. Jaffé, A. (2023). *Reflections on the Life and Dreams of C.G. Jung*. Einsiedeln, Switzerland: Daimon Verlag.

Jeromson, B. (2005). "Systema Munditotius and Seven Sermons: Symbolic Collaborators with the Dead." *Jung History*, Vol. 1:2.

Jung, C.G. (1953-1983). *Collected Works*, ed. Sir. H. Read, M. Fordham, G. Adler, W. McGuire. 20 volumes. Princeton, NJ: Princeton University Press.

_____. (1899/1983). "Thoughts on the Interpretation of Christianity, with reference to the Theory of Albrecht Ritschl." *The Zofingia Lectures*. Supplementary Volume A of the Collected Works of C.G. Jung.

_____. (1912). *Wandlungen und Symbole der Libido*. Leipzig and Vienna: Deuticke Verlag.

_____. (1916/1960). "The Transcendent Function." *Collected Works*, vol. 8.

_____. (1916/1976). "Adaptation, Individuation, Collectivity." *Collected Works*, vol. 18.

_____. (1916/1991). *Psychology of the Unconscious. Collected Works*, Supplementary Volume B.

_____. (1921/1971). *Psychological Types. Collected Works*, vol. 6.

_____. (1925/1989). *Analytical Psychology: Notes of the Seminar Given in 1925*. Edited by William McGuire, Princeton, NJ: Princeton University Press.

_____. (1929/1967). "Commentary on 'The Secret of the Golden Flower.'" *Collected Works,* vol. 13.

_____. (1931/1934/1966). "The Practical Use of Dream-Analysis." *Collected Works*, vol. 16.

_____. (1930/1966). "Richard Wilhelm: In Memoriam." *Collected Works*, vol. 15.

_____. (1931/1966). "Problems of Modern Psychotherapy." *Collected Works,* vol. 16.

_____. (1931/1966). "The Aims of Psychotherapy." *Collected Works*, vol 16.

_____. (1936/1960). "Psychological Factors Determining Human Behaviour." *Collected Works,* vol. 8.

_____. (1937/1969). *Psychology and Religion. Collected Works*, vol. 11.

_____. (1944/1953/1968). *Psychology and Alchemy. Collected Works*, vol. 12.

_____. (1946/1966). "Psychology of the Transference." *Collected Works*, vol. 16.

_____. (1947/1960). "On the Nature of the Psyche." *Collected Works,* vol. 8.

_____. (1950/1969). "Foreword to the I Ching." *Collected Works,* vol. 11.

_____. (1952/1960). "Synchronicity: An Acausal Connecting Principle." *Collected Works*, vol. 8.

_____. (1952/1954/1969). *Answer to Job. Collected Works*, vol. 11.

_____. (1952/1969). "Foreword to White's 'God and the Unconscious.'" *Collected Works*, vol. 11.

_____. (1952/1976). "Religion and Psychology: A Reply to Martin Buber." *Collected Works*, vol. 18.

_____. (1955-1956/1963). *Mysterium Coniunctionis. Collected Works,* vol. 14.

_____. (1961). *Memories, Dreams, Reflections.* Recorded and Edited by Aniela Jaffé. New York: Random House.

_____. (1961/1976). "Symbols and the Interpretation of Dreams." *Collected Works,* vol. 20.

_____. (1966). *Two Essays on Analytical Psychology. Collected Works,* vol. 7.

_____. (1976). *The Symbolic Life. Collected Works,* vol. 18.

_____. (2009) *The Red Book: Liber Novus.* New York and London: W.W. Norton & Co.

_____. (2009). *The Red Book: Liber Novus. A Reader's Edition.* New York and London: W.W. Norton & Co.

_____. (2020). *The Black Books.* 1913-1932. 7 volumes. New York and London: W.W. Norton & Co.

Kapleau, R.P. (1980). *The Three Pillars of Zen.* New York: Anchor Books.

Kerényi, K. (1941/1950). *Das Ägäische Fest.* Wiesbaden, Germany: Limes Verlag.

_____. (1944/1955). "The Mysteries of the Kabeiroi." J. Campbell (ed.), *The Mysteries.* New York: Pantheon.

Kerr, J. (1993). *A Most Dangerous Method.* New York: Knopf.

Kirsch, J. (1982). "Carl Gustav and the Jews: The Real Story." *Journal of Psychology and Judaism,* 6, No. 2, pp. 113-43.

Kirsch, T. (1998). "Jung and Tao." *The Round Table Review,* Vol 7, No. 3.

Lammers, A. (1994). *In God's Shadow: The Collaboration of Victor White and C.G. Jung.* New York and Mahwah, NJ: Paulist Press.

_____. and Cunningham, A. (eds.). (2007). *The Jung-White Letters.* London and New York: Routledge.

Liebscher, M. (ed.). (2015). *Analytical Psychology in Exile: The Correspondence of C.G. Jung and Erich Neumann.* Princeton, NJ: Princeton University Press.

Madden, K. (ed.). (2016). *The Unconscious Roots of Creativity.* Asheville, NC: Chiron Publications.

Marcus, P. and Rosenberg, A. (eds.). (1998). *Psychoanalytic Versions of the Human Condition.* New York: New York University Press.

McCormick, F. (1962). *Carl Gustav Jung – 1975-1961: A Memorial Meeting.* New York: The Analytical Psychology Club of New York, Inc., pp. 10-16.

McGuire, W. (ed.) (1974). *The Freud/Jung Letters.* Princeton, NJ: Princeton University Press.

_____. (ed.) (1983). *Jelliffe: American Psychoanalyst and Physician; His Correspondence with Sigmund Freud and C.G. Jung.* Chicago and London: University of Chicago Press.

Meier, C.A. (ed.). (2001). *Atom and Archetype: The Pauli/Jung Letters.* Princeton, NJ: Princeton University Press.

Neumann, E. (1950/1994). "The Moon and Matriarchal Consciousness." In *The Fear of the Feminine.* Princeton, NJ: Princeton University Press.

_____. (1954/1959). "Creative Man and Transformation." In *Art and the Creative Unconscious.* Princeton, NJ: Princeton University Press.

_____. (1959). "A Note on Marc Chagall." In *Art and the Creative Unconscious.* Princeton, NJ: Princeton University Press.

_____. (1959/1979). "Georg Trakl: The Person and the Myth." In *Creative Man.* Princeton, NJ: Princeton University Press.

_____. (1960/1989). "The Psyche as the Place of Creation." In *The Place of Creation*. Princeton, NJ: Princeton University Press.

_____. (1960/2016). "'*Dear, dear Olga!*' – A Letter to Olga Fröbe-Kapteyn." In *Turbulent Times, Brilliant Minds*. (Eds.) E. Shalit and M. Stein. Asheville, NC: Chiron Publications.

Neumann, J. (1960/2016). "A Letter from Julie Neumann to Olga Fröbe-Kapteyn." In E. Shalit & M. Stein, (eds.), *Turbulent Times, Creative Minds. Erich Neumann and C.G. Jung in Relationship (1933-1960)*. Asheville, NC: Chiron Publications.

Rennstich, K. (1998). "Richard Wilhelm." In *Biographish-Bibliographisch Kirschenlexikon*. Band XIII. Verlag Traugott Bautz.

Rowland, S. (2013). *Jung as a Writer*. London: Routledge.

Samuels, A. (1985). *Jung and the Post-Jungians*. London: Routledge.

_____. (1993). *The Political Psyche*. London: Routledge.

Schlamm, L. (2006). "C. G. Jung's Visionary Mysticism." *Harvest* 52:1, pp. 7-37.

Schwartz-Salant, N. (1989). *The Borderline Personality: Vision and Healing*. Asheville, NC: Chiron Publications.

Shamdasani, S. (2003). *Jung and the Making of Modern Psychology*. Cambridge: Cambridge University Press.

Stein, M. (1985). *Jung's Treatment of Christianity*. Asheville, NC: Chiron Publications.

_____. (1992). "Power, Shamanism and Maieutics in the Countertransference." In *Transference/Countertransference*, ed. N. Schwartz-Salant and M. Stein. Asheville, NC: Chiron Publications.

_____. (1992). "The Role of the Anima/Animus Structures and Archetypes in the Psychology of Narcissism and Some Borderline States." In *Gender and Soul in Psychotherapy*, ed.

N. Schwartz-Salant and M. Stein, Asheville, NC: Chiron Publications.

_____. (1995). "Introduction." *Jung on Evil*. Princeton: Princeton University Press.

_____. Stein, M. (2022). "Acts of Imagination: The Creation of the (Inner) World." In M. Stein (ed.), *Jung's Red Book for Our Time,* Vol. 5. Asheville, NC: Chiron Publications.

Stern, P. (1976). *C.G. Jung: The Haunted Prophet*. New York: Dell.

Urban, E. (2005). 'Fordham, Jung and the self: a re-examination of Fordham's Contribution to Jung's conceptualization of the self'. *Journal of Analytical Psychology*, 50:5, pp. 571-594.

Van Eenwyk, J. (1991). "The analysis of defences." In *Journal of Analytical Psychology* 36:2.

Wehr, G. (1987). *Jung: A Biography*. Boston: Shambhala Publications.

White, V. (1952/1965). *God and the Unconscious*. Cleveland: The World Publishing Co.

Wili, W. (1944/1955). "The Orphic Mysteries and the Greek Spirit." In J. Campbell (ed.), *The Mysteries*. New York: Pantheon Books.

Index

M

N

O

P

Pathology 11, 27
Patriarchal stage 116
Pauli, Wolfgang 79, 91, 160
Phanes 191, 206, 207–215, 222–225, 229, 231
Philemon 132, 133, 170, 176, 191–194, 196, 197, 199, 200, 210, 211, 215, 226, 229, 230, 242, 248, 251–256
Primordial stage 109
Privatio boni 34, 35, 48, 54–56, 73, 174, 175
Projection 15, 21, 22, 126, 236
Psyche 1, 3–11, 13–16, 18, 23, 24, 26, 27, 61, 64, 65, 68–71, 74–83, 85, 87, 95–97, 99, 104–106, 108, 110–112, 115, 120, 121, 126–129, 140–142, 146, 160, 161, 169, 176, 178, 187, 197, 213, 215, 216, 220–222, 224–229, 231, 237, 240, 243, 244, 250
Psychoanalysis 11, 12, 32, 47, 48, 50, 51, 91, 172, 173, 176, 182, 188, 202, 221, 246
Psychogram 221, 222, 224, 227, 228, 233, 235
Psychotherapy 1, 94, 96, 98, 100, 124, 236, 237

Q

Quaternity 140, 146, 174
Queen 49, 140–143

R

Relationship 10, 20, 21, 31–33, 36, 47–53, 57, 61, 65, 66, 71, 74, 76, 90, 91, 93, 94, 98, 124, 147, 153–159, 161, 163, 172, 198, 202, 219, 242, 244, 254–256
Rowland, Susan 43
Rosarium Philosophorum 250

S

Sacred 74, 87, 123, 125, 138, 145, 183, 248
Salome 91, 128–131, 169 , 243, 244
Samuels, Andrew 268
Schwartz-Salant, Nathan 23

INDEX

www.ingramcontent.com/pod-product-compliance
Lightning Source LLC
Chambersburg PA
CBHW020340270326
41926CB00007B/258